CHARLES FORT

OTHER BOOKS BY JIM STEINMEYER

Hiding the Elephant

The Glorious Deception

CHARLES FORT

The Man Who Invented
the Supernatural

Jim Steinmeyer

JEREMY P. TARCHER/PENGUIN

a member of Penguin Group (USA) Inc.

New York

JEREMY P. TARCHER/PENGUIN
Published by the Penguin Group
Penguin Group (USA) Inc., 375 Hudson Street, New York, New York 10014, USA •
Penguin Group (Canada), 90 Eglinton Avenue East, Suite 700, Toronto, Ontario M4P 2Y3,
Canada (a division of Pearson Canada Inc.) • Penguin Books Ltd, 80 Strand, London
WC2R 0RL, England • Penguin Ireland, 25 St Stephen's Green, Dublin 2, Ireland (a division of
Penguin Books Ltd) • Penguin Group (Australia), 250 Camberwell Road, Camberwell, Victoria 3124,
Australia (a division of Pearson Australia Group Pty Ltd) • Penguin Books India Pvt Ltd,
11 Community Centre, Panchsheel Park, New Delhi–110 017, India •
Penguin Group (NZ), 67 Apollo Drive, Rosedale, North Shore 0632, New Zealand
(a division of Pearson New Zealand Ltd) • Penguin Books (South Africa) (Pty) Ltd,
24 Sturdee Avenue, Rosebank, Johannesburg 2196, South Africa

Penguin Books Ltd, Registered Offices: 80 Strand, London WC2R 0RL, England

Most Tarcher/Penguin books are available at special quantity discounts for bulk purchase for sales
promotions, premiums, fund-raising, and educational needs. Special books or book excerpts also can be
created to fit specific needs. For details, write Penguin Group (USA) Inc. Special Markets, 375 Hudson
Street, New York, NY 10014.

Library of Congress Cataloging-in-Publication Data

Steinmeyer, Jim, date.
Charles Fort : the man who invented the supernatural / Jim Steinmeyer.
p.   cm.
Includes bibliographical references and index.
ISBN: 978-1-58542-640-9
1. Fort, Charles, 1874–1932.   2. Parapsychologists—United States—Biography.
3. Supernatural—History.   4. Curiosities and wonders.   I. Title.
BF1027.F67S73   2007   2008005961
001.9092—dc22

Printed in the United States of America
1   3   5   7   9   10   8   6   4   2

BOOK DESIGN BY MEIGHAN CAVANAUGH

For my brother and sister,

Harry and Susan,

from "the little kid"

CONTENTS

AUTHOR'S INTRODUCTION

And science is a turtle that says its
own shell encloses all things.

In *Technopoly,* Neil Postman's book about the way we think about technology, the author recalled one of his students suffering a hot, muggy day in a room without air-conditioning. When the student was told that the thermometer read ninety-eight degrees Fahrenheit, he quickly replied, "No wonder it's so hot!"

Human beings are nitwits.

We process information in notoriously idiotic ways—which explains the persistence of carnival operators, telephone psychics, used car salesmen, advertising executives, and politicians. Despite the common perception, they don't always need to be crooked, because we're perfectly capable of watching their skills and misinterpreting them—adding the skewed angles ourselves. Abraham Lincoln may have been technically right when he said, "You can't fool all of the people all of the time," but there's no pride in so vague, or so small, a proportion of success.

One of my favorite constructions is the reassuring phrase "That makes sense." Nothing actually "makes" sense, and, more often than not, sense is assigned in retrospect. Because something occurs or exists, we comfort ourselves that it has been perfectly explainable and predictable. The clouds painted on the television weatherman's map demonstrate how today's rainstorm "made sense"; an obscure business hiccup explains that Wall Street's sudden dip "made sense." For centuries, physicians were bleeding patients; the sun was circling the earth; and priests were offering human sacrifices: these similarly "made sense." We search for the formula of understanding—we assume that the world is rational and understandable—and we convince ourselves that there is a simple way in which it must all make sense.

Psychologists tell us that our brains love to form patterns—assembling information to draw larger conclusions. Our pattern-making abilities are usually offered as proof of highly evolved human thought. But it is that fondness for patterns—the habitual need to look at pieces and infer a larger picture—that causes problems. If you picked up a quart of paint and, instead of merely asking the color, wondered if it were tartan, polka-dot, or striped paint, you'd have the same analogy.

Recognizing our faults, we've gradually evolved the scientific method, a system of checks and balances, taking bits from Aristotle, Bacon, and Descartes. It's a way of looking at data, conducting experiments, and drawing conclusions. But despite our best intentions and the hallowed status of the scientific method, it can still be subject to individual foibles and pitfalls. It is a process that human beings thought of so they could think about things in reliable ways, because humans have such unreliable tendencies when it comes to thinking about things. In other words, it's the best we'll do under the circumstances.

The author Charles Fort wrote, "I confess to childish liking for making little designs, or arrangements of data, myself. And every formal design depends upon blanks, as much as upon occupied spaces."

At a time when people were desperate for patterns, Charles Fort insisted that we should wonder about the patterns we'd been given, and beware the blanks.

CHARLES FORT was a frustrated fiction writer who became obsessed with a new kind of story.

"Before the first manifestation of Dadaism and Surrealism," wrote Louis Pauwels and Jacques Bergier in their book *The Morning of the Magicians*, "Charles Fort introduced into science what Tzara, Breton and their disciples were to introduce into art and literature: a defiant refusal to play at a game where everybody cheats, a furious insistence that there is 'something else.'"

"Strip yourself of custom, habit, education, the conventionalized mental clothes of millions of years and presto! You are a candidate for wonders," according to Fort's friend the journalist and poet Benjamin De Casseres.

> *Here Fort, as everywhere in his marvelously beautiful and brain-stimulating books, puts on the seven-league boots of intuitive apprehension. He is a man done with clumsy apparatus of thought, the wires, the pulleys, the cranks and winches of reason and standardized experience. Poets and seers carry the patterns of infinity in their souls. Science tags along thousands of years behind.*

"Fortean," as an adjective, can apply to a general class of oddities, and Fort's name surfaces in discussions of the paranormal. But "fortean" usually suggests a cool, wry, open-minded analysis of these mysteries. Today the author is heralded as a godfather of supernatural writing, and even his staunchest critics admire him as a genius of a crank. He's inspired science fiction stories, served as an example to generations of later authors, and appeared as a character in a comic book.

But in writing the actual story of Charles Fort, I'm describing a confluence of specific oddities. Of course, the story includes his notoriously unsettling data, which he relentlessly pried from libraries in New York and London. But it also involves the social climate in which Fort wrote, the audience he was writing for (both his friends and his many unknown readers), and the particular character of Charles Fort. Coincidentally, all of these elements were able to combine—the right time and the right place—to produce four memorable and influential books.

Fort offered the final fillip.

> Or that there are no coincidences, in the sense that there are no real discords in either colors or musical notes. That any two colors, or sounds, can be harmonized by intermediately relating them to other colors or sounds.

In other words, we've simply been missing part of the pattern.

THROUGHOUT HIS CAREER, Fort assiduously avoided definitions and classifications, so I'm convinced he would have objected to the title "The Man Who Invented the Supernatural."

For example, he was uncomfortable with the notion of "invention" and wondered whether Watt really invented the steam engine or the Wright brothers invented the flying machine. In his book *New Lands,* Fort wrote, "One of the greatest of secrets that have eventually been found out was for ages blabbed by all the pots and kettles in the world—but that the secret of the steam engine could not reveal itself until came the time for its co-ordination with the other phenomena and the requirements of the Industrial Age."

Similarly, Fort argued with the word "supernatural." It was a word, he wrote in *Lo!,* "that has no place in my vocabulary. In my view, it has no meaning, or distinguishment. If there never has been, finally, a natural explanation of anything, everything is, naturally enough, the supernatural."

The generation before Fort, the Victorians, were in love with various aspects of the supernatural, including mind-reading, mesmerism, and spiritualism—and often gave these phenomena the patina of scientific study and analysis.

What Fort invented was our modern view of the paranormal. He worked as a pure agnostic; rather than building up his phenomena to the status of miracles, he tore down the hallowed traditions of religion and science. After Fort, it was no longer possible to discuss these subjects without debating the nature of reality. After Fort, the supernatural was no longer associated with religiosity, but was presented as a natural, if unexpected, part of our world: those nagging "believe it or not" facts suggesting that our belief system is at best misguided and at worst conspiratorial. As De Casseres wrote of Fort's accomplishments, "There is something tremendously real, annoyingly solid about Fort. His is the first attempt in the history of human thought to bring mysticism and trans-material phenomena down to (or maybe lift it up to) something concrete."

Readers are still arguing whether Fort pointed out the foibles in our thinking or exploited them. Just as he suggested that a particular moment had been steam-engine time, it's important to realize that his timeless supernatural mysteries were gathered and published at a precisely supernatural time in history. By the early 1920s, Americans were discovering that the world was a strange place.

Charles Fort could demonstrate that it was even stranger than anyone suspected. Frogs fell from the sky. Blood rained from the heavens. Mysterious airships visited the earth. Dogs talked. People disappeared. He asked why, but, even more vexing, he asked why we weren't paying attention.

Taking his cue from Fort, author Damon Knight speculated, "If there is a universal mind, must it be sane?" It wasn't the myriad of Fort's phenomena that stunned readers, but one underlying suggestion that human beings have always found to be hair-raising: The world is actually irrational.

— *Jim Steinmeyer*
Los Angeles, California
November 2007

Meek young men grow up in libraries, believing it is their duty to accept the views which Cicero, which Locke, which Bacon, have given—forgetful that Cicero, Locke and Bacon were only young men in libraries when they wrote these books.

—RALPH WALDO EMERSON

Some circumstantial evidence is very strong, as when you find a trout in the milk.

—HENRY DAVID THOREAU

But the Damned Will March

You can oppose an absurdity only with some other absurdity.

No one knew what to make of *The Book of the Damned*.

It appeared on the shelves of bookshops across America in January 1920. At Brentano's Bookstore on Fifth Avenue in Manhattan, the cardboard cartons containing *The Book of the Damned* had arrived from publishers Boni & Liveright during the Christmas rush. They were quickly pushed into the storeroom with other new titles, to make room for the illustrated children's picture books and popular romance novels that were displayed as ideal Christmas gifts. As the year 1920 began, as the tinsel garlands and glass ornaments were removed from the front window and packed away, the Brentano's clerks rearranged their displays, offering the latest books. In addition to *The Book of the Damned*, there was Blasco Ibañez's latest spy novel, *Mare Nostrum;* a collection of H. L. Mencken's acidic essays, *Prejudices; Theodore Roosevelt's Letters to His Children;* Siegfried Sassoon's poems about the Great War, *Picture-Show;* and *Memories of Buffalo Bill*, by the Wild West star's wife. The cartons were unstacked and sliced open, releasing the pungent odors of hide glue and printer's ink—the promising smell of new books.

Boni & Liveright was an upstart publishing house, but they had distinguished themselves several years earlier with a line of prestigious reprints under the title of the Modern Library—books by authors like Oscar Wilde, Robert Louis Stevenson, and Henrik Ibsen, each bound in imitation leather and economically priced at sixty cents. Unfortunately, the first Modern Library books were manufactured using cheap fish-oil glue, and on a warm sunny day the books fairly reeked. Publisher Horace Liveright quickly changed the formula for later editions, but the firm suffered years of jibes about their fishy odor.

Liveright's latest book had no such problems. The cover price was one dollar. It was a fat little volume covered in bright red fabric and adorned with neat gold stamping: the title, *The Book of the Damned*, the author's name, "Charles Fort," and a pretty little decoration of a planet spinning merrily amid a cluster of stars. On a flap of the dust jacket was an endorsement from novelist Theodore Dreiser— "It is wonderful"—and a promise of what was inside:

> *In this amazing book—the result of twelve years of patient research—the author presents a mass of evidence that has hitherto been ignored or distorted by scientists. . . . Things that [seem] incredible support the author's argument, which he develops with strong touches of sardonic humor and flashes of sheer poetic insight.*

Nothing else identified the contents as fantasy, religion, science, or philosophy. The attention-grabbing title presented an arresting mystery, and the modest paper wrapper made it all the more beguiling: simple block letters and swirling gray and pink shapes suggesting planets, surging lava, and a solar eclipse. Customers stopped, picked up the book, and turned it over in their hands. With side-long glances, they cracked the cover to peer inside. They wondered if the author was promising immorality or criminality, hedonism or atheism—in 1920, it was now possible to find any of those between the covers of a new book.

The Brentano's clerks were equally anxious about the contents and studied the response of the shoppers. Boni & Liveright was known for quality authors and interesting publications. But the clerks were disappointed to find that reactions to Charles Fort seemed to depend upon where the book fell open. Some customers smiled, as if discovering a joke, and then slid the book back onto the shelf. Others opened the pages to encounter a thicket of facts arranged in clumps of prose—scholarly citations with publication names, dates, and volume numbers. With a frown, those readers closed the cover and continued browsing. But many seemed quickly hypnotized by the contents, turning page after page as their jaws slackened and time seemed to stand still. Glassy-eyed, they paid the dollar, hurrying *The Damned* across a counter and into a bag, scurrying from the store with the package under their arms.

Examining the book carefully, readers found no helpful introduction to set the tone or explain the author. With chapter one, they were thrown headfirst into an unsettling polemic, Fort's tossed gauntlet that seemed to defy all of science.

> *A procession of the damned. By the damned, I mean the excluded.*
>
> *We shall have a procession of data that Science has excluded.*
>
> *Battalions of the accursed, captained by pallid data that I have exhumed, will march. You'll read them—or they'll march. Some of them livid and some of them fiery and some of them rotten.... There*

are things that are theorems and things that are rags; they'll go by like
Euclid arm in arm with the spirit of anarchy. . . . Many are clowns.
But many are of the highest respectability. . . . The ultra-respectable,
but the condemned, anyway. The aggregate appearance is of dignity
and dissoluteness; the aggregate voice is a defiant prayer; but the spirit
of the whole is processional. The power that has said to all these things
that they are damned, is Dogmatic Science.

But they'll march.

The author then launched into a mystifying twelve-page quarrel with traditional science. He explained that our knowledge of the world is dependent on drawing arbitrary boundaries around things that are of a continuous, boundary-less nature: as if defining red and yellow as distinct things, yet not accounting for orange-ness. He insisted that there is no such thing as a definition; there is nothing to define. He hinted that Newton's three laws were merely articles of faith and Darwinism was a bald tautology. He believed that all things were reaching for truth, beauty, and definiteness by seeking to be more real than other things.

At first this summing up may not be very readily acceptable. At
first it may seem that all these words are not synonyms. . . . By
"beauty" I mean that which seems complete. Obversely, that the in-
complete, or the mutilated, is the ugly.

Venus de Milo.

To a child she is ugly.

When a mind adjusts to thinking of her as completeness, even
though, by physiologic standards, incomplete, she is beautiful.

A hand thought of only as a hand, may seem beautiful.

Found on a battlefield—obviously a part—not beautiful.

The author labeled himself an "intermediatist," recognizing that there was no way of positing absolutes or coming to conclusions. According to his formula, established science was a sham, for science didn't actually concern itself with "prying into old bones, bugs, unsavory messes," but was seeking reality by actively excluding all the data that did not fit with its present organization.

> *The amazing paradox of it all: That all things are trying to become the universal by excluding other things. . . . In this book, I assemble some of the data that I think are of the falsely and arbitrarily excluded. The data of the damned. . . . They will march.*

Starting with chapter two, *The Book of the Damned* took a different perspective, as if viewing the world through the opposite end of a telescope. Hailstones have fallen as big as hen's eggs. Or two-pounders. Six-pounders. A lump of ice fell in India "the size of an elephant." Snowflakes the size of saucers, or even bigger. Fort gave the citations: from the *Monthly Weather Review, Report of the Smithsonian Institution,* or *Nature,* all within the last few decades.

Stones had fallen from the sky. Not meteors; stones. Pebbles, rocks, boulders. Rains of pollen. Yellow rains. Black rain and black snow. Red rain. Fort gave many examples of red rain, and admitted that scientists often explained it as dust from the Sahara. But there are also accounts of blood from the sky, "thick, viscous red matter."

A fall of fish from the sky in India, 1836. Flakes of beef from the sky in Kentucky, 1876.

As his chapters progressed, the facts piled up, each adorned with citations. "Manna" from the sky in 1829, a mysterious substance that was eaten by the sheep and could be ground into flour and made into bread. Spiderwebs descending and covering miles of the English countryside. But "there is no record of anyone, in England or elsewhere, having seen tons of spider webs going up." Salt, slag, cinders, coal. *Philosophical Magazine*'s account of fossils that had been found inside meteorites.

By chapter seven, Fort hit his stride: living frogs and toads falling from the skies.

> *See* Leisure Hours, *3-779, for accounts of small frogs, or toads, said to have been seen to fall from the sky. The writer says that all observers were mistaken: that the frogs or toads must have fallen from trees or other places overhead.*
>
> *Tremendous number of little toads, one or two months old, that were seen to fall from a great thick cloud that appeared suddenly in a sky that had been cloudless, August, 1804, near Toulouse, France according to a letter from Prof. Pontus to M. Arrago (*Comptes Rendus, *3–54).*
>
> *Many instances of frogs that were seen to fall from the sky.* (Notes and Queries, *8-6-104); accounts of such falls, signed by witnesses* (Notes and Queries, *8-6-190).*
>
> Scientific American, *July 12, 1873: "A shower of frogs which darkened the air and covered the ground for a long distance is the reported result of a recent rainstorm at Kansas City, Mo."*

Fort puzzled over his many accounts: He had never found a report of tadpoles falling, only grown frogs. "It is so easy to say that small frogs that have fallen from the sky have been scooped up by a whirlwind," he offered. But then again, "there is no regard for mud, debris from the bottom of pond, floating vegetation, loose things from the shore—but a precise picking out of frogs only. . . . Also, a pond going up would be quite as interesting as frogs coming down. It seems to me that anybody who had lost a pond would be heard from."

He followed with several pages of accounts of fish falling from the skies. Some fish were hard and dry; some small, some large. Sometimes the fish covered a large area and flopped atop rooftops, sometimes they all fell within a mysteriously small area on the ground.

The author paused to speculate. Perhaps there was an invisible "Super-Sargasso Sea" suspended somewhere overhead, "derelicts, rubbish, old cargoes from inter-planetary wrecks; things cast out into what is called space by convulsions of other planets. . . ." It was a sort of junkyard where gravity didn't apply, or worked in unexpected ways. And then, with a shrug, he changed his mind, refusing to offer any explanation.

> Or still simpler. Here are the data. Make what you will, yourself, of them. . . . We have expressions: we don't call them explanations. We've discarded explanations with beliefs.

Recounting falls of lizards, snakes, and eels, insects of various kinds, and worms, his data proceeded for pages and pages before the author changed his mind again.

> Genesistrine. The notion that there is somewhere aloft a place of origin of life relatively to this earth. I should say, myself, that Genesistrine is a region in the Super-Sargasso Sea, and that parts of the Super-Sargasso Sea have rhythms of susceptibility to the earth's attraction.

Fort dithered over several subjects as the chapters progressed. Comets seem to defy predictions. Meteors are stranger than we suspect, and often tied to terrestrial phenomena. Mysterious lights or airships were often seen in the sky, long before any sort of airship had been invented. A scientist had explained a fall of dried leaves on a village in France—the leaves went up in a storm several days earlier. But Fort was mystified that dried leaves could remain suspended in the air for days or weeks, and then return to the earth together, in one spot. "In November, 1918, I made some studies upon light objects thrown into the air. Armistice Day," he dryly remarked. "I made notes upon torn up papers thrown high into the air from windows of office buildings." Recounting the falls of blocks of ice from the skies—the size of bricks, the size of boulders, or even larger—he offered an opinion. "That large blocks of ice could form in the moisture of this earth's atmosphere is about as likely as that blocks of stone could form in a dust whirl." Returning to accounts of blood dripping from the sky, he suddenly had another inspiration.

> . . . *that our whole solar system is a living thing: that showers of blood upon this earth are its internal hemorrhages.—Or vast living things in the sky, as there are vast living things in the oceans.—Or some one especial thing: an especial time: an especial place. A thing the size of the Brooklyn Bridge. It's alive in outer space. Something the size of Central Park kills it.*
>
> *It drips.*

What was the reader to make of these perspectives? The author wrote in sentence fragments, as if trying to jam in as many notes, dates, and phenomena as possible. At times he chose to jolly the reader through the dense material. "A whopper is coming. Later it will be as reasonable, by familiarity, as anything else ever said," or, "Short chapter coming now, and it's the worst of them all. I think it must mean that the preceding chapter was very efficiently done. . . ." Or, sneering at scientific categories, he offered an example:

> *An elephant can be identified as a sunflower—both have long stems. A camel is indistinguishable from a peanut—if only their humps be considered. Double inclusion: or it's a method of agreement that logicians make so much of. So no logician would be satisfied with identifying a peanut as a camel, because both have humps: he demands accessory agreement—that both can live a long time without water, for instance.*

Sometimes his weird suggestions—monsters or floating islands, from a kind of medieval cosmology—were constructed to accommodate the latest paragraph of data. He seemed to be making it up as he went along. Or, even worse, he was deliberately tugging his audience in the wrong direction. For example, after wondering why mysterious aircraft were visiting the earth and monitoring us, the author suggested:

> *I think we're property. I should say we belong to something. . . . That something owns this earth—all others are warned off. . . . Pig, geese, cattle. First find out they are owned. Then find out the whyness of it.*

At other times he lapsed into first-person plural that sounded deliberately overblown:

> *We have a datum and we give it an interpretation in accordance with our pseudo-standard. At present we have not the delusions of Absolutism that may have translated some of the positivists of the*

nineteenth century to heaven. . . . We do not insist that our data and interpretations shall be . . . shocking, grotesque, evil, ridiculous, childish, insincere. . . . We ask only whether data and interpretations correlate.

At the end of *The Book of the Damned,* the chapters grew shorter, the pace of the data quickened, and Fort indulged in fewer speculations. It was as if the footfalls of his excluded facts overwhelmed even the author, drowning out his voice. Or perhaps the author no longer felt a need to organize and lead the parade; he was content to stand on the curb with his awestruck readers, indifferent, paring his fingernails.

The final chapter, twenty-eight, was a detached report of an eerie mystery discovered by the residents of Devonshire—"all of south Devonshire." They awoke on the morning of February 8, 1855, to find mysterious hoofprints pressed into the freshly fallen snow throughout the villages and for miles into the countryside. "That they were hoof-like marks, but had been made by a biped . . . generally eight inches in advance of each other." The tracks were found in many unaccountable places, in gardens enclosed by high walls, and up on the tops of houses as well as in wide-open fields. Fort quoted contemporary accounts in *Notes and Queries,* the *Times* of London, and the *Illustrated London News.*

TODAY WE REMEMBER the 1920s as the decade that roared: F. Scott Fitzgerald's libertines, mobsters, and flappers, all accompanied by an exciting new jazz beat and washed in bathtub gin. But the daring notions of the twenties were rareties. The decade actually began with whimpers, not roars, with staunch conservatism and a frightening, pull-the-covers-over-your-head cynicism about the way the world was working.

Terrorists delivered bombs in packages on the streets of Washington, anarchists planted explosives on Wall Street, and civil liberties were tightened around thousands of citizens suspected of Communist sympathies. America banned alcohol and cynically withdrew from world politics. Fundamentalists debated the theory of evolution in court. Every day, newspapers were filled with reports on political machinations, psychic phenomena, or scientific discoveries that seemed to portray the world as a strange and dangerous place. More than any other book, more than *The Great Gatsby* or *The Waste Land*, it was Charles Fort's *Book of the Damned* that whispered to its readers, "Welcome to the 1920s."

THE *NEW YORK TIMES* despised it: "[Any] conclusion . . . is so obscured in the mass of words and quagmire of pseudo-science and queer speculation that the average reader will find himself either buried alive or insane before he reaches the end."

Ben Hecht, reviewing it for the *Chicago Daily News*, loved it with the same analogy: "For every five people who read Charles Fort, four will go insane. Charles Fort has delighted me beyond all men who have written books in this world."

Life magazine wrote, "Hamlet, visited with Ophelia's madness, might find this effort wholly satisfying."

H. G. Wells was nonplussed by author of *The Book of the Damned:* "Fort seems to be one of the most damnable bores who ever cut scraps from out-of-the-way newspapers."

H. L. Mencken thought Fort must have been a particular kind of fool: "He seems to be enormously ignorant of elementary science."

But Theodore Dreiser respectfully disagreed: "Fort is not enormously ignorant of anything. . . . To me no one in the world has suggested the underlying depths and mysteries and possibilities as has Fort. To me he is simply stupendous."

THE BOOK WAS certainly schizophrenic. Early reviews commented on the wild polemic in the first chapters as if that were the author's purpose. But for readers, it was the later chapters—the chilling accounts of unexplained chaos and Fort's damned facts—that were so memorable. There's no question that Fort had written a new kind of ghost story for the smug, modern readers of the 1920s—in which it is the cold, hard data that haunts.

As the first great book of oddities, the first attempt to collect, systematize, and marshal these ragged annoyances, *The Book of the Damned* became the gospel to later writers on the paranormal. It became a model for an entire branch of literature, and an inspiration to a burgeoning field that became known as science fiction. Over the next dozen years, Fort followed with three additional books. His accounts of mysterious airships formed the canon when, decades later, this phenomenon became a public obsession as Flying Saucers or UFOs. Charles Fort created the word "teleportation," inspired the term "Bermuda Triangle," and popularized accounts of spontaneous human combustion, visions of cities in the sky, the *Mary Celeste* mystery, or Kaspar Hauser.

But if *The Book of the Damned* was never intended as gospel in a religious way, it certainly proved to be so in a literal way—"good news" about the world for its strangely pessimistic and private author. And, like any true gospel, it attracted disciples who were happy to assign holiness as they massaged and misinterpreted the original message.

After all, the text invited plenty of speculation. Fort had a distinct and ambiguous way of storytelling. For nearly three hundred pages his voice nagged at his audience: his whispers of advice over the shoulder of the reader, his relentless, staccato presentation of the data, and the peculiar way he seemed to keep readjusting his cosmology, while always insisting that none of it mattered. Was he really serious? Could the whole thing be a joke? He wrote with all the fidgety syntax of a tenured college professor, all the literary swagger of an established crank. Various readers and reviewers—even those who loved the book—seemed unsure whether they'd stumbled across the work of an unheralded genius or an undiagnosed madman. Most pulled their punches by offering praise for the book but confusion when writing about the author.

Ben Hecht: "Mountebank or Messiah, it matters not. . . . If it has pleased Charles Fort to perpetuate a Gargantuan jest upon unsuspecting readers, all the better. If he has in all seriousness heralded forth the innermost truths of his soul, well and good."

The *New York Tribune:* "No imaginative fiction writer could conjure up stranger visions than Mr. Fort creates in his collection of mysterious happenings . . . calculated to confuse any Horatio and his philosophy."

Booth Tarkington: "People must turn to look at [Fort's] head as he walks down the street; I think it's a head that would emit noises and explosions, with copper flames playing out from the ears."

Both Hecht and Tarkington asked the question plaguing all the readers who had closed the back cover of *The Book of the Damned*. They were struck with one profound, rattling mystery that seemed to be marching louder than any other, one annoying obsession that had elbowed its way to the front.

"Who in blazes is Charles Fort?"

Toddy's Nose Bleeds
So Readily

May 15, 1890, at Messignaldi, Calabri, the fall of blood from the sky—But later, in the same place, blood again fell from the sky.

He could recall the disillusion distinctly. "The boy next door told us that there is no Santa Claus; he had pretended to sleep and had seen his father arrange gifts around him," Charles Hoy Fort wrote of his boyhood in Albany, New York. Charles was the oldest son of a successful Albany family, born to inherit his father's place in a wholesale grocery. He was a chubby, thoughtful Victorian boy who was alternately spoiled lavishly or punished mercilessly. He was more curious than most, more troubled by self-doubt and, it seems, more mystified by the world around him and his place in its hierarchy.

We had never thought to doubt Santa Claus before, but had a feeling that, doubt as we might, the boy was right. Then torments like religious unrest. Kind, jolly old Santa Claus coming down chimneys was too beautiful to give up. But no one could possibly come down our chimney. Then the reindeers, Prancer, Dancer and the rest, skim-

ming from roof to roof. We could not give it up; it was too beautiful.
But we had to; reindeers cannot skim from roof to roof. Oh, don't
take from us any more of our beliefs! Perhaps heaven and the angels,
too, were only myths.

He was nicknamed Toddy in his youth to distinguish him from
his father, Charles Nelson, who was the second generation of Fort
grocers. The family name actually should have been Liberte. Back
in 1683, it was Jan Liberte, a Dutch settler, who acquired land on
the shore of the Mohawk River north of Albany, New York—near
the town of Latham. It was a modest fort at nearby Canastigione—
a tiny construction of logs and sod that offered occasional protec-
tion against the French or Indians—that gave the family its new
name. Jan Liberte became known as Jan La Fort, Jan Van Fort, or
John Fort.

One of John's sons, Nicholas, established a rope ferry across the
river at a spot that became known as Fort's Ferry. The cluster of
homes there became a well-known hamlet, and the family continued
to operate the ferry into the twentieth century, when the river was
dammed for the Barge Canal and the area was flooded.

Five generations later, Peter Van Vranken Fort was born at Fort's
Ferry in 1821—the Van Vrankens were another well-established
Albany family. But rather than remain a ferryman, Peter moved to
the city. Peter Fort had little imagination or learning, but was a
successful entrepreneur. He worked in Herkimer, New York, owned
and managed the Fulton Hotel in New York City, then established
his own wholesale fruit and grocery store in Albany. A collection
of stern granite buildings topped by formal mansard roofs, Albany
was proud of its reserved Dutch heritage. By the mid-1800s, it
hummed with pragmatic business and corrupt politics—the stuffy

little state capital that, they told themselves, controlled America's great metropolis.

Peter V. Fort's library at home was filled with pretty, bright leather-bound copies of Ruskin and Carlyle; he loved books but puzzled over these volumes, as they were intended for show. At his food warehouse on Eagle Street in Albany, he kept two offices. One was a businesslike office for clients; in addition to the grocery, Peter owned various properties and loaned money usuriously. Upstairs was a crowded private office, the walls filled with romantic little paintings, the shelves jammed with demijohns and the well-worn books he enjoyed rereading—biographies, histories, a thick dictionary, and dozens of books on travel, including accounts of Arctic explorations. Here Peter spent the afternoons laughing and smoking with his good friends, sampling his own inventive concoctions of alcohol and fruit juice.

His first child, Charles Nelson Fort, was born in Albany in 1849 and followed his father into the grocery business—P. V. Fort and Son. Charles Nelson was a small, vain man with a crisp waxed moustache and a natty wardrobe, in the style of the Victorian era. In the early 1870s, he married Agnes Hoy, the dark-haired daughter of a successful Albany hardware merchant. On August 6, 1874, at four in the morning, their first son, Charles Hoy Fort, was born.

Two years later, on November 7, 1876, a second son, Raymond Nielson, was born. Again, two years after that, on November 11, 1878, Agnes gave birth to a third son, Clarence VanVranken. But the bright, healthy young family suffered a tragedy just after Clarence's birth. The Fort relatives recalled that Charles and Agnes were invited to the Governor's mansion for a holiday ball. Agnes's friends feared that the glittering social event, a tempting evening out, would be too strenuous for the young mother, who was still recovering from the strain of Clarence's birth. In fact, she contracted an infection that quickly developed into pericarditis, an inflammation around the heart; she died on January 2, 1879. Agnes Fort was only twenty-five years old.

Charles Nelson Fort moved his sons—aged four, two, and two months—to a house at 53 Philip Street in Albany. The widower could afford servants to tend to the cooking and cleaning, and a housekeeper for the children. The housekeeper was a middle-aged lady named Elizabeth Wassen who loved and pampered the Fort boys. But if their businesslike father expected that the loss of their mother would instill a new sense of maturity—that Charles, Raymond, and Clarence would grow up quickly—he was disappointed. The three boys took their time with their childhood, became absolutely devoted to one another, and suspicious of their father's stern discipline.

> [Some] thought that the Law School was built for a large number of serious looking young men, who left with still more serious looking books under their arms and then went over to the Cottage. But it wasn't. It was built with steps for us to play on and stone blocks for us to jump from. All along were houses built with windows, not to look from, but for us to climb to. Gates for us to swing on, hydrants for us to leap over, fences and stoops for us to hide behind. Why things were could be of no interest to us. For we know: everything was for us.

The house on Philip Street had a nursery on the top floor, which had been fitted with swings and a seesaw for the brothers. But they naturally preferred walks through the park, races through the neighborhood, treasure hunts, fights, or the adventurous chores for which Mrs. Wassen recruited the boys.

Coming home from school in an autumn afternoon. Piles of flowerpots and window gardens scattered around. Mrs. [Wassen] calling for us to help for all we were worth; for Jack Frost was coming. Digging and transplanting for all we were worth, helping to get our friends into the house before Jack Frost could catch them. Speaking to the geraniums, telling them to have no fear, for we were taking them to a place where they'd be safe all [Winter]. Of course they could not understand us, you know; but at the same time, they could understand us. Then great excitement! Jack Frost was only a mile away. All four of us working desperately, getting all the plants in, just as Jack Frost peeked around the church steeple.

Toddy's perceptions of his childhood—that is, Charles Fort's memories—were recorded a dozen years later, when the author was in his twenties, in an unpublished manuscript titled *Many Parts*. Only fragments of *Many Parts* have survived, written with an odd, childish literary swagger. Fort wrote in first-person plural. Throughout, Charles was "We." Raymond was "the Other Kid." Clarence was "the Little Kid." Mrs. Wassen was called Mrs. Larson. And his father was always referred to as "They."

At the dinner table, we were not allowed to speak. They could not bear to hear our voices. Once, feeling the restraint, we giggled nervously. They looked over the newspaper, saying, "Who's that?" The Little Kid started to tell. He kept quiet. The Other Kid answered that he had heard nothing. We said, "I did it." Mrs. Larson would have told anyway; we wanted credit for truthfulness.

"Go upstairs!" We rising slowly, eating pie as we rose. We going up inch by inch, pie going down inch by inch. Couldn't bear to leave that pie. And this was defiance to them. Jumping from their chair, catching us by the collar, hitting us in the face with their open hand.

Fort believed that his father struck "in passionate outbursts," and the punishments described are brutal.

> *In Mrs. Lawson's room one day. She was teaching us our Sunday school lesson; it was about Moses and the rock. They strolled in, brushing their hat, looking into the mirror to see that the necktie was all right, very particular with every detail of their appearance. Then Moses smote the rock. But they flurried us; we could not pronounce, "smote." An easy word, but we said, "smut." Told to read it over; again we said "smut." More flurried; unable to use our brain; saying "smut" still again, because our lips formed that way and we had no brain. To them, we were showing dogged meanness. They struck us in the face.*
>
> *"That's smote," They said. "Now do you understand what smote is? Say smote."*
>
> *We whimpering, "Yes, sir; smote." Our brain had cleared; perhaps something had flashed into it to make it work. Probably not; it was right to beat us when we were bad.*

Not surprisingly, Charles, Raymond, and Clarence were never comforted by their father's authority, and offered no respect in return. In their imaginations, they wished they could.

> *. . . beat him into insensibility; no, we'd have the little kid of a big, noble-looking man do the beating, for three against one would not be fair. Anyway, all our dreams seemed to end in violence in some form.*

Similarly, Toddy had quickly reasoned away religious or scientific authority. "When a small boy, we puzzled over inconsistencies in the Bible, and asked questions that could not be answered satisfactorily," he later wrote, "sometimes puzzling right through a game of baseball." Although he said his prayers and made his confessions to Mrs. Wassen to clear his conscience, Toddy was too analytical, too tormented to make a commitment of his beliefs.

We almost liked Sunday school, especially as there were some very good books in the library. Religion as an emotion was strong in us, though, quite as strong, was a resisting of this emotion. Sometimes, all that wanted to be Christian were called upon to raise their hands. A throbbing and an urging would almost overcome us with a seeing of beauty in what were called upon to be. But our hand would never go up, as if a feeling of sternness withheld us from what seemed an indecent advertising of feeling.

In school, his science teachers seemed to offer simple explanations for the world. But Toddy learned to doubt their answers as well.

There did seem to be something wrong with about every experiment. Professor demonstrating that in a vacuum a bullet and a feather fall at equal speed. The bullet falling first. Teaching us that black is the absence of color and white is all colors. Mixing colors. Producing a brownish grey. Putting a black cloth and a white cloth out in the sun on window sill snow. As black absorbs heat, the black cloth should sink in the snow. White cloth making a decided impression; black cloth not a trace that it had been there. Very hard to teach truths when truth won't come out right.

THE FORTS MOVED AGAIN, to a fashionable, five-story brick home at 253 State Street, just a block from the new State Capitol building. In 1886, the widowed Charles Nelson Fort announced that he would be marrying Blanche Whitney, from a prominent Albany family: her father was the secretary of the gas company. Toddy and his brothers were indulged as Blanche attempted to win their affections.

> *"You collect stamps?" our new mother asked. "If you'll tell me where to get them, we'll go now." And all together we cried where an old collector of stamps lived. And to the old collector we went, trying not to be too greedy, making our new mother's admission fee into the family as reasonable as we could. And then walking back with her, thinking it would be very bad manners to leave her in the street, though we very much wanted to get back to the album with our new stamps. And on our way back, the first thing we said was, "She's all right!" Denouncing all that had lied about her. And we'd defend her; and we'd do everything chivalrous. We all excited. Just what wouldn't we do?*

Their new mother was only accepted into the boys' world as long as they greedily accepted her gifts. Young Charles was an inveterate collector. He treasured his stamps for the romantic lands they represented: "for a few cents, something from Africa; little square bits of Japan; trifles that seemed a part of Peru." When the brothers were forced to work at the family store on Sundays, Raymond and Charles ordered stamps from various dealers, hiding in the office and mailing off orders by using the company stationery. "They would wonder where all the envelopes were going . . . we had the wisdom and self-control that a true criminal has not; so we were never caught."

"Paper soldiers had marched into our lives," Fort recalled. He and Raymond hoarded battalions of paper soldiers, investing the heroes with awards for bravery in their pretend battles, or humiliating the losers. Charles collected birds' eggs, feathers, and nests, finally learning taxidermy to mount his own specimens of birds, and then formally labeling them and cataloging his collection. When he was given an air gun, he scoured Albany for still more samples: robins, crows, or sparrows. "When that air gun was in our hands we had no civilized instincts and our mind could hold nothing but intent to kill." He later added a collection of minerals, first by digging stones from the streets around Albany, then by buying or trading rock samples. He fussed over each entry and guarded them jealously. It made him sick to have to trade any sample with a schoolmate.

Young Charles dreamt of achieving great things, "something that seemed wondrous and better and meant for us." Mostly, he was anxious to be grown up, with all the vague dreams and specific obsessions that entailed. No more rations of goose grease or oatmeal . . .

> But some day we'd be a man; looking forward to that far-distant, twenty-first birthday. Then we could have all the chili sauce that we should want. We had some sort of an idea of a chili sauce spree. Celebrating with our friends; opening bottle after bottle. Awful debauchery; more bottles. On our twenty-first birthday, there would be little heard but the popping of chili sauce bottles.

When his grandfather asked Charles what he wanted to be when he grew up, the boy knew to avoid the question. But on one occasion, when Peter V. Fort asked, "Fell, haff you decided yet?" obviously, the correct answer would have been "A wholesale grocer." But

Fort abruptly answered, "A naturalist." Peter Fort furrowed his brow and disappeared into his study to consult the dictionary. After reading what a naturalist was,

> *Our grandfather looked pained, for our dreams startled him. He had his own dreams. Which were of a great grocery house founded by him, going down the generations, his eldest grandson some day the head of the family and important among things in barrels, things in bottles, and things in cans.*

THE BOYS' TIME in the store should have been their introduction to business, but the Saturday afternoons spent working in the storeroom inevitably felt like punishment. Charles and Raymond were told to scrape old labels off cans and replace them with Fort and Son labels. They went about the work, "rebelling and grumbling and shirking," until Toddy gave up and sat in a corner. Raymond, always more pragmatic, soldiered on sullenly for a time.

> *Then both of us lazy. Sliding down the elevator cables, exploring from loft to loft. Exploring through canyons of boxes piled high. Breaking into cases, taking out cans. Eating a few cherries, then having a light lunch of peaches; trying a little asparagus, going on to apricots. Hammering cans flat so that we could take them out in our pockets. Then lazy and not bothering; just throwing cans out on the roof. Throwing a plum pudding can with too much force. It rolled. It would fall in the street right by the side door. We ran back to our scraping, but the elevator cables were moving. Scraping furiously, but*

hoping anyway. Cables glimmering up, and then the rust spot that
meant that the elevator was a floor away. Tall hat appearing. Their
face, chest, arms . . . still, we hoped.

Free access to the Fort canned goods suggested a plan to run away from home. Biff Allen, a schoolyard friend who had been tormented by his mother, organized the scheme. He had heard that boys could get a job as elephant drivers in Upper Burma for eighteen dollars a week. Charles and Raymond, disgusted with their father and besotted by images of elephants, natives, and turbans, quickly agreed. They sold their stamp collection to raise money for the trip and made surreptitious raids on the Eagle Street store, collecting canned provisions that were hidden in Biff's garret—"more groceries than we could possibly have carried."

Clarence, the "Little Kid," heard the details of the plan, but realized that he'd be left behind. "We told him that he was a good Little Kid, and we should always remember him when away off in foreign climes. 'Foreign climes' too much for him; making awful faces, trying not to cry." To his credit, he never told on his big brothers. The plotters arranged to leave at four o'clock one morning. As Charles and Raymond tiptoed out of their room, they went into Clarence's room to see him once more.

Fast asleep, but all his clothes were on, and he hugged a bundle
under one arm. We wavered at this; but India is no place for small
boys. So, we kissed him goodbye; and the Other Kid kissed him good-
bye. We wanted to have some kind of a ceremony over the little,
sleeping kid. Wanting to pray that he should be happy and should be
the good businessman that we could never be. But the Other Kid said,
"Come on."

Creeping down the stairs, passing Their hat on the rack in the grey hall. Wanting to be mournful and sentimental over the hat, going away forgiving everyone for everything. But the Other Kid said, "Come on."

Lingering in the street to take a last look at our home. And the Other Kid said, "Come on."

Biff didn't show up. The next morning he wove an elaborate excuse, and the plot to run away dissolved. Raymond explained that Biff had probably organized it all to gather winter provisions for the family, who were on a small income. Charles refused to believe such scheming.

But pickles on the table whenever we went through Biff's dining room. Playing in the yard, and embarrassed by stumbling over lobster cans. Soup cans everywhere, we pretending not to see.

THE BROTHERS played recklessly and invited trouble. Charles's poor eyesight meant that he became a "spectacle-wearing boy," and he feared that he would seem weak and ineffective to the other boys. But he was tall and husky with powerful fists, unafraid of a battle on the playground or an adventure in the streets. Later, the author marveled at his boyhood adventures.

[We] three found an old revolver of large caliber; snapping the rusty old revolver at one another. Just happening to aim at something else when it went off; nothing left of the something else. Slipping on roofs, but catching a projection just before going over. Beams and

stones falling in [a derelict building] just where we had been a second before. Run over more than once, we lying quiet between wheels or runners. Breaking through the ice, someone throwing a skate strap to us. Here we are still. That in all this world there should be more than two or three grown men seems remarkable.

Fort carried scars on his forehead, from these childhood injuries, for the rest of his life. During another prank, an inevitable misadventure, Charles accidentally burned a fence in the back garden. His father wanted him to answer for his crimes, but by now Charles had become completely numb to his punishments.

"Why do you do these bad things?"

"Just for fun." Our stiff body was there; we were somewhere else, or had ceased to exist.

"Now tell me; try to think and don't be afraid; why do you do these bad things?"

Our lips formed, "Just for fun." They struck us savagely; blood gushed from our nose. Then we were there.

Said Mrs. Larson, "Toddy's nose bleeds so readily."

They went away; but we were there. A wild, mad we. Running up the stairs, blood all over. Running into the spare room, throwing ourself upon the bed, rubbing our nose all over the counterpane. A dirty, groveling, little beast, crazed to get even and doing damage was the only way to get even. Rubbing our nose on the lace curtains, making the room a horror room. Gurgling hysterically and then just sodden, not caring what should be done with us. In fact, wishing they would kill us, for suicide had been in our mind from the earliest days. Trying a sharp rap on our nose to renew the supply, for the truth is that nosebleeding was an ailment of ours.

Throughout childhood, when Toddy's world seemed unpredictably harsh or wildly beyond his control, he was capable of matching the absurdity.

They went out and, when the other kids came up, we were leaning over the banister, letting blood drip into the lower hall to do damage. We knew it was dirty work; had as much sense of decency as a grown person. Only, just then we were a little beast.

Littleness That Was No Longer There

The fate of all explanation is to close one door only to have another fly wide open.

Fort found school difficult. He studied French and German. He loved history—but only of certain romantic eras—enjoyed geography, and was proud of his compositions, which he filled with two-dollar words. But he had no sense of mathematics and often his grades were dire. The intense society of the classroom made him uneasy. As he grew up, he found himself tongue-tied around the girls his own age, helplessly anxious to impress and appear worldly. Invariably he stumbled through these conversations and then second-guessed each encounter. It was much easier to speak with older girls or his female teachers—who volunteered their friendship to the shy, clever boy without the confusing game of having to woo them.

When he was thirteen, Charles met a young lady named Anna Filing. She was four years his senior. Her parents, John and Catherine Filing, were from Ireland, and Anna was born in Sheffield, England; the Filings had immigrated to New York when she was nine years old. Anna came to Albany to live with relatives, and, for a short period of time, she may have worked as a cook in the home of Charles's grandfather, John Hoy. Anna was fascinated with Charles's romantic and imaginative interest in faraway places. They became good friends.

Charles wanted a grown-up suit of clothes like the other boys at school had, a real suit with long pants. A group of boys at school had suits of nubby black cheviot wool—"the black cheviot caste," Fort described them—and he longed to be part of this group of schoolyard sophisticates. Charles and Blanche Fort spent richly on parties and their evenings out on the town; his father dressed in expensive clothes and hosted parties of Progressive Euchre, inviting Albany's elite. "We knew They were prosperous. But one of the [employees] in the store had a son dressed better than we and the Other Kid."

Instead, his parents decided to buy Charles a cheap brown suit with faint yellow stripes. "The menagerie that was we then included a zebra." It didn't fit properly, with Charles's chubby legs stretching the seams, and the brown dye rubbing off onto his hands. Within a few weeks, he had pushed through the seat of his trousers and found himself walking sideways in the classroom, keeping his back toward the blackboard. "No one mending us."

Up in our room, looking at thread and needle, but feeling it beneath us to do any sewing. Progressive Euchre downstairs; costly prizes; everything always done on a scale that was costly. We upstairs, trying to sew rags together. And succeeding very well, we thought. Sitting down. Swish! Worn out cheapness could not keep those big, fat legs in. So we pounded a chair, just as, when a little boy, we pounded chairs.

•   •   •

BUT THERE WERE ALSO advantages to his size. "Though They continued to beat the others, They struck us no more after the time We had forced them almost to the floor." So the punishment changed, incredibly, to imprisonment.

> No longer beating us, but locking us in a little dark room, giving us bread and water, sentencing us to several days or several weeks in solitude. Three times a day the door would be opened, and bread and water would be thrust into darkness.

The brothers instinctively looked after one another.

> Three times a day a bundle would come down the airshaft. At the table, the other kids would sit with handkerchiefs on their knees, slipping in things when no one was looking. So well did we take care of one another that when two were serving terms, the free one would be the starved one.
>
> Books coming down the airshaft, and matches to light the gas with. We in prison and They turning the gas fixture so that we should be in darkness. A monkey wrench coming down the airshaft. Then singing to make the time hasten. Melancholy songs, we the unfortunate little boy. Then singing patriotic songs, half defiantly because of the noise we were making. About "Let freedom ring." Adding, "Freedom don't ring here." Hearing our new mother, under the airshaft, laugh at this. Then we, too would laugh, for we could never be mean when others were not.

• • •

RAYMOND, THE MIDDLE BROTHER, was cloddishly well be-
haved and incurious about most things. There was no doubt that he
had inherited a skill for business and would join his father at P. V.
Fort and Son. He monopolized trading games with Charles and
always seemed to gain the upper hand.

Clarence, the Little Kid, idolized his siblings and was jealous of
their attention. He didn't develop his own interests; he greedily tried
to share theirs. He developed a twitch in his eye, which seemed
exacerbated by his punishment. But like many mistreated children,
he aped his father, exhibiting an icy cruelty that surprised his brothers and terrified his parents.

> *The Little Kid was punished oftenest of all. He'd do outrageous
> things, without much interest in what he was doing. Mrs. Lawson
> would make him stay in the yard to play. Sitting at the window,
> sewing, looking out at him. The Little Kid would want to do some-
> thing wrong. He'd do something a little wrong, such as stepping
> among the plants to find out whether he was watched, knowing by the
> tapping of the thimble on the glass. No tapping. Mrs. Lawson having
> a caller. Little Kid luring the very little kid next door to the fence.
> Reaching under, starting to pull his neighbor through a space about
> big enough for cats. Very little kid screaming; Little Kid pulling
> away on a very little leg. Parents crying to him; Little Kid pull-
> ing away without excitement; very little kid coming through with a
> jerk, most of his clothes scraped off.*

In 1888, when Clarence was ten, his father informed him that
he had reached the limit of his patience and was sending him to

Burnham Industrial Farm in Canaan, New York. Burnham Farm, founded by Fredrick Burnham and his wife, Catherine, in 1886, was a refuge for "wayward" boys that emphasized work and discipline to make them fit for society. Later it became famous as the Berkshire Industrial Farm. Charles Fort recalled their farewell.

> *"We are indeed three brothers. . . ." It was too much for the Little Kid. He leaned up against a fence post, and put up his arm. He didn't want us to see him cry. And it was too much for us, for we were looking at the Little Kid, with his little arm up.*
>
> *Our same old madness; some of it because we were seized upon, some of it to impress the others. Crying that we should kill Them. Butting our head against a post. Butting and falling in frenzy, trying to kill ourself or whatever the post meant to us. The Other Kid looked on, disapproving; the little kid stood erect, not a sign of anything at all on his space.*
>
> *They took the Little Kid away.*

Early in Burnham Farm's history, ten-year-old boys were the youngest accepted, suggesting that Charles Nelson Fort may have been planning his son's confinement: Clarence's birthday, not a particular offense, was the final reason he was sent from home. The incident rattled Charles.

> *Evening. Going into the dining room. We had been crying all afternoon, and felt that if there were the slightest reference to the Little Kid we should break down. And we and the Other Kid paused in the doorway. For we saw something. What the Other Kid saw was a smaller table; a leaf had been taken out. This was sensible to the Other Kid; the table had been too large anyway. He went to his chair to eat his supper, which is what he had gone down to do.*

*What we saw was the meaning of a vacant chair in the leaf that
had been taken from the table. Littleness there brought to us littleness
that was no longer there. We could not move and we could not speak.
Just standing there, the Other Kid looking at us as if wondering what
new flightiness could be the matter with us.*

They looked from the newspaper; we had feared that look once.

We said, "Oh!" just softly, because we were choked and quivering.

CHARLES'S COLLECTION was still lovingly spread across the
shelves and tabletop in his room—minerals, stuffed birds, eggs, and
little bottles of formaldehyde with the organs of various small
animals, all labeled with printed paper slips. But he had lost interest.
He was outgrowing it, and the sensation confused him. "Something
was slipping from our life; it distressed us." When bottles were
knocked aside by a football—the sort of accident that would have
reduced him to tears—he was surprised to find that he didn't care.
When the collection was covered with dust, he vowed to spend a
day cleaning, but never did. He forced himself to go hunting, to
assemble a new catalog, to have new labels printed, but found it all
dreary work. He tried to collect autographs instead, sending away
to Amiens, France, for an autograph from Jules Verne. Verne responded with a letter of precise handwriting in French and a neat,
tight signature.

Gradually Fort realized that it was his own writing that intrigued
him. "There were luring and wonderfulness in this feeling of creative instinct; seemed god-like to take a pencil and then let things
happen." He kept a diary, thinking that he would fill it with pro-
fundities, but was disappointed when he could only manage to describe the most prosaic incidents.

There was a temporary truce offered by his father. Charles was naturally suspicious.

We and the Other Kid were pretty poor property, something like waste property that, if cultivated, might after a while pay its own taxes. They arranged to take our new mother and their really valuable property—the commanding appearance—to a fashionable resort. And then arranged for us, having us join the Y.M.C.A. to send us for a month to the camp on Lake Champlain.

Charles was almost fifteen years old. Realizing that he'd have a real adventure that summer, Charles befriended his father, visiting his room to play chess, talking about fishing and hunting, "everything forgotten and forgiven at last."

Charles and Raymond shared a glorious summer with twenty other boys, hiking, canoeing, and camping under the stars. "Everything we had longed for. . . . We'd think of the little girl in the next block. If she could only see us, we were sure she would be quite stupefied with admiration, for we had walked where Indians had walked, we were on familiar terms with a real guide, and we had seen bear marks on a tree." It was a revelation to a city boy. Charles was struck with the godlike vistas of the green fields, hills, and the river, the graceful camaraderie of the older boys around the campfire, and the mysterious, beautiful sound of their voices in harmony, which was new to him: "Not singing straight alone, all the same way, but one going down and one going up."

Wonderful things for us to write about in our diary, we breathing picturesqueness, trying to impart some of the picturesqueness. . . . These are the things that made us go away somewhere to write in our diary. Urged to write of darkness and light left behind. Having an

*impression of the way singing made us feel. Writing of pouring mo-
lasses into Crayley's shoes.*

HIS SCHOOLWORK was still uneven, but Charles had joined the
literary society. His interest in writing fascinated his uncle, John
Hoy, who always asked to see what Charles had been writing. John
was Agnes Hoy's younger brother; he was about a decade older than
Charles and treated him as a younger brother. Charles, in turn, was
honest with John: "We had always told the truth about our worthless self when he had asked us." John realized that the boy, just
sixteen years old, was pessimistic about taking his final high school
examinations. He asked him, "How would you like the newspaper
business?" Charles answered, "Oh, all right," later explaining in his
memoirs, "By which we meant that nothing could be more attrac-
tive to us."

John Hoy was a boyhood friend of the editor of the Albany
Argus, and put in a good word for his nephew. "Go around to
the *Argus,*" he told him. "There won't be much of anything in it for
you at first, but it will give you an idea, and some day we may get
you down to New York. Just keep your rubbers on, and you'll not
slip up."

One of his first tests was to interview local ministers, listing the
upcoming sermons that would be offered that weekend. Fort meekly
asked how to proceed. "Ministers? Directory!" the editor snarled at
him. "Look in the directory!"

Charles sat at a desk, paging through the Albany city directory,
starting with the A's and poring down each column, looking for the
designation of clergyman and writing their addresses on a list. Then

moving on to the B's. "Searching for ministers among housepaint-ers, blacksmiths, widows." Late in the afternoon, the editor grabbed the directory and, with a sigh, opened it to the back, showing a list of churches and clergymen. All afternoon, Charles went from min-ister to minister, delighted by the work and fantasizing about the important assignments that awaited him.

He carefully wrote up his interviews, eliminating repetitive words and trying to puzzle out synonyms for "and." The next morning he handed in his first assignment to the copy editor, who glanced at it and quickly handed it back, saying, "The puzzle editor isn't in just now. Perhaps you'd better write it over."

The editor called him into his office to explain the problem. Charles's scrawl was hopeless; he could never succeed with such sloppy handwriting. So the editor suggested that the boy cultivate a big, rounded script. "He had known poor writers to produce leg-ible work in that way." It worked perfectly for Charles, who carefully rewrote his story, "making each letter as large as a bean." For many years, until he began using a typewriter, Fort had two distinct hand-writings. His own notes and letters to friends were written with a sloppy, almost illegible cursive. His manuscripts used a childish handwriting of oversized, round letters, with each period circled like a bull's-eye, the mark of an experienced newspaperman.

With his usual obsession, Charles now could think only as a reporter. He terrorized his stepmother at meals by quietly recording bits of her gossip, surreptitiously scrawling in a notebook in his pocket and then translating the information into newspaper col-umns the next day. Blanche Fort was afraid to speak in front of him. "They, irritated and scornful, refusing to believe that we could write anything, thinking that someone had patched it up for us."

Charles's galumphing enthusiasm only irritated his father, who now realized that his son had rejected the grocery business. This was a personal insult. It was only made worse by John Hoy's involvement—the other branch of the family. Charles Nelson Fort merely thought of his son as John's "experiment." "They sneering at anything undertaken by 'that young John,' as they called him." The atmosphere in the dining room was once again caustic. "We'd long for encouragement," Charles wrote. "They'd shake the newspaper at us; just as when a little boy, talking was forbidden at our table." Charles was nearing adulthood, but could not speak while his father quietly read the *Argus*—the paper his son had been working at all day.

CHARLES RETURNED to the Y.M.C.A. camp that summer at Lake Champlain, and it gave him a knowing, insider's feeling to revisit the old places from the previous year. Now, in addition to collecting beautiful, romantic notions in his head, he was attempting to translate them into sentences. At the *Argus*, the editor had told him casually that, should he "get up a good story, he'd be glad to have it."

All the way back on the train car, Charles struggled with a pencil and paper. "Our mind was confusion; incidents, characters, scenes were all mixed up. Making our most pretentious effort in writing, trying to tell not only what we had seen but what we had felt." He decided to describe paddling a war canoe with a group of other boys, crossing the dark waters at night, singing in unison.

He cobbled together a short humorous story that hinted at his reverie—"pictures of rain storms far off in Vermont hills; their coming then seen in roughness advancing over smooth water; the splashing of rain drops sweeping from blots and swirls down upon us." The editor looked over the page and said, "Execrable!" Fortunately, the editor was talking about the handwriting, not the story. When it was published the following day, Charles was treated to pats on the back and grudging compliments from the seasoned reporters. He'd arrived. "You keep your rubbers on, and we'll have you down in New York yet," his uncle John repeated, proudly pasting his nephew's story in his scrapbook.

AT THE NEWSPAPER, Charles Fort was rewarded with a "beat," covering the Surrogate's Court every morning. "Uneasiness. We knew not how to address the Surrogate." As always, it was the social niceties that flummoxed the boy. He wavered between obsequious, Victorian pleasantries that he'd observed and the elbow nudging of his tobacco-stained colleagues at the *Argus.* "Your Honor" seemed un-American and hopelessly grand. So for several days he mumbled a greeting, hoping that "Mmm-mmm" could be interpreted in the right way.

Sauntering into the County Clerk's office with "the briskness we admired so much," he called across the desk. "Ah! Fine morning!" Charles said. "How's everything this morning, old man?" The clerk quickly looked up and snapped at the young reporter, "Don't you get so fresh!"

Charles was just seventeen, but he now smoked a pipe, sampled cheap port or an occasional beer, and followed a friend into an Albany betting parlor. "Having no difficulty to get in, for our slow, old city was a wide-open town." The rattle of the chips and the sharp cracks of the balls on the pool table were temptations, and his first gambling excursion led to a grand night on the town. He could appreciate that he was now strutting, anxious to be all grown up.

Fried oysters and bottles of beer! Leaning back, smoking cigars! And we tipped the waiter! Waiter holding our overcoat, reaching under to pull down our undercoat! There was nothing left except to walk out, chewing a toothpick, and then have our shoes shined outside. . . . Awfulness.

ONE NIGHT Charles misjudged the time and returned to his family's home at 253 State Street after ten o'clock. He was locked out. He knocked on the door. No answer. He pounded again and again, but the lack of response inside was clearly intended as a message.

So he calmly paced the front of the house, selected a fist-sized cobblestone and smashed the ornate red stained-glass doorway. Then another stone, and another, to make sure that every bit of glass had been knocked from the frame. He nonchalantly reached around and opened the knob, stepping inside.

His father sent him into the basement to sleep with the servants. There was no new punishment that could be devised for Charles, no torture that could be felt through his thick scab, built up from layers and layers of discipline. For a week, he was refused meals with the family. The servants were forbidden to offer him any food.

Several days later, Charles slouched sullenly in his chair as a plate of cake was being passed across the table. He was tired of it all. He made a quick grab for the plate, snagging a slice. His stepmother tried to pry it away from him. Charles cocked his arm and hurled the cake into her face. And in an instant—upturned chairs, screams, and thrown food—his father's stern, Victorian household erupted like a volcano, spilling over with all the tension that had been bubbling under the surface.

Charles Fort tumbled through the hallway, grabbed his coat, and pushed his way through the front door, now roughly repaired with planks of wood. He slammed it one last time.

We Wrapped the Piece
of Cake to Keep Always

To investigate is to admit prejudice; that nobody has ever really investigated, but has sought positively to prove or disprove something suspected in advance.

Charles left his father's house and arrived on the doorstep of his maternal grandfather, John Hoy, the retired hardware merchant. Hoy was warm and sympathetic, agreeing to take in the young man. Charles's bachelor Uncle John, who had arranged the job at the newspaper, was now living in the same house in Albany, as grandfather Hoy had been trying to gather the family together again.

Charles Nelson Fort was in a bind. His son was just seventeen, not of legal age; as an apprentice at the *Argus*, he couldn't support himself. But it was now obvious that father and son could not live together under the same roof. The successful grocery wholesaler grudgingly made arrangements with John Hoy to pay the boy's board until he was an adult: eighteen years old.

In return, Charles agreed to resume his education—hedging on his potential as a reporter, balancing his newspaper work with schoolwork.

But first, Charles was obsessed with a new adventure. After the family sent Clarence away to Burnham Industrial Farm three years earlier, they had virtually ignored his fate. Now out of his father's house for good, Charles felt a burning desire to see Clarence, "the Little Kid," and commiserate with him as the other proud, disowned son. He went on his mission to Burnham Farm in the early winter of 1891. *Many Parts*, Charles Fort's childhood memoirs, described the trip, and his aching, flickering emotions.

> *Missing several trains, which would make it difficult to get back by evening. We didn't care. "All aboard!" We hastening to the train; or no, we "bustled" like a traveling man. We were in the Berkshires, familiar ground, because we had been there with our grandfather, yet strange and interesting, for this time we were traveling alone. Little hills piled on big hills, looking like shop-worn chocolate drops, with their brown patches and sow-covered spaces. Sitting out on the steps, to have everything closer to us. Telegraph wires that were white cables with a break here and there where sparrows had rested. Whiteness weighing down greenness, as snow covered evergreen boughs hung low.*

Fort deliberately bought a ticket for a station beyond his stop. "You see, we wanted to do some real detective work. No one expected us, but we seemed to think it clever to go into the village not from its station but from the station three miles away. So it was night by the time we had walked back; thus likely there would be the worst trouble of our life at home. We didn't care. It would be very pleasing to stay all night in a hotel."

The next day Charles appeared at Burnham Industrial Farm, politely asking to see Clarence V. Fort. He had turned over this visit again and again in his mind, creating a maddening melodrama that left him completely confused. "You see, we could not tell what we might do when we should see the Little Kid after not having seen him in such a long time. In our hip pocket there was a revolver. We had always felt contempt for auxiliary weapons, but Biff Allen had pressed this revolver upon us."

Charles waited in a small office and a few minutes later Mrs. Dean, a helpful proprietress at Burnham Farm, stepped through the door with Clarence.

Just as little as ever, but sturdy as ever, showing not a sign of ill-treatment except his twitching eye caused in his own home.

All we said was, "How are you?"

All the Little Kid said was, "Pretty well, I thank you," just as if I were a stranger. But he sort of leaned towards us. And we were seized upon because of that sort of leaning. Our arm around him, having him sit beside us. Littleness seeming to send a sense of bigness tearing through us. And our flightiness was upon us. We wanted to shout and to struggle. In our mind, we were already in the doorway, our arm around this little kid, battling with the whole village.

Said Mrs. Dean, "I quite envy you your trip through the Berkshires; at this time of year they must be beautiful."

Said we, "Yes, but I'd like to have come earlier; I'd like to see the maple leaves in Autumn."

Charles was now a burly young man, nearly six feet tall, with pince-nez glasses and wavy brown hair. He looked respectable and successful, far older than his seventeen years. But standing at Burnham Farm, he could still sense all of his adolescent emotions, and he had trouble deciding if he was a boy or a man.

After a formal call, we said we should have to go. Little Kid asking that he might walk to the station with us. Mrs. Dean fearing not; he had lessons to make up. Little Kid saying nothing, never pleading for anything denied him. We telling him to be a good boy and study hard, and then going away. But with a depressing, out-classed feeling. How easily Mrs. Dean had made nothing but a formal call of our detective mission, easily turning us from battles to Autumn leaves.

We lingered in the village, dissatisfied with tameness instead of adventure, more and more displeased with the uneventfulness of everything. We would see the Little Kid alone; we would find out how he was treated. So we waited until dark, then went again to the house. Looking at the lights, wondering which light he was near. And then we saw him. Up in his room, moving around near the lamplight; a trellis underneath.

We crept over the lawn. And three pebbles at the lamplight. Little Kid opening the window, making not a sound. He knew; this Little Kid always knew. Whispering down to us, "Wait a minute."

But we wanted a picture. We climbed the trellis, thinking that climbing this trellis was the most interesting picture we had ever been in.

Little Kid coming back, greeting us at the window. He handed us a piece of cake. Why, this poor, foolish Little Kid thought we were hungry! And that did move us. His going down to steal for us, as we had so very often stolen for each other. We wrapped the piece of cake in a paper to keep always.

It reminded him of the fateful slice of cake that had been denied him on State Street, of the prized linen-wrapped packages of food that had been dangled down the airshaft to his improvised prison.

Little Kid wanting to go to China, Singapore, anywhere with us, whispering that two miles down the track we could catch a freight car without trouble. But we thought the hotel would do. Both of us stole down the trellis.

Up in our room. We ordered drinks, soda for him and port for us. Feeling that it was wrong to have him see his big brother drinking, but quite unable to resist having him see his big brother drinking. And smoking a big cigar, murmuring something about, "The beastly quality of these country weeds." The little kid hinted that he smoked cigarettes, having learned to smoke in the Industrial Farm, as he would never have learned at home, for we and the Other Kid would have trounced him well for it. Then we were severe with him. Little Kid very respectful, pleasing us that he should recognize the vastness of difference between seventeen and just only thirteen.

And now tell us everything; you must not be afraid, for you know whom you're talking to and everything will be used in your favor and against our common enemy. Is anyone ill-treating you? If there be . . . ! Great excitement! Pounding of the table. By this and by that if anyone's unkind to you, there'll be. . . . Dear me, a whole massacre in five minutes.

Little Kid unmoved.

The tirade slowed and stopped, replaced with only rational, adult-sounding words. Charles felt impelled to be responsible, and urge responsibility. He put on his coat and escorted Clarence through the snowy countryside back to Burnham Farm, watching from the road as the Little Kid shimmied up the trellis and disappeared into the glowing window without looking back. Charles returned to Albany the next day. There's no record that the two brothers ever met again.

•   •   •

PETER VAN VRANKEN FORT, Charles's grandfather who founded the grocery warehouse on Eagle Street, died in December, 1891,
of tuberculosis. That month, Raymond and Charles stood mutely
at the side of the grave at the Albany Rural Cemetery, several miles
north of the city. His grandfather had secured an impressive plot
of land for the family grave beside a pond. The family erected a tall
granite column with a mourning goddess atop it—befitting one of
Albany's successful businessmen.

The family store, P. V. Fort and Son, passed to Charles's father,
Charles Nelson Fort. The grandfather's will included allowances for
his three grandsons in the form of property in Albany that could
be rented for income. The money would have been particularly useful to Charles, who would soon come of age. But invariably, the
Fort family money had been arranged to frustrate any of Charles's
ambitions. Contingent legacies in the will meant that a court-
appointed guardian, Matthew J. Wallace, supervised the boys' inheritance. The properties promised to earn very little, or they
required constant upkeep.

For Charles, there was no more interest in foreign stamps or bits
of minerals. Instead, he now used his spare time hunched over a
desk, sending out manuscripts. His latest story would be carefully
copied and mailed to local literary magazines or newspapers in
oversized envelopes with a prominent return address. "To Editor:
If enclosed contribution is not deemed worthy of remuneration,
please return in addressed envelope. Respectfully, C. H. Fort."

Every story accepted or rejected inspired him to send more and
more manuscripts, in ever-wider geographic spirals. He was soon

mailing stories to New York City, and a newspaper syndicate there purchased several of them. They were published in various papers around the country, making Charles a celebrity among his friends.

Raymond Fort recalled that the early stories were based on "some schoolboy prank or an expedition in the country." The camping trips continued to provide inspirations. Fort massaged the facts, exaggerated the humor, added a twist, and turned these everyday incidents into the sort of amusing column fillers that were quickly devoured by editors. "We would all have the pleasure of reading about ourselves in a magazine," Raymond wrote. "He always used our real first names."

His uncle John's prediction had been true: after several years in journalism, Charles had earned a small scrapbook of stories and real credits toward a newspaper career. As he continued to submit stories, he was surprised to be offered a modest position as a reporter at the *Brooklyn World.*

The job was especially appealing because it would bring him to a thriving borough of New York City; just across the Brooklyn Bridge was the center of the American publishing industry. Even better, the *Brooklyn World,* founded in 1883, was an edition of the *New York World.* Charles would have an opportunity to contribute stories to a Manhattan newspaper.

He was now a year behind in school, and by the time he had turned eighteen in 1892, there was no reason to remain in Albany. The *Brooklyn World* job paid eighteen dollars a week, and Fort quickly accepted, leaving high school in Albany without his diploma.

A PHOTO OF CHARLES FORT from this time shows a proud, serious young man in a three-piece wool suit, one hand casually in his hip pocket and another holding a rolled sheet of newspaper at his side. He is a reporter. Fort had grown a walrus mustache; with his full face and bright, narrow eyes squinting through glasses, he resembled a taller, chubbier Theodore Roosevelt—the former Rough Rider and future New York Police Commissioner, who had not yet announced his intention to run for president.

The best record of Fort's days in Brooklyn may be a series of short stories he composed several years later, based in a Brooklyn newspaper office. Even if Fort's stories were fictionalized, a reader can easily recognize Charles Fort as the narrator. For example, one story is about rewriting a reporter's assignment, a sad tale about sailors burying a pet dog. "No one would know, for I can write with two hands," Fort explained, "my naturally ornamental style and the cultivated newspaper hand of fat, squatty letters easily read." He also boasted of his own skills at pathos. "I have written stories that have brought tears to my eyes. I have written stories that have made me exclaim to myself, 'After all, you must be a pretty good fellow to have such depth of feeling as this!'"

Fort described the typical activity of the Brooklyn office:

> The copyreader looks up at the ceiling and remarks in his impersonal, mechanical way, "Don't prefix 'Mr.' to a name of a man of no importance."
>
> Young Bingler, who is learning the business, squirms, fearing that this advice has been overheard by the city editor. And how Bingler hates this copyreader, who seemingly addresses no one, but means him every time.
>
> "Begin at the bottom of the first page and leave room for the head to be written."
>
> And Bingler eats a lead pencil as his shortcomings are advertised by this dragon, who corrects everyone else's copy silently.

The managing editor comes down from his coop upstairs, which
he shares with an artist. He believes in encouraging us occasionally.
He looks at a group of us and says, "That was a good story of yours
in this morning's."

Four of us, greatly flattered, bow and say, "Thank you, Mr.
Bluneum," each annoyed by the conceit of the three others.

The predominant joke in Fort's stories was that reporters were
usually trying to put one over on the editor, do as little work as
possible, and be paid as much as possible. When a stranger stumbled
into the office with a story, Fort explained why certain reporters
might ignore him.

We were on salary and were not straining our eyes for extra
work; we never saw callers who might have stories that someone
would be sent out on. But young Bingler, who was "on space," looked
interested. The more he wrote the more he was paid, and that boy had
a vocabulary that would astonish if not pain you. For "mundane
sphere" he was paid twice as much as for "earth," so polysyllabic he
always was—and of a man slipping on a banana peel could write a
book. A generous young fellow, but space-writing makes one so mean
that he had been known to turn Smith into Smithers for three more
letters. You can figure out that gain yourself; sixteen hundred words
to the column, and for a column four dollars and a half.

Dramatic criticism in Brooklyn, according to Fort, invited
indolence.

I learned that every female inhabitant of Brooklyn was an ama-
teur actress, and every male inhabitant sang in a male quartet. Every-
body in Brooklyn belonged to a lodge of some kind, and every lodge

gave a theatrical performance when it had no one to initiate and had nothing else to do. In small theaters and large halls, and small halls and every kind of a hall this vice broke out. We were pestered with it. Gilt-edged cards, with cupids or masks on them, came in every mail and most of our night assignments were theatrical performances—for hopeless actresses and hopeless tenors would buy many copies of the newspaper with their names in it to send throughout the country to everyone they had ever known.

When programs were sent, we would not bother to go to a performance, but would just make a list of the participants and write our criticisms at home. It is very easy to be a dramatic critic. Start with the first name on a program and write, "Creditable rendition" after it; go on with, "Lifelike interpretation," and tack on to someone else, "Dramatic intensity." When we had nothing else to do, we wrote out a dozen criticisms in advance, and then filled in with the names from night to night.

When asked to report on a minister's sermon, Fort's narrator admits, "We wrote our own." It was always easier than the actual reporting.

The day before, I had been sent to [write up] a lecture on Abraham Lincoln, somewhere miles away in the Eastern District. Naturally, I walked merely over to the library and, asking for a biography, wrote my own lecture, which was creditable enough to the lecturer, for I took more pains than I should have taken with veritable extracts.

A PLAN WAS HATCHED in the offices of the *Brooklyn World.* Two other reporters, friends of Fort's, quit to start their own newspaper in the sleepy community of Woodhaven, deep in Queens. Somehow they had assembled financing for the venture. Charles was recruited for the plan and nominated for the job as editor. It's hard to imagine that he was, at eighteen, the most experienced of the group, or that the shy boy from Albany could convincingly bark out story assignments.

Their *Woodhaven Independent* was founded in 1893. The newspaper limped along for several months before disappearing completely. Raymond later thought that the problem was that Charles and his partners "ran afoul of some of the local big shots," but this may have just been an optimistic way to describe the failure.

In Fort's later stories about work in a newspaper office, Woodhaven came in for a particular ribbing. He wrote of one reporter, a brilliant faker who has decided to take the afternoon off, sitting in the saloon beneath the newspaper office. He used the bar telephone to call upstairs to his editor. "Where am I? Out in Woodhaven. There's nothing in this story except a tip that leads out past Jamaica. Shall I bother with it? No? Well, I'll be back in an hour; though perhaps it may take me a little longer, as there's a pretty hard road ahead." The reporter stepped outside, dirtied his shoes—to simulate the muddy terrain of the countryside in Woodhaven—and then returned to a leisurely hour of beer drinking before going back to the office. Woodhaven was a place where nothing happened, and newspapermen knew it.

Fort had been besotted by his quick rise in the newspaper world. Twenty years later, he recalled his successes to a friend: "I was only seventeen, up in Albany, when I sold things to a New York syndicate. When I was only eighteen years old, I wrote stuff for the Brooklyn edition of the *World* that made quite a little star of me for a while. I wasn't twenty when two of the fellows of the *World* started up the *Woodhaven Independent* and made me editor of it. If some damned thing didn't have me, I'd have been a success at twenty-five, anyway."

What had him in a stranglehold was his romantic notion of experience.

AS HE WAS GROWING UP, Fort's sense of the picturesque was oddly analytical. It seemed that the notion of having adventures—the process—was much more important than the actual adventures. In *Many Parts*, he described his feelings.

> *Floundering in the snow, staggering and fighting, calling to the other, small boys, "Come back ye cowards!" Very much liking the "ye"; it seemed as if right out of a storybook. Crying things we had read, our mind filled with much reading. But it was not courage; it was our joy in the picturesque, we seeing gallantry and romance in our defiance. And we had a mania to fight with larger boys, because of the glory that would come to us if we should triumph.*

Similarly, he was able to construct surprises for himself. The idea of a surprise was more delicious than a real surprise.

> *We'd put candy away and pretend to forget it, just so that we could run across it some time and be surprised to find it. Telling ourself we had thirty cents in our bank, when we very well knew we had fifty cents, then trying to lose track. Just trying to surprise ourself.*

If that didn't work, he was happy to imagine a surprise for someone else. During a camping trip, Charles kicked up leaves, hoping to find Indian artifacts, "wishing some Indian had been so thoughtful as to leave lying around a few old relics." When there weren't any, he took matters into his own hand.

> *We'd be thoughtful; stealing away during a rest to bury whatever we could find in our pockets, even pennies, for someone to find maybe a thousand years later and be pleased with.*

With the same logic, his mission to see Clarence had become a pretend mission. The older brother valiantly performed his sweetly immature melodrama. The "Little Kid" was far more worldly and rational. Once Charles had acted out his part and salved his conscience, his little brother, his audience, was sent back to Burnham Industrial Farm.

AFTER TWO YEARS as a reporter in New York City, Fort feared that he'd reached his limit as a writer. He'd been confined to a small world of experiences in Brooklyn or Woodhaven. "I became a newspaper reporter," he later wrote of this time, "and instead of collecting idealists' bodies in morgues, Sunday school children parading in Brooklyn, greengoods men and convicts in jail, I arranged my experiences. I pottered over them quite as I had over birds' eggs and minerals and insects." He realized that real writers drew on a wealth of experience—they recounted faraway places, exotic people, and unexpected adventures with confidence. He had none of that capital.

Fortunately, Matthew J. Wallace, the boys' guardian, had succeeded in renting the property in Albany, and Charles Fort was now earning twenty-five dollars a month from his grandfather's estate. It would have been difficult to live on that amount in one of the less reputable areas of New York. Charles decided to use that stipend—just eighty-three cents a day—and travel around the world, seeking out new sensations and viewpoints.

> *All this to accumulate an experience and knowledge of life that would fit me to become a writer; wanted to know cowboys and day laborers; sailors, queer boarding house people; clerks, sea captains, vagabonds—everybody. I would get together a vast capital of impressions of life, and then invest it.*

Deliberately, he assigned no distinct design to the exercise: neither a finish line, nor a goal. He was nineteen years old, and would now "wander with a definite purpose."

Blue Miles, Green Miles, Yellow Miles

Ships from other worlds have been seen by millions of inhabitants of this earth; exploring in the skies of France, England, New England, and Canada.

In 1893, Charles Fort could have seen the world the way that millions of Americans were seeing it, by taking a train to Chicago and touring the Columbian Exposition in Jackson Park. The collection of classical palaces, Victorian mansions, and midway exhibits offered fascinating collections from far-away countries: a display of cannons from Germany's Krupp Gun Company; an Elizabethan dining room from Great Britain; wood carving from India; artifacts from the Vatican museum. Early that year, when he was still working as a newspaperman, Fort must have been tempted to travel to Chicago; the Columbian Exposition was a plum assignment. But now, as a committed world traveler, he wasn't interested in artistic recreations or sideshow exhibits, but only in the real thing.

His friends discouraged him. His brother Raymond, Uncle John, and his fellow reporters in Brooklyn all thought that it was a foolish plan, especially for someone like Charles, who could be fretful and uncomfortable in social situations. He had been on the verge of solid work in New York, and it seemed a dangerous time to neglect his career.

But as Charles thought about traveling—aimlessly, spontaneously, to gain experiences that might be useful in his writing—he found the idea energizing. In retrospect, it sounded like a grown-up version of his boyhood scheme to run away with Biff Allen and become elephant drivers in Burma. It was as if all of the wild energy of Charles's boyhood would now be directed toward getting from city to city in search of adventures. Charles "got the wanderlust," Raymond later recalled, and nothing would stop him.

Through Matthew Wallace in Albany, Fort arranged a system where he could indicate where he was headed and then have his monthly twenty-five dollars mailed ahead, awaiting him in general delivery at the post office of the next city. It was a gigantic game of musical chairs—dashing to Wallace's envelope of money before the music stopped. By building in this sort of chase, Charles only added to the excitement.

Late in 1893, he left New York City by rail, with a small grip filled with clothes in one hand and a small roll of bills in his pocket. Standing at the train station and looking over the destination board, he realized that it was a simple, practical decision to head south, where the weather would be warmer. He stopped in Richmond, intrigued with the remnants of the sweet, antebellum sensibilities, which seemed so foreign to a New Englander. Fort was fascinated to meet real "Southern negroes, with their tatters and turbans," a distinct and intriguing subculture within America. He watched a guard barking orders at a chain gang on the side of a road—a series of workers "linked like zebra sausages."

Fort befriended traveling salesmen and hoboes, inquiring about where they were going, deciding at the spur of the moment to join them. He headed farther south, to Jacksonville, Florida, and then over to the coast to enjoy the sunshine and sand in Tampa, where he watched the pelicans flying in wide circles over the beach. He slept in train yards, improvised meals with cans of corned beef around a campfire, or pocketed sandwiches to accompany his nickel beer. He became adept at living on pennies a day.

Making it a point to be interested in everything and anyone, he circled back to Mobile, meeting two young photographic salesmen who had been abandoned on the road by their boss. Now several months into his adventure, Fort was down to his last fifteen cents. He knew he had twenty-five dollars waiting for him in New Orleans, if only he could get there. He bought crackers and cheese with his last few coins, and he and his two friends jumped aboard a nighttime freight train headed to Louisiana. They sat on the catwalk along the tops of the cars, clattering through the warm swamps. Fort dreamily admired the scenery: "Black night and the yellow swath of the headlight; glimpses of the gulf surf in long, white lines; the fluttering of hanging moss on the trees around us."

When the train stopped at a watering station, a brakeman came aboard and marched the length of the catwalk, discovering the three hoboes sitting in the darkness. Unsure of their fate, Fort meekly offered the last of the crackers and cheese. The brakeman waved off the food. "Oh, that's all right!" he told them. The three travelers looked at each other and then looked back at the brakeman. "Then we can get to New Orleans, can we?" Fort asked. "Sure, you'll get to New Orleans; don't let that worry you." "Most amiable brakeman," Fort later recorded, "an addition to the fund of characters; would write about him some day." But it was too good to be true. Once the train was back up to steam, the brakeman explained:

The only thing is that you'll have to do your ten days, sweeping
the streets, in the chain gang. The cops get ten dollars a head for every
hobo from a freight car, but you'll get to New Orleans; don't let that
part worry you.

Fortunately, several miles outside of New Orleans, there was a
shriek from another engine and the freight had to stop suddenly.
The three men took their cue and jumped from the train, tumbling
along the siding and grateful that they'd made their escape.

Fort left his friends in New Orleans, picked up his money, and
felt salvation for another month. He pottered around the city in the
sunshine for several days, working his way to the docks. For six
dollars he was able to travel up the Mississippi on a slow-moving
boat, making his way to Louisville. But he felt guilty for such ex-
travagance and economized in Louisville again, fishing for his dinner, sleeping under the stars in the shipyard.

Sleeping one night on a pile of cypress lumber; don't know why,
because cotton bales and molasses bales were plentiful; awakened
away in the night by a nibbling feeling at my ankles; a roustabout
trying to steal the shoes from my feet.

CHARLES FORT HAD constructed meticulous rules for himself
during his travels. "An obsession with me," he later wrote, "didn't
attempt to write anything while preparing; didn't look for a single
job or diversion of any kind; nothing but such planning of how to
get from Jacksonville to Tampa . . . and how to live the month out
there." Previously he'd tried to keep a notebook filled with ideas for

writing, but invariably he was disappointed by the halting, awkward nature of these notebook entries. So, during his travels, he kept no journal. His point was to experience the adventures first-hand, allowing them to mix and mingle in his imagination to form vivid memories.

As a sign of his new obsession, he had learned to think of his journey as an accumulation—the same way he had once meticulously accumulated birds' eggs, or feathers, or minerals. It was an adult version of stamp collecting. He was assembling bits of faraway places. Fort was comforted by collections: things that could be counted, sorted, and rearranged into different combinations. Now he was collecting miles.

> *Treasuring and hoarding my experiences, a miser in miles. Gloating over them—like, "Now I've got fourteen-thousand eight hundred and seventy-five; blue ones, with white foam scattered on them; green miles, through palm trees; yellow, over sandy stretches; black miles, of nights on top of freight cars. Now, if I can get from Mobile to New Orleans, that will make an extra fifteen thousand. Up the Mississippi, to Louisville, will be sixteen hundred more.*

A fragment of a letter from this time demonstrates how Fort noted every mile as an achievement. He was probably writing to his friend Anna Filing in New York, and speculating about when he'd return home again. "I'm in Louisville now," he reported. "First 1400 miles from New Orleans and about 800 [to] New York. I'm doing the best I can to get there."

Fort was pleased to find that the "Letters of warning to me [were] becoming fewer and ceasing." Or, perhaps, his friends were simply frustrated trying to chase him from city to city across the country. For several months, he watched the rough circle that he was forming on the map, and considered ending his travels and returning to New York: "No hardships; picturesqueness transmuting everything; maybe within a few months I could begin to use the material I was collecting."

He didn't stop, but returned to Brooklyn just long enough to arrange for the next leg of his travel. While in the South, he'd met a cowboy and heard about the opportunities for cattlemen on cattle ships to England. Ships left from New York loaded with consignments of cattle; often a ship would have two consignments, with two separate cattle bosses supervising the herds. The cattle were herded into pens for the journey. Workers were taken on for every voyage to help handle the animals, tie them in place, and feed them through the journey. These workers paid five dollars for the privilege, and for one-way transportation across the Atlantic. During their boyhoods, two other American authors, Sinclair Lewis and Will Rogers, also worked on cattle ships for their passage overseas.

To Fort, it was too wonderful an opportunity to miss, even if the work was hard and the bosses strict. He applied at a pier on the Hudson, exaggerated his experience, emphasized that he was strong and fit, and paid his five dollars. In a later short story set on a cattle steamer, Fort had one of the hired cattlemen explain that it was his job to get "as much work as you can get out of trash that pays its five dollars apiece to get over the ocean, instead of getting pay for their labor." At the end of the journey, the cattle were taken off the ship in Liverpool, and Fort found himself, gloriously, in England.

Perilously short of funds again, Fort was pleased when a squire and a "gentleman-farmer" in Liverpool took in the stranger and offered him boarding. The quaint little garret that the squire offered appealed to Charles's sense of romance. "Just the sort of garret that had often longed for; and two rats who had not a trace of snob-bishness in them."

The gentleman-farmer seemed insistent on making something of his American visitor. "Don't know which, gentleman or farmer," Fort later admitted. He was probably impressed to hear that his visitor was a "cattleman." But Fort "didn't know much about work in those days." Leaving the first morning for his office in Liverpool, the squire gave Charles "a pair of spurs to polish; mentioned a garden, with weeds in it, perhaps, or said something about a hoe somewhere."

When the squire returned late in the day, Charles was still intently polishing the spurs. "Lost a good home on account of it," Fort shrugged, "and two rats who weren't inclined to draw social distinctions."

He passed through Lancashire on a Sunday, and found that he had just three ha'pence, the price of a pint of mild ale.

> Stopping at a public house; had never heard of the Sunday law, by which one who has come a distance greater than three miles may get a drink. "Where'd you come from?" the publican. "From New York." "Bli'me! You've come far enough!" Drawing one.

Now out of funds again, he was headed to London, where he hoped to find another envelope of money waiting for him. Late at night he fell asleep under a culvert. "Rush and roar of the passing trains, tracks three feet away. Rush and roar that, under the bridge, became frenzy; peacefulness and comfort; had found in the dark, some kind of soft material to lie on." When he tried to get up in the morning—"never liked getting up in the morning"—he had more trouble than usual. He'd fallen asleep on the contents of a broken tar barrel, and his shoulder was now stuck to the ground. "Never since caught a fly on flypaper; sympathy."

Fort deliberately kept no record of his journey beyond the vague impressions of hardship or wonder that lingered in his memory. In London he visited Poets' Corner at Westminster Abbey. It seemed a portentous notion for a determined, aspiring writer. He lingered in London, touring government buildings, museums, and libraries, admired the ale, and indulged in roast beef when the bankroll was replenished. Then he tramped through the English countryside and worked his way back to Liverpool. In September 1894, he boarded a passenger ship, the *Ohio*, bound for Philadelphia. According to the ship's log, Charles H. Fort was "a reporter" who was "returning home in Brooklyn, New York."

BACK IN BROOKLYN, Fort was only a former reporter, with no money and no prospects; he had only "plans for a thousand here and five thousand there when the time should come for the investing of all this accumulating capital."

He felt he still wasn't ready. After a year on the road, he'd acquired a knack for travel and a taste for life on the road. Still too impatient to sit at a desk and stare at a blank sheet of paper, he set out again, this time headed north.

Fort signed on for odd jobs that would get him from one place to another: dishwasher, fireman, or stoker. In the summer of 1895, in Nova Scotia, he boarded a ship that left the Bay of Fundy, sailed across to the Firth of Clyde, and arrived in Glasgow, Scotland.

From there he was determined to see London again, so he purchased a ticket for a train headed south. During the trip, he stopped
at a station to get out and buy a sandwich.

> Got out and worried over ham or chicken—train gliding away;
> all the doors locked. Oh my! My! Compartment with own luggage
> long gone by, and train going faster. Sudden energy; great presence of
> mind in emergency—head first through a window and the projecting
> chest of the austere and pompous kind of an elderly Englishman.
> Broke his eyeglasses, knocked his book out of the window, spilled the
> bottle of cold tea he was drinking. Had done enough damage to raise
> anybody's indignation. The Englishman's resentment: "Sir, this is a
> most undignified entrance!"

After a full year of scrapes and misadventures on the road, Fort
had also learned to be nonchalant.

> Never mind; had the sandwich. London; luggage never recovered.
> Never mind; bought another collar.

He traveled west, through Wales and Ireland, and then returned
to London, taking a menial job to raise money. He went to the
steamship agency and purchased a ticket for South America. It was
only when he arrived at the dock that he realized that the agent had
made a mistake and booked him on a ship to South Africa. The
agency was willing to change the ticket, but Fort, suitcase in hand,
thought over the matter and realized that it made no difference to
him. He boarded the ship for Cape Town, South Africa. He slept
in the "fo'c's'le" of the ship, officially the "forecastle" or the point
of the bow, rocked to sleep by the undulations of the prow and the
rumble of the waves against the hull. On the journey south, he

stopped at Tenerife and St. Helena, which he fondly recalled from his history books:

> *Not only where Napoleon had been, but an African island, where cocoanuts, dates, olives and bananas grow wild, just like the pictures in the geographies. The things I was seeing! The mania and the sensuous abandon of it! Doing not another thing in the world but storing away experiences and impressions.*

He must have remained in South Africa for months. It was an exciting time there. Not only was Cape Town a thriving metropolis, but the country also crackled with the dangerous conflict of British imperialism and the Transvaal Republic. Charles met soldiers of fortune, buccaneers and filibusters who were left over from the first Boer War, or were crowding into the country, awaiting the next sparks of revolt.

Raymond Fort recalled receiving a letter from his older brother while he was living in South Africa near the end of 1895. Somehow he'd managed to be challenged to a duel by a Frenchman. It's hard to imagine Fort's offense, or that his bashful, "kicking the dirt" mannerisms couldn't have appeased the aggrieved Frenchman. Perhaps the notion of a duel inflamed Fort's romantic fantasies.

He'd never handled a sword and had only an amateur's experience with guns. He accepted the challenge and informed the Frenchman's seconds that he'd decided upon "fists."

Fort had befriended a prizefighter in South Africa, who may have encouraged Fort in this clever decision. Charles had been a good fighter as a boy, and was tall and powerful with large fists. When his French challenger objected, Fort knew he'd made the right decision, as he had the definite advantage of weight and reach. He held his ground, insisting that the weapons used be fists or the challenge be withdrawn. The fight took place. It took only minutes for Fort to pummel his opponent.

Over the New Year, 1896, Fort was in the British Colony of Cape Town during the famous Jameson Raid. Paul Kruger was the president of the South African Republic. A raid on Johannesburg in the Transvaal, to be led by Leander Starr Jameson, was planned late in 1895. More than likely Joseph Chamberlain, the British Colonial Secretary, was behind the raid, hoping that it would spark an uprising that would lead to British rule in the Transvaal.

But as the politicians second-guessed the plan, Jameson and his force of six hundred men grew impatient. On December 29, 1895, Jameson crossed into the Transvaal. The British realized that they couldn't support the raid and quickly disavowed it. The raid was a complete disaster, and the raiders were captured days later.

Fort remembered "the excitement of Cape Town" as the city waited to hear the results of the raid. "Factory whistles blowing at midnight." He claimed that his friend, the prizefighter, brought his belt back to Cape Town with a bullet hole in it, a result of the skirmish. Today the Jameson Raid is remembered as one falling domino that led to the Second Boer War of 1898. Rudyard Kipling's poem "If" was reportedly based on the life of Jameson. The famous line, "If you can keep your head when all about you / Are losing theirs and blaming it on you," was a reference to Jameson's honor and Chamberlain's duplicity.

Early in 1896, Fort boarded a ship that crossed the Atlantic to South America, and then went up the coast to New York. Finishing two full years of travel, he took stock of his "tangled line on the map." Fort's family remembered that the end of his trip was precipitated by an illness—more than likely malaria. Careless about his health, the recurring bouts of fever and chills finally persuaded Charles to leave South Africa and return home.

I had thirty-thousand, many-colored, vividly diversified miles hoarded; experiences, impressions, hundreds of characters, the world's scenery. Nothing more to see; everything in life known; only twenty-one years old, but now for the work of a master!

IN NEW YORK CITY he found Anna Filing, the petite friend from Albany whom he had befriended eight years earlier. Annie was happy to hear the tales of his adventures; she was intrigued by his plans for stories. But she took particular satisfaction in quietly nursing him back to health when his fevers returned, or cooking solid, nourishing meals of meat and potatoes—offering the kind of simple support he hadn't received since he was a little boy. Anna's domestic tasks were second nature to her, and Charles took particular comfort in her help and friendship.

Charles Fort had been overwhelmed by sights and sounds, but had no better instinct about writing: no understanding of how to put his impressions on paper or tease apart the jumble of adventures into engaging stories.

He had imagined the grand tour as running toward something—a career as a great writer. But the vague, unfocused nature of his travel suggested that he was also running away from something. Before he would be able to sit down at the typewriter, Fort would need to assemble the pieces of his life again—his family, friends, and career.

SHORTLY AFTER HIS RETURN, according to Fort, he met an old man in New York who was confined to his rooms. The man had been paralyzed on one side of his body and shared a small apartment with his wife and daughter. Perhaps it was an acquaintance through the *Brooklyn World*, or a neighbor. During his visit to this man, in an effort to be sociable, Fort good-naturedly launched into an account of his travels, boasting of everything he had seen and learned. The man listened wistfully, and then responded:

> *I, too have always had that interest in life. When I got on the [train] cars, I thought that at last I had got where I could study and understand human nature; such opportunities; the thousands of people on and off, every minute; all ages, occupations and temperaments; here was a wealth of material for me. Lord! Lord! Such a mistake. You don't want to know something about everybody, but everything about somebody. I never began to learn about my life until I was cooped up here with my wife and Maggie.*

Somehow, this brief bit of kitchen-table philosophy had more of an effect on Charles Fort than anything he'd experienced in the previous two years. That night, as he bumped down the street in Brooklyn, contemplating the familiar illuminated tenements and dark storefronts, he realized that the old man was absolutely right, and he'd been wrong. He had already outgrown his latest collection.

> *Then I, with my thirty thousand miles, and the hundreds of characters; the impressions of houses, roads, waves, coasts and people! One cannot ignore a truth when one has passed through all the errors below it. The toppling of the structure that two of my best years had gone into. Pelicans at Tampa, Poet's Corner in Westminster Abbey, the bow of a vessel cutting the waves at night time. All gone, and no*

investing of capital; I knew that one should not scatter one's self upon all life, but center upon some one kind of life and know it thoroughly. Romances that would have to be solidified into the doings of some little group of commonplace people. Nothing more of the headlights of engines in Southern forests, but the lighting of the fire in Mrs. Murphy's back kitchen; Mamie Murphy, and her young man, and a few neighbors.

Thus ended my first lesson. It takes me about two years to learn anything.

The man's advice must have had a particular effect on Fort because, at that moment, he knew the person with whom he could spend the rest of his life.

CHARLES FORT proposed to Anna Filing in October 1896, when he was twenty-two years old and she was twenty-six. She accepted. "I always loved him," she told a friend years later, "but I never thought I would marry him." The couple pooled their resources to move into a neat, simple apartment on the East Side of New York, at 170 East Thirty-second Street, near Third Avenue.

On October 26, 1896, Charles and Anna stood in front of the Bride's Altar at New York's Episcopal Transfiguration Church, the "Little Church Around the Corner," on Twenty-ninth Street near Fifth Avenue. The church was founded in 1848 by Reverend George Haughton, whose famously open-minded parish was well known for ministering to the actors in the nearby theater district in Manhattan. The seventy-six-year-old Haughton presided at the ceremony.

When they heard the news, Charles's parents made it clear that they disapproved of the marriage. They remembered Anna as the simple Irish-English immigrant who had lived in Albany. As Charles Hoy Fort was part of an important family of businessmen, they were convinced that their son had married beneath him.

By now, Charles Fort really didn't care what they thought.

SIX

We, Then a Great Famous Man

Take care, O reader, with whom you are amused, unless you enjoy laughing at yourself.

Anna Fort was a proud homemaker, a good cook, and a curious neighbor who made friends with the other renters in their apartment house. She had a warm, quiet manner and was naturally gregarious in a way that Charles was not. Part of Anna's youth had been spent in New York City, and she was comfortable with the metropolis. Charles tended to see the city as an outsider, fascinated with its museumlike collection of characters.

For their honeymoon, the couple traveled to the Maine coast. Charles was not much of a drinker. When he was a young man, he once overindulged in a bottle of port and always remembered the scared, unsettled way it had made him feel. But he enjoyed his beer, and after two weeks in Maine—a completely dry state—he was anxious to wet his whistle. "He went out to buy tickets for [the ferry to] Canada," Anna remembered, "and was gone the longest time. He had thirty dollars with him. After hours and hours I heard his voice." Charles had a soft bass voice, and seldom raised it above a whisper, so it was odd to hear him in such an animated conversation. Anna looked out the window and saw her new husband staggering around on the street, arm-in-arm with a man in overalls. "You never saw such a drunken boy," she said. Anna ran down to the street and grabbed her husband by the shoulders, "spanking him all the way upstairs."

They traveled to St. John's, Newfoundland, in Canada, and hiked up and down the hills. By November, the weather in Newfoundland was getting cold, so the couple decided to pack their bags and return to New York City.

In their apartment on Thirty-second Street, Fort handled the finances. Anna did the shopping, prepared the meals, and managed the laundry and household chores, leaving Charles to quietly write at the kitchen table during the days. Friends remembered her as a sweet, birdlike lady, just over five feet tall, who devotedly buzzed around her husband. She enjoyed singing, and Fort occasionally joined her in harmony. During his travels, he had also learned to play the guitar. He called her "momma" or "Annie." She called him "poppa" or "Charlie." She was the only person who called him Charlie; to everyone else, he was Charles.

Years later, a friend described Anna as a literary dullard: "She never dreamed what went on in her husband's head, never read his or any other books." But this was an overstatement designed to emphasize Fort as an isolated, lonely genius. Charles often read her stories or chapters as he was working on them, asking her how she thought "it would pan out" or "how it sounded." He valued her opinion and we can recognize her point of view in a number of characters in his fictional stories. Throughout their life together, she was the first judge of his writing.

• • •

MANY NEW YORK newspapers published supplements, and were always looking for bright bits of fiction, either sentimental or comic, to fill their pages. An increasing handful of "second-tier" literary magazines, like *Argosy* or *The Black Cat,* were looking for pulp: punchy, imaginative tales of fantasy.

Fort was still unsure of his abilities, but he wrote out story after story in his round, easy-to-read handwriting and sent them off to the editors. Rejections were common, and a story sometimes needed to be resubmitted to various publications, perhaps six or eight times before it was accepted or Fort decided that it was a failure. When a story sold, it may have paid a penny a word: often no more than twenty or twenty-five dollars. To make a living, a writer needed a continual parade of stories, moving from magazine to magazine— under consideration, rejected, or accepted—with new stories continually joining the collection.

Fort's occasional successes couldn't support the couple, and he depended upon the checks from Albany. Unfortunately, Matthew Wallace had difficulty collecting the rent and was forced to pay for a number of repairs on the Albany house. In a poor economic market, it was difficult to find good tenants, Wallace explained. When Fort inquired about selling the house, Wallace advised against it.

Desperate for a real job, Fort resolved to join the army during the Spanish-American War, but they wouldn't accept him because of his poor eyes. The couple economized by moving to cheaper lodgings. They settled just west of Longacre Square—later renamed Times Square—at 686 Eighth Avenue. It was a tenement apartment at the edge of a notorious collection of tenements called Hell's Kitchen. The wash sink was down a flight of stairs, and the bath-

room was down the hall. Anna was stoic about their new surround-
ings; Fort, after his years of travel, felt no need for luxuries. In
between writing stories, he began making notes about his childhood
memories, and in 1899 the idea of an autobiography, the book he
titled *Many Parts,* became his latest obsession.

FORT WORKED on his first draft of *Many Parts* between 1899 and
1901. The manuscript may have signaled his dissatisfaction with
the endless string of magazine stories, and also his determination
to earn real money with a book. Perhaps it also represented his lesson from the paralyzed old man in the apartment: study familiar
subjects in depth.

Many Parts seems remarkable for the tightrope performance of
the author: always about to fall into sentimental nostalgia, but invariably righting itself with bracing honesty. It was, after all, written
by a man in his early twenties—it's hard to imagine that he could
summon wistfulness for his childhood.

Fort added to the arch, mysterious style by substituting aliases
for family members, friends, or even the local newspaper (the *Argus,*
which became the *Democrat* in his manuscript), suggesting that Fort
realized the book would cause offense. He was not simply recording
his boyhood recollections, but was minutely examining them and
coming to terms with his youth. *Many Parts* prickled with all the
misplaced romance, achingly disproportionate concerns, and confusions of childhood.

> *We learned something new every day. And across the street was
> a family even more interesting. For it had not only a General, but
> an Irish setter in it. We could never be so important as all that, but*

some day we might be a Colonel and own a pug. And there were
little boys up and down the street; but none of them was friendly.
We taking a sleigh away from a little girl, just to be acquainted.
Trouble. Pushing another little girl into a snow pile; perhaps she'd
speak to us. More trouble. Knocking a little boy's hat off; that might
lead to acquaintance. Little boy beating us fearfully. Oh, we'd just
have to go away and be a hermit somewhere.

The title, a friend later reported, was taken from Shakespeare's
As You Like It: "All the world's a stage, and all the men and women
merely players. They have their exits and their entrances, and one
man in his time plays many parts." But the surviving fragments of
Many Parts offer only one painful part for the author—a shy, curious
little boy in a tortured relationship with his family.

We sitting in the little window, writing our name and date on
the white wall, adding, "Imprisoned here for doing nothing," which,
we believe, is the view of most criminals. It would please us to write
these things, feeling that many years later we, then a great, famous
man, should like to come back and look at them. Often we'd have this
feeling that the great, famous man would like to see relics of his child-
hood. Raising boards and nailing them down with paper soldier or
heroic marbles down under; slipping treasures down cracks between
walls and floors. Our mind was filled with our reading of great
men; positively we should be one of them.

IN MARCH 1901, Annie was admitted to the German Hospital
at Seventy-seventh Street and Lexington Avenue. There's no record of
her illness. One receipt from the hospital shows a $14 bill, but notes

from Fort to his wife suggest that the illness extended over days or weeks. Charles's correspondence was composed with the same round, easy-to-read handwriting that he was using to complete *Many Parts*:

> *I have just returned from the hospital, where I learned that at least the dread and uncertainty are over. I don't remember about walking up, my suspense and fears were so great, and I don't know down which avenue I returned, my relief was so inspiring, though tempered by the thoughts of the condition in which you must be. The doctors told me it is doubtful if I can see you. . . .*

Three days later, he wrote again to Annie, still in the hospital, telling her that he'd received a little good news from Wallace. After a long period, one of the tenants had finally paid.

Anna recovered, but the medical expenses and Charles's work on *Many Parts* left the couple dangerously short of funds. Fort completed the book that same month and sent off copies to publishers. Now desperate to sell it, he used his handwritten copy as well as a typewritten copy, so two separate publishers could consider the manuscript at the same time.

Late in March, Harper Brothers rejected the book. "Damn their eyes," Fort wrote in his journal. The following month, Cassell and Company turned it down. As the copies were returned to him, he quickly posted them to new publishing houses. It was rejected that summer by Stokes, Appleton, Doubleday, and Houghton Mifflin.

HE TRIED ANY JOB that would pay the bills. For eight months he washed dishes in the kitchen of the Metropolitan Hotel, earning a letter of recommendation: Charles Fort "made himself useful in the kitchen" and was "honest and sober." (In a later story, one of Fort's characters exclaims, "I'm tired to death of working hotel kitchens for six a week and taking every chef's abuse!") He applied at the Grand Central Employment Agency, and was turned down for a job as a watchman at the Hotel Buckingham. He worked as a joke writer and attempted to sell ideas for little household gadgets and novelties. A pawnshop ticket from October 1902 shows that Fort received thirty-one cents for "two suits."

Fort hadn't given up on *Many Parts*, and spent evenings rewriting and editing. The final draft, 80,000 words, has not survived, but a sheet of paper with the table of contents hints at the author's changes.

Only one chapter title, "In Flight from Adoption," seemed to directly match the original manuscript; it may have been the story of Fort, Raymond, and Biff Allen almost running away from home. Other titles, like "Making Her Debut," "The Return of Ambition," "A Concert Garden Failure," and "The Opinion of Critics," suggested that the new draft no longer centered on a claustrophobic childhood in Albany, but was broader in scope and friendlier.

Unfortunately, Fort still failed to sell the book. Harper rejected it a second time in June 1904. Broadway Publishing Company was only interested in producing it if the author would assume half of the costs, $450.

Years later, in his journal, Fort speculated about his failure. "My book *Many Parts* was simply the work of an immature metaphysician, psychologist, sociologist, et cetera, trying to express in a story. Also, individualism, or [style], not only interfered and made me not easily readable, but gave me a satisfaction or elation that held back development."

· · ·

DEJECTEDLY, Charles returned to writing stories, pulling out his notebook of ideas, revising and rewriting previous efforts—the neglected pile of papers that had been sitting in their apartment for the past few years. He had tried to avoid story writing, feeling uneasy about his abilities, the tight efficiency necessary for each story, and the salesmanship it took to impress in a thousand or two thousand words. But he now looked upon it as a desperate, necessary way to pay the bills. Lightning struck. Fort's experience and resolution made a formidable combination. He sold several stories with surprising ease, by early 1905 his name on the manuscript earning recognition and respect from the editors of monthly pulp journals.

Throughout 1905, Charles Fort placed about a dozen short stories—roughly one every month—to various magazines and newspapers. It was still a painfully slow way to make money, seldom more than twenty dollars at a time: a receipt from the *Popular Magazine* shows that Fort was paid thirty dollars for two stories that ran in the summer of 1905. But the acceptance letters represented the sort of praise he had always treasured and seldom received. Those letters were addictive.

Some of his plots recycled familiar themes and may have fictionalized incidents from the failed *Many Parts*. For example, Fort's thirty-dollar stories for *Popular Magazine* were about camping. Although they're humorous, exaggerated tales of city boys bumbling their way through rural adventures, they fall into an easy rhapsody that was clearly based on Fort's memories of Lake Champlain.

Sometimes the twenty were boys, and sometimes they were very young children. Everything pleased them; idly leaning head down over

the side of a boat to look under at deep light from the side now shad-
owed; thrusting sticks into the water, just to see an angle spring into
a straight line by refraction; feeling the electric thrill of a fish not
caught but nibbling.

. . . he sang with a voice ridiculously high; Marcy joined in with
a voice awesomely deep and rumbling. Voices were roaring and growl-
ing and grumbling old songs, there in the very old woods, evoking
feelings as old as is the feeling that comes with any kind of music
when greenness is overhead, and underfoot is the brown of green that
has fallen. He amazed himself. Never before had it occurred to him
that he had so much poetry in him.

Some of Fort's most engaging stories were set in a Brooklyn newspaper office, inspired by his work on the *Brooklyn World.* In "I Meddled," the narrator recalls his relationship with a terrible amateur actress in Brooklyn named Madeline Firscape.

I became acquainted with Madeline and, when she pretended fear
of me because I was "one of those awful critics," I was as charmed
as any ordinary reporter would be to be called a critic.

Madeline was ossified on the stage; she had no joints and spoke in
shrill tones, like chalk rubbed on slate. She walked like scissors, and
her gesticulations were as unmeaning as the fluttering of a family
wash in the wind. But, instead of fairly dividing "creditable rendi-
tion," "lifelike interpretation" and "dramatic intensity" among the cast,
I lavished them all upon Madeline and would have bestowed other
phrases upon her had I had any more in stock—for she called me a
critic; and to Madeline Firscape, body and typewriter, I belonged.

One character named Fryhuysen, an incredibly dishonest reporter, first appeared in a June 1905 story in the *Popular Magazine,*

"With the Assistance of Fryhuysen," and then reappeared in other newspaper tales. In this story, Fort explained his point of view:

> If you were a bricklayer, likely enough you would believe in bank presidents or United States senators or carpenters. You would have a small opinion of bricklayers. I knew one bricklayer who said, "I'd rather be a roofer; every man in my union is mean enough to stare at people coming from pawnshops." A carpenter said, "Plumbers are pretty good fellows, and for some reason bricklayers are a decent sort, but every carpenter I ever knew would eat turkey sandwiches before a starving family."
>
> Said a plumber, "I wish I'd started in with the plane and saw; carpenters are the right sort to work with, but I never knew a plumber who wouldn't shovel snow on a freezing cripple."
>
> Every man seems all contempt for his own kind, because he knows his own kind best. Outside his experience, he believes that virtues in moderation may possibly exist. But take one with nothing outside his experience. Take one who knows everything, sees everything, and goes everywhere. The newspaper man, of course. A newspaper man must be a cynic without reserve.

Fort treated all his characters with indulgent, loving cynicism. He didn't write love stories, or moral little tales with traditional happy endings. Much of the humor came from a gentle sense of larceny: someone trying to subvert the system and get away with something. The dialogue was often rich and funny; the characters were colorfully odd.

A FORMULA FOR a number of his stories was to present an inexplicable mystery, and then explain it all with a twist at the end.

Two stories were set in the American Museum of Natural History; in "Mystery in the Museum," the narrator, one of several street-smart young men, comments naïvely on the exhibits and shrewdly on the public filing past the glass cases.

> *"See the girl in yellow, how intent she is in examining those old skulls!" says Skinny. "And how the lady with the white feather is studying spears and arrows!" The girl in yellow gives three little dabs at the lace at her throat; the lady with the white feather smooths her hair above her ears. Then me and Skinny is cynics! The female sex was only studying and examining and intent upon their own reflections in the giant cases; looking where there's zoology, but seeing nothing but whether their hats is straight.*

The jewel collection at the museum presents a temptation when the museum is closed. But the would-be thief is undone by a haunting, painful annoyance that seems to chase him down the darkened halls. The last sentence of the story reveals that he has upset a working display of honeybees.

"Jed's Big Scheme" ran in *Argosy* in May 1905. It was a perfect *Argosy* tale, a weird story about a lazy local farmer who suddenly came into money.

> *Walking into the store in which he was so well known, he ordered five cents worth of crackers and paid for them with a five-hundred dollar bill, which Wilkins would not change. "Well, here's the smallest I have," said Jed. A hundred dollar bill.*

His neighbors discovered, to their horror, that he had found a practical way to change the face of a pig so that it resembled a person, and was selling the animals to sideshows around the country: "The Pig with a Human Face."

The *New York Evening Post* purchased a Fort story called "The Tropical Parts of New York," which later ran under the title "Ignatius Cassidy in a Greenhouse." It was a short, witty tale about a warehouseman who has handled wholesale groceries, but finds unique fascination in examining exotic plants—particularly the banana palm—in a New York greenhouse. He takes a menial job offered by the "head gardener, or arboriculturist, or horticulturist, for words thrive and grow fat in a greenhouse." But he is surprisingly foiled by a silly mistake with the banana palm. The story offers a few reminders of Fort's adventures: working in a wholesale grocery and studying the flora of St. Helena.

One of Fort's oddest tales, "How Uncle Sam Lost Sixty-four Dollars," ran in *Black Cat.* It's easy to imagine the tale as a parody of Fort's own impoverished travels. Simon Bobbles, an eccentric New Yorker, is determined to visit a friend in San Francisco. But, he complains, "It costs money to travel!" He puts a two-cent stamp on his forehead, writes an address across his coat, and sits atop a letterbox. When the postman arrives and contemplates the problem, Simon announces, "I can't move and by rights I can't talk, either. I'm mail." The postman carries him over his shoulder to the post office. "I'm always first class goods," Simon tells him. "I'm sort of a ward o' the government and must travel luxoorious. I'm mail and I can't walk."

By law, the two-cent stamp takes him to the address in San Francisco, where his friend is asked to pay the additional postage. But his friend objects. "He ain't worth it. Sorry, Simon, but you know you aren't worth anything like sixty-four dollars." Simon is carried back to the San Francisco post office and placed in the dead

letter office. There, a clerk tears off his coat (the "envelope"), discovering his return address written on a card, so Simon is returned
to New York. "There's always a way of doin' things," he declares.

Another story purchased by the *New York Evening Post* in May
1905 drew on Fort's experience aboard a cattle ship during his first
trip to Europe. "A Cattleship Mystery Solved" was written in first
person, filled with the lingo of an expert:

> *Most likely most of youse wasn't never in the business, but the
> first work is to tie the cattle to a headboard that runs along the front
> of a pen. The cattle swarms down a gangway, wild, scared and crazy,
> crowding and turning so that when a pen's full some is lodged with
> their tails to the headboard. . . . We're cracking corn and teasing out
> baled hay all morning, and then it's chuck-time. The cattle deck's quiet
> when all of a sudden, it's pandemonium. There's bullocks gored and
> there's leaping and crazy scrambling, all the more curious seeing
> cattle at sea is usually half seasick.*

The ship is plagued by stampedes at curious times, and the
mystery is finally solved when the author explains that an ill-
tempered hand had brought a bright red shirt aboard. "For a red
shirt ain't no article wanted on no cattleship."

IT WAS PROBABLY the realistic dialogue of the "Cattleship"
story that earned Fort a letter from the publishing house Street and
Smith. Theodore Dreiser, the new editor, had been reading Fort's
byline in other journals with jealousy, and finally inquired whether
he'd submit stories for their flagship publication, a pulp journal

titled *Smith's Magazine.* Toiling away on the kitchen table on Eighth Avenue, Fort had come to think of his stories as rent checks. He was oblivious to any new admirers in the publishing world.

Dreiser later recalled Fort's work:

> *They were the best humorous short stories that I have ever seen produced in America. Some of his writings suggested mental clowning, but they were realistic, ironic, wise and, in their way, beautiful. And among ourselves—Richard Duffy of* Tom Watson's, *Charles Agnew MacLean of* The Popular Magazine, *and others—we loved to talk of him and his future: a new and rare literary star.*

Dreiser realized there was something special about Charles Fort. Dreiser asked to meet him downtown at *Smith's* office, urging the writer to bring stories for consideration. Fort demurred. His usual procedure was to send his stories; he didn't want to have to brush off his old wool suit and squeeze into the vest, or spend the pennies for a clean paper collar. But no, Annie insisted, he had to go, and the occasion called for a new shirt. Nothing but a new shirt would do for a meeting with an important man like Theodore Dreiser.

Anybody Could Write a True Story

If the gods send worms, that would be kind, if we were robins.

One morning in the spring of 1905, Charles Fort walked down to Seventh Avenue at Fifteenth Street, entered the offices of Street and Smith, and asked to see Mr. Dreiser. It was the most important meeting of Fort's life. Dreiser recalled it years later:

> And a figure, almost a duplicate of Oliver Hardy of Laurel and Hardy, now came briskly forward. To this day, when I see Hardy I see Fort as he was then—that unctuous, ingratiating mood, those unwieldy, deferential, twittery mannerisms were Fort's then. He stood with his hat in his hand and said, "Ah, you wrote me, I believe. I am Charles Fort." And with the tone of his voice added to all else, I knew that I liked him and that I would like him, and that somehow he was the embodiment of the charming thing that I had read.

The comparison of Fort to the comedian Oliver Hardy was especially perceptive. The joke behind Hardy's performance is a character uneasy in any interaction, terrified that the shopgirl may be his social superior. He covers his insecurity by aping the Victorian courtliness of the previous generation, becoming more ridiculous. Similarly, Fort could quickly revert to the thirteen-year-old boy from Albany, fidgeting with his tie, shuffling his feet, trying to adopt the adult niceties that could pull him through the situation.

"I asked him to sit down," Dreiser later wrote. "We began an inquiry into his affairs solely because I was intrigued." Fort resisted the pleasantries.

> At first, his replies were almost inconsequential. Yes, he was interested in short story writing. Yes, he thought he might do something I might be interested in—maybe not. Anyhow, he thought he didn't want to waste my time so he brought a couple of things with him. He fished in a rather outstanding coat pocket in which he usually kept his fists and produced two short stories, written on undersized sheets of paper of a faded yellowish tint. He said shyly that I might look these over, and if they didn't interest me he might try something else. I tried to keep him in the office and talk some more; but as I decided afterward, he was too nervous and shy to stay, and he made his way out.

Fort told him nothing about his personal life; he never even said he was married. Dreiser, more class conscious than Fort, tried to fill in the pieces. "He had told me that he had just completed a trip around the world, that he had been to South America, in Cape Town, and so on. I judged from this that he was single and of some private means." Fort must have been confused about someone showing so much interest in his work; this was a new and mystifying compliment. He knew that Dreiser was an editor of popular journals and a successful author of magazine stories. Fort didn't know at the time—barely five hundred people across America knew—that he had been talking to one of the generation's most important novelists.

HERMAN THEODORE DREISER was just three years older than Charles Fort. He was born in August 1871 in Terre Haute, Indiana. His mother, the former Sarah Schanab from an Ohio Mennonite family, was the warm, hopeful center of the family. Dreiser's father, John Paul Dreiser, was a Roman Catholic German immigrant, and, like Fort's father, an uncompromising disciplinarian. But John Dreiser, a sometime mill worker, was also hopelessly unemployable, and his family of ten children was sloppy, poverty-stricken, and chaotic, an embarrassment to their midwestern neighbors.

The hero of the family was Theodore's oldest brother, Paul, who had run away to join a medicine show. Later Paul worked as a blackface minstrel, singer, songwriter, and vaudevillian under the name Paul Dresser. When Theodore was nine years old, Paul reappeared miraculously at the family home in Sullivan, Indiana—fat, happy, bedecked in a fur coat and a silk hat, offering his latest songs for the family's amusement, peeling dollar bills from a thick wad of money to pay their debts. "He was like a warm, cheering fire," Theodore later recalled.

But even Paul's largess was erratic, based on his high living. When Theodore was sixteen, he left home and moved to Chicago with dreams of success in the big city. He was tall and scrawny; his ears stuck out, and he spoke with a stammer. He found only a series of low-level jobs that disgusted him: as a dishwasher, hardware clerk, a driver for a laundry, and a bill collector. In 1892, when he was twenty, Dreiser took a job at the *Globe*, "the poorest paper in Chicago." Like Fort—who was writing for a Brooklyn newspaper at exactly the same time—Dreiser learned from a sympathetic editor, John Milo Maxwell, who mercilessly slashed at his stories with a blue pencil. "This is awful stuff!" Maxwell told him. "Now you probably think I'm a big stiff, chopping up your great stuff like this, but if you live and hold this job you'll thank me."

Dreiser's prose could be muddy, and spelling and punctuation required special attention. But he loved writing and, maybe more importantly, was willing to rewrite. Theodore earned a recommendation to a first class St. Louis paper.

Covering a story about St. Louis schoolmarms visiting the 1893 World's Fair in Chicago, Dreiser met a pretty young teacher, Sara Osborne White. Her family had nicknamed her Jug, for her shiny, jug-colored auburn hair. She was twenty-four years old, two years older than Dreiser. Months after their return to St. Louis, Theodore Dreiser proposed marriage, and Jug quickly accepted. Dreiser suspected, almost immediately, that the engagement was a mistake. He was obsessive and insatiable about his relationships with women, plotting one pursuit after another. Throughout his life, he had little sense of romance, but only a romantic, dreamy sense of conquest. Sara White returned to her hometown outside St. Louis and Dreiser left town for Ohio, in search of a better salary before they were married.

IN THE SPRING OF 1894, Dreiser traveled to the tiny town of Weston, Ohio. Another St. Louis reporter had convinced him that they should purchase the Weston newspaper, the *Wood County Herald*.

It was, coincidentally, almost the same plan that had ensnared Fort the previous year in Woodhaven, New York: inexperienced reporters taking over a small-town paper. But when Dreiser saw the sad little town and the dusty newspaper office, he balked, moving on. After jobs in Toledo and Pittsburgh, he settled in New York City.

The great metropolis fascinated and terrified Dreiser. He found small assignments at Joseph Pulitzer's *New York World* and wrote magazine stories. Eventually he swallowed his pride and marched into the offices of Howley, Haviland and Company, a music publisher on Twentieth Street. The "Company" was Dreiser's brother Paul, who had written a long string of successful songs for the firm. Theodore proposed that they publish a monthly magazine to promote their songs; a rival music publisher had become successful with a similar publication. Paul thought it was a great idea, and Dreiser was installed as editor in a small office. His salary started at $10 a week, and *Ev'ry Month*, a collection of editorial ramblings, short stories, book reviews, and songs appeared in October 1895.

The magazine was a success, but Dreiser found the atmosphere at Howley, Haviland oppressive. Grandly and naïvely, Dreiser wanted the pages to bristle with philosophy and thought-provoking articles. The partners wanted him to promote music and "tickle the vanity and cater to the foibles and prejudices of readers." No doubt the bigger-than-life presence of Paul also made him uncomfortable. One day in the office, when Paul pulled his belly up to a piano and tried to hammer out a new song, he asked his little brother, a sometime poet, for help. Theodore carelessly suggested some lyrics about the Wabash River in Indiana, where the Dreiser family grew up. The following year, "On the Banks of the Wabash," Paul's latest song, was a nationwide hit.

After two years at *Ev'ry Month*, Theodore quit to write for magazines, specializing in interviews with famous men, profiles of historical figures, or articles about industry. "I have an easy pen," he boasted. Unlike Fort, Dreiser was writing for first-class magazines like *Cosmopolitan* and the *Saturday Evening Post,* writing nonfiction and earning close to $100 a week. He brought Jug back east, refusing a family wedding but marrying her in a quiet ceremony in Washington, D.C., in December 1898—more than five painful years after he had first proposed.

The following summer, Arthur Henry, a friend of Dreiser's from the *Toledo Blade* newspaper, suggested that they both begin writing fiction. Dreiser penned some short stories, and, urged on by Henry, started a novel. As he recalled, he picked up a piece of paper and started with the title *Sister Carrie.*

Penning the first chapters, Dreiser later recalled, he "thought it was rotten." But Henry cheered him on, and Dreiser gained confidence. The plot was loosely based on his sister Emma, who had lived in Chicago in the 1880s. Emma had eloped with a married man who had stolen money from his bosses to finance their trip.

Sister Carrie was an astonishing, disconcertingly modern book. Its characters respond to inner urges and desires, barely acknowledging any governing morality. But the text was also filled with Dreiser's fascination with life in the big city; his famously rambling prose provided gritty accounts of the fashions, sights, and sounds of society, including the colloquial speech of its main characters.

The book was rejected at Harper's, who were disdainful of its "reportorial realism." But it was quickly accepted at Doubleday, Page. Unfortunately, Frank Doubleday was traveling in Europe when the deal was signed. Upon his return, Doubleday took proofs home to read. He hated it, convinced that the book was immoral and unprofitable—the tale of an ambitious young girl who has two illicit relationships, with a traveling salesman and an embezzler.

Worst of all, the author seemed oddly tolerant of these transgressions.

"Excellent as your workmanship is," a partner at Doubleday wrote to Dreiser, "the choice of your characters has been unfortunate." Doubleday asked to be released from their agreement; they offered to find another publisher for Dreiser or make amends. Arrogantly, Dreiser chose to hold Doubleday to their contract, which left the success or failure of the book in the hands of the publisher. The firm printed and bound the contracted minimum, one thousand books, and gave it cursory distribution. A number of reviews were favorable, and a few praised its greatness. But a year after its publication, *Sister Carrie* had sold fewer than five hundred copies, netting its author $68.40.

Dreiser was ruined financially and near a nervous breakdown. Attempting to reestablish a career, he sent Jug to her family in St. Louis. Dreiser developed insomnia, pain in his fingertips, stomach trouble, and uncontrollable weeping. In a big-city contretemps that seemed taken from the pages of *Sister Carrie,* a year after the publication of his book, Dreiser found his vision impaired and suffered a maddening impulse to walk in circles, which, he later wrote, "was nothing more or less than pure insanity." He was renting a miserable $1.25-a-week six-by-eight-foot room in Brooklyn, living on carefully rationed meals of bread and milk, and pacing the East River, staring into the icy waves. "It would be so easy to drop in. The cold would soon numb me—a few gulps and all would be over."

As usual, it was Paul Dresser who offered salvation, paying Theodore's way to William Muldoon's sanitarium in upstate New York. Muldoon had trained wrestlers and boxers; he was now running a camp for wealthy city folks who were too drunk or too rattled to go on with life.

Five weeks of strenuous exercise and healthful food were restorative. Jug returned to her husband, and Dreiser took a job of manual labor, working in the carpentry shop for the New York Central
Railroad. He returned to newspaper work and, in 1904, applied at
Street and Smith, the pulp magazine publishers. They hired Dreiser
to edit their new flagship magazine, *Smith's*. He was earning $35
a week.

He discovered Fort's stories in another Street and Smith publication, the *Popular Magazine*. Fort's realistic stories of rough-and-tumble
dockworkers and stevedores reminded Dreiser of his own hardships:

> *I had been in contact with the slums and every other phase of*
> *New York, for that matter, for years. The regions, the characters, the*
> *incidents that Fort's stories concerned were things I had observed, but*
> *from a different angle. These were essentially my streets, my docks,*
> *my loafers, my failures. Yet nevertheless, here they were set forth in*
> *an entirely new light. These were almost lovingly dealt with, and so*
> *understandingly. All the little social and emotional and financial*
> *problems as intimately set forth as though the people themselves were*
> *talking. Here was the sunlight, rain, clouds of dust, the smoke of tugs*
> *blackening the housewives' wash, the noises and smells natural to the*
> *crowded, violent life he was describing. And as I read I wished that*
> *I had been with this man when he was loafing and meditating over*
> *these trivial and yet enticing lives.*

WHEN FORT WAS STANDING in Dreiser's office at Street and
Smith, the crumpled stories that he pulled from his coat pocket
consisted of "When We Were Vicariously Virtuous," a tale of his

newspaper days in Brooklyn, and a tenement story about a "police-man accidentally drawn up to the roof." "When We Were Vicari-ously Virtuous" particularly interested Dreiser. After reading it, he wrote to Fort:

> This [newspaper] story of yours is clever in its way, but you have put too much in it for our purposes. I think if you had left out everything except the story of the neighborhood which the reporter wrote up . . . it would be suitable. However, I know that these things are hard to change and you are at liberty to suit yourself about re-turning it.

He added a postscript: "If you come into this office some time soon, I shall be most pleased to see you."

"When We Were Vicariously Virtuous" was later run in *Smith's* as "Fryhuysen's Colony." It's difficult to tell if Fort made the cuts suggested by Dreiser, for the story still contains a subplot involving "vicarious virtue," and was published a full year after Fort submitted it, suggesting some sort of backstage tussle. It features the dishon-est reporter Fryhuysen, who had already appeared in a story in the *Popular Magazine.*

> "Did I ever tell you how I got my job here?" asked Fryhuysen. "I got it on the strength of the most realistic and beautifully repulsive little story you ever read. It was a fight, for five hundred a side, between a bulldog and a Negro, who fought the brute on hands and knees. Of course, there was no truth in it, but anybody could write a true story. We said: 'You ought to go to some nice, quiet, psychopathic ward and have your mind scraped for imagining such things.' This boastfulness of his was always irritating; it seemed so amateurish."

When Fryhuysen is given an assignment to find some interesting Sunday story down at the docks, of course he returns with a whopper, a story about a squatter's colony.

> "I've got in descriptions of odd houses pieced together with old doors and roof tin. There's a cave dweller in it, and the other characters are great. There's the old woman with the seventeen goats, and the one-legged sailor. And not a word of it is true. I just went to Jennings' and shot pool and came back to write the first thing I could think of."

The article is published, but the story is so perfect that the editor, Old Buttons, begins to smell a rat. He asks Fryhuysen to escort him and the staff artist to the docks and introduce him to his squatters. As the three approach the docks, the reporter grows glum.

> "I don't know what to say," Fryhuysen whispered, as they walked down a long block to the riverfront. "I might as well confess."
>
> "What?" cried jolly Old Buttons. "Whispering in company? Shocking manners, Fryhuysen. Ah, here we are! Then it's just around the corner? This is the corner you mentioned?"
>
> "It is," said Fryhuysen, faintly. All three wheeled around the corner of a tall fence.
>
> There was the one-legged sailor. He sat in front of a house queerly made of old junk and old woodwork. The goats were there; the queer old woman and the cave dweller. Just as described was everything. Humiliated Fryhuysen hung his head. He had boasted of his imagination, but this time, perhaps for the novelty of it, had written things that only existed. Pitiable was his chagrin.

. . .

SOMETIMES FORT'S STORIES were a little too realistic. Dreiser must have been especially chilled to read "I Meddled." It ran in December 1905 in the *Popular Magazine*, originating down the hall from Dreiser. In a 1905 letter to Fort, Dreiser pointed out that his stories were being read "for both *Smith's* and the *Popular*," so Dreiser might have considered the story.

In "I Meddled," Fort's Brooklyn reporter insists that small-town dramatic critics never bothered to attend performances; they just wrote generic reviews filled with two-dollar adjectives, and then inserted the names of the actors.

In 1893, when he was a dramatic critic at the *St. Louis Globe-Democrat*, Dreiser had done exactly this. Attempting to review three shows on one night, he was also assigned to investigate a streetcar holdup on the opposite side of town. He wrote his reviews based on press releases, filling them with trenchant observations about the cast. The next morning, he discovered that a rainstorm had prevented two of the shows from arriving into the city. Rival newspapers used the reviews to ridicule the paper's editor, Dreiser's boss: "This latest essay of his into the realm of combined dramatic criticism, supernatural insight, and materialization, is one of the most perfect things of its kind." Dreiser left a note of resignation and slinked away. He was embarrassed by the incident and only admitted it many years later, in a 1922 book.

THROUGHOUT HIS LIFE, Fort translated every serious interest into a collection. As a boy, it was paper soldiers, and then stamps, birds' eggs, or minerals. When he became interested in short-story writing, he collected images.

Fort constructed dozens of small pasteboard boxes, simulating pigeonholes. He filled them with slips of paper, each scrawled with a metaphor or simile. Fort kept a pocketful of tiny paper slips and a stub of a pencil in his vest pocket; he carefully recorded these images as they occurred to him. Soon the boxes filled the mantel, were stacked on the dresser, and pushed against a wall of Charles and Anna's Eighth Avenue apartment.

The distinctive images shine like little jewels in Fort's stories.

A skinny man taking a chair: *By a series of angles, just as you would fold up a metal ruler by its joints, an angle at his ankles, an angle at his knees, another at his waist, he sat down.*

A fat lady in the tenements: *A cherry on a plum on an apple! All three impaled upon a skewer to hold them together. That should give you some idea of Mrs. Pillquit's figure.*

And an Irish laborer: *He was log-shaped; he seemed as big around at his ankles as at his chest, and, although he wore collars, it was because everyone else wore collars, and not because his neck was perceptible.*

A lady carrying a bundle of wet laundry: *Out and away and back home with her big white turnip and its pouter-pigeon effect, too bulky for her arms to go around, her chin lost in fluttering turnip-tops.*

A frowsy landlord: *Face spattered with red spots, as if every one-thousandth drink had rung up and registered itself there.*

Workmen unloading a shipment of fruit: *Watermelons were undulating in a green streak from a cart to the rear of Leonidas Marcy's store. Men in a line caught melons with a sharp slap on each*

side, and turned just in time to catch another, with catching and
throwing in one motion.

A sea captain's forehead: *Exactly five wrinkles in it, as if*
it had been pressing upon banjo strings.

To Fort, the notes represented not only achievement but also
ownership. When he was tired of writing, he could sort through the
slips, looking for new inspirations or rearranging them in new orders. Soon he had twenty-five thousand of these notes, and, like any
collection, he began obsessing over it. "I worried when I thought
of the possibility of fire," he later wrote. "I thought of taking the
notes upon fireproof material."

FORT DEVELOPED a knack for tenement stories. One of his
earliest, a boardinghouse tale called "Not Like Mother's," ran in the
February 1906 *Smith's* magazine.

> *Mrs. King's boarding house come up to all my notions of society*
> *that I read of in the Sunday papers. There ain't much scrapping in*
> *the halls, and all there is, is done subdued and gentle by the ladies,*
> *and not one of them says to another lady, "Come down in the yard*
> *and I'll lick you!" None of that! Only a harmless little clinch by the*
> *hall rack once, and the lady that done the biting didn't cause no*
> *hurry-up call, as her teeth was only counterfeits.*
>
> *That's why I just couldn't comprehend when Alonzo Grudgger*
> *begun his kicking. Him kicking in that society boarding house, which*
> *had its day beginning and ending with the same two sounds you*
> *couldn't mistake, was you on a desert island—the dropping of shoes*

all around you at half-past ten at night, and the song of the chopping bowl at six in the morning.

Dreiser was now sure that the "strongest vein" for Fort was tenement and waterfront stories; he wanted more of these, but he cautioned Fort to avoid too much style, and simply tell "the straight away story."

> *Out of last bunch of short yarns you submitted I am retaining "How Murphy Won by Losing," which I wish to consider a little longer. The others I am returning. Would you let me know how you are getting on the dock yarns, which you were going to look up? I would like to see you attempt something in that line as I think you could do it well.*

But he found only one of the dock stories satisfactory, and again advised Fort about his style: the "diary idea is entirely unnecessary." Dreiser purchased several "Lannigan stories" (presumably stories based on Irish immigrants). He returned "Miranda's Honeymoons," curtly explaining that he liked the character of the gas man, but was "not so pleased with the temperament of Miranda." He wanted Fort to "make Miranda a more pleasing type," and then "send the story to me again."

Fort was shy but also stubborn. As a freelance writer, he must have found Dreiser's fussy notes an annoyance and his needy, back-and-forth correspondence exasperating; after all, he was only being paid $25 for each story. Dreiser undoubtedly intended this as flattery to his new friend, reminding him of Arthur Henry's literary cheerleading that had inspired *Sister Carrie*. Dreiser's thoughts were still directed toward novels. "I am an editor at present," he wrote to an admirer, "but am longing to do one thing, write." *Sister Carrie* had been received with success in England; Dreiser was arranging a new American edition of the book, and had already begun work on his second and third novels. He lured Fort downtown for another conversation: "I want to talk to you about some idea I have, which may prove of interest to you."

Dreiser told Fort that he was wasting his time with magazine stories. He should be writing a novel. As Fort sat in his office, twiddling his thumbs, the editor talked him through the process: Fort had a knack for interesting characters and distinctive dialogue. He simply needed to develop his dramatic storytelling.

"You ought to devote yourself to the novel which I spoke to you about," Dreiser wrote Fort in October 1905. "Do not forget that is the next important thing for you."

EIGHT

Leaping Out of a
Window, Head First

Is life worth living? I have many times asked that question, usually deciding negatively, because I am likely to ask when I am convinced that it isn't.

In Fort's stories, the sharp, colloquial conversations seem too real to be pure inventions, and must have been inspired by the chatter of his neighbors up and down the tenement steps. Similarly, it is easy to glimpse Anna on the periphery of many stories, efficiently going about her housework and pausing to exchange gossip.

"Those That Are Joined Together," from the April 1906 *Tom Watson's Magazine*, is typical:

> It would surely please you to look at Mrs. McGibney when she
> worried; left forefinger beginning over the fingers of his right hand;
> left forefinger lodging on the right little finger, Mrs. McGibney paus-
> ing to look into space, counting up to assure herself that the butcher
> had not cheated; forefinger beginning again and dealing with the grocer,
> this time; another fixed look into space to be sure the grocer had not
> imagined a can of tomatoes or a pound of flour. It would please you

because you would know that not one penny, worked so hard for by
McGibney, would be wasted. When Mrs. McGibney bustles—ah, now
that is pretty! That means a very keen sense of responsibility, nothing
shirked, nothing that will make McGibney's comfort neglected.

Mrs. McGibney plays adviser to a quarreling couple, and each
arrives to tell her their troubles. Of the couple's meager belongings,
both man and wife prize the tintypes "taken one almost impossible
happy day at Coney Island." Anna treasured one of these cheap
Coney Island tintypes for many years; it showed Anna and Charles
just after their wedding.

From a story, "Ructions":

Sinks in houses like this are very much like wells in Oriental
countries—meeting places, gossiping places for women. Mrs. Lunn at
the third-floor sink; Mrs. Delaney at the next sink; Mrs. Weasel
at the first-floor sink.

And pretty Mrs. Delaney, the motorman's wife!—starting to run
up to the sink above, but feeling that something more interesting might
be said at the sink below. Starting, then, to run down to the first sink,
but feeling that Mrs. Lunn would be less guarded in her utterances,
as she was not likely to stay in the house very much longer.

All three women suffering intensely! One must gossip, but one
must have some excuse, if only the borrowing of a match, to approach
the relief of gossiping. Trust them for that when it was necessary to
their happiness to discuss Mrs. Bonticue! All three of them up and at
it. "Outrageous!" "Oh, scandalous! Never heard of such carryings-on
before!" Turning on the water, to at least pretend to fill a kettle.

These housewives in "Ructions," from *Tom Watson's,* May 1906,
form the supporting cast. The star is a battle-axe of a tenant named

Mrs. Bonticue, who wreaks revenge on the landlord when she thinks she's being dispossessed. The character was popular enough to appear in a second story, "Mrs. Bonticue and Another Landlord," the following month.

"And Now the Old Scow May Slant As It Pleases," from *Smith's*, October 1906, hints at Fort's familiarity with manual labor during his impoverished travels.

> *The* Mary Fallon *of Haverstraw lay at her pier—stanch old brick-scow, brick-dust ground into every beam—tied with great hawsers, so that she should remain true and not go flirting away with the tide. Each laborer threw seven bricks at a time to the driver, who was most dexterous and played a game of skill that any baseball catcher might envy. You could sit and count all day; certainly you could sit—we say sit, because one always sits when bathing in the idle comfort of watching others toil—sit, week in and week out, and never see him take eight bricks at a time. He slaps down his hand upon a row of bricks, without looking at it, and by instinct, his hand always slaps upon the seventh brick. The seventh is deftly plucked out and placed over against the first, so there is room at each end of the seven for a hand.*

The captain marries a sweet girl; she tries to put up with the housekeeping in their cabin on the scow, the clouds of red dust and the precarious tilt of the vessel as a ton of bricks is removed from one side against the dock, before then the ship is reversed to unload the opposite side. Her pretty porcelain vases and knick-knacks tumble off the mantle. "The greater the slant the greater her distress, casting back anxious glances but believing that, after all, there would be an escape this time. Then the familiar crash."

Perhaps the strangest of Fort's stories was called "A Radical

Corpuscle." A white blood cell pauses in its artery long enough to deliver a philosophical rant, about the universe—the man they inhabit—and their purpose in life.

> *"Fellow leucocytes, do you know why we are placed here in this Man?"*
> *"To get all we can out of it!" answered a sleek, shiny corpuscle.*
> *The others laughed good-naturedly, agreeing that this was their sole reason for being.*

Although the sentiment was a reminder of Fort's childhood in Albany, "Everything was for us," it also hinted at Fort's later insights. The agitator leucocyte argues that the Man calls his own world the Earth. "He is a white corpuscle to the earth. He says the moon causes the tide. Perhaps. Then the moon is the Earth's heart." The crowd shouts him down, rejecting his philosophy.

> *"He says we were made for the Man!" jeered the few leucocytes who gave the distasteful doctrine another thought. "But we know, and have every reason to know, that this Man was made for us!"*

In March 1906, the ideas only served as an early science fiction tale in *Tom Watson's*. It was a taste of Fort's amazing inside-out cosmology that later became his calling card.

FORT'S WARM, QUIRKY STYLE suggests an author brimming with self-confidence, but he wasn't. His notebook reveals that he was plagued by doubt, fretting over bits of advice, and using self-analysis to teach himself about writing.

*Not yet reached the top because not yet made every possible mis-
take. Every improvement is only doing something done before but with
more concentrated power. In each step something suffers; plot, character, style, human interest. That in all my mistakes, I have gone in
the right channels, but in every wrong detail.*

Everything wrong is a low plane of something right.

*Hoff [another editor] says, "You don't mean that, do you? That
you think you have no dramatic instinct?" It makes an impression on
me; I'm not yet ready to take dramatic up.*

*Dreiser says, "Why don't you give us something dramatic?" That
speaks, because I am ready.*

*Last of August, utter inability to write, but feeling of gathering
power, feeling of not writing, because won't stoop to level of former
productions. Feel have reached the limit of good work for one cent a
word. Feel can't any more write sordid stuff of such low people.*

Been a carpenter of a writer; be an artist now.

*Can't sit still. Jump from chair. Realize that fault has been pet-
tiness of theme. My style is right for action and excitement. "Ructions" went because fits that style.*

Perhaps Fort's most significant note appeared in an entry at the
end of October 1906:

*Am cutting suggestions from the papers, and broadening field of
note taking. [Now cutting] in earnest and with system.*

In April 1906, Dreiser left Street and Smith to edit *Broadway*
magazine, an established publication in search of a larger audience.

He was anxious to include Fort's stories. Two Fort pieces appeared in *Broadway* in the summer of 1906, "The Discomfiture of Uncle McFuddy," a dock tale of a runaway boy, and "The Rival Janitors," about tenants auditioning for the job of tenement janitor—because the position offered free rent. The *Broadway* stories were similar to Fort's previous formulas, and may have been brought over by Dreiser from the *Smith's* office. When Dreiser lured Fort to see him at *Broadway*, he was surprised to find the author still reluctant and mysterious:

> *He said he had changed his method. He had a new idea as to how his stories should be written. Since I could not imagine any method he might employ that would make his work unsatisfactory to me, I begged him to let me see them. He now presented his ideas in a straight dialogue with so little description as to almost eliminate the loveliness of the atmosphere in which previously his characters and their troubles were bathed. Not only that, but in the story offered me he had fixed his attention on a sodden slum group whose temperaments and conduct were almost unbearable.*

The editor felt that the story was artistic, "wonderful, but impossible." It must have been "Had to Go Somewhere," the last of Fort's short stories, which was eventually published in *1910 Magazine* in February of that year. An astonishingly bleak story, it is told in snatches of dialogue and vivid, hellish descriptions, as if a cruel joke on the fashionable, family-oriented publications that had been employing Dreiser:

> *The crowded back room of a junk shop, all worn-out-looking and badly patched with shadows from a long rag of flame of a tipless*

gas-burner. Against a flickering wall, a table for two musicians, their handwritten music in notebooks, leaning upon bottles of cheap red wine—against the opposite wall, baled rags surmounted by a black bale, insecurely poised, pointing downward like the head of a big, black dog on watch; part of a broad, scarlet petticoat hanging from it like a monster dog's tongue. Junkman's family and neighbors sitting on flat, oval-shaped objects on the floor, in an irregular line from table to bales. "Sure," someone was saying, "we must go somewheres this night."

There are no personalities and no story. Fort describes a drunken bacchanal of the lowest strata of society. As faceless neighbors stumble into the room, they drink, argue, or sing loudly along with the music. They whirl, stumble, and tip over furniture.

A young lady, sitting on a link of the horse-collar chain beside a young gentleman, combing his hair with her hair-comb, his arms bearishly about her; in her lap a flask of whiskey, cigarettes, and matches. "Yes, I'll recite for youse—light it for me!" Putting a ciga-rette in the young gentleman's mouth. "When I was in the Tombs, I used to see Solinski, the murderer, every day. Once at noon, I seen six murderers playing ball."

"Now, if yez'll all be quiet, I'll recite!" Young lady reciting "The Face on the Barroom Floor," but forgetting it, starting something about two violets and a brook. "Aw, here!" to the young gentleman, "light this for me."

The reader's only surprise—Fort's trick ending—makes the story all the more dire. In the last lines, the revelers collapse in inebriated heaps as a lamp is knocked over and extinguished.

In the darkness, the watchman's lantern shone like a sullen-fierce
monster's eye. Scrambling, shrieking, swearing, someone shouting:
"A Merry Christmas and a Happy New Year!"

When Dreiser suggested modifying the story, lightening its tone, he feared Fort's reaction. The author just shrugged. It was all he had at the moment, he said. He was no longer interested in writing short stories. "But listen, Fort," Dreiser recalled telling him, "you have a gorgeous gift for this. This is not just story writing in your case. A book of these stories will make you." "Well, that may be so," Fort answered, looking down at his hands, "but I am not interested in being made that way. It isn't really what I want to do any more."

Too shy to admit it, he had actually adopted Dreiser's suggestion and now was obsessed with the idea of writing a novel, unable to contemplate the jolly, innocent stories he had composed for magazines.

But Fort was tenaciously concealing one more secret from his friend. If Fort's childhood had inspired the camping stories, his travels provided the dock yarns, and his apartment life in New York had suggested the colorful tenement stories, Dreiser should have wondered how the author managed to write so world-weary a story as "Had to Go Somewhere." Charles and Anna Fort were now miserably, hopelessly poor.

THE MAGAZINE CONTRIBUTIONS were part of the problem. Stories took a long time to sell and Fort had difficulty collecting his money. Correspondence shows that Dreiser was no better than any other editor. In November 1905, he accepted a Christmas story about lonely reporters, "Christmas Waifs," but it didn't run until January 1907, after Dreiser left the magazine. He brought Fort down to the *Broadway* magazine in August 1906, to encourage him to rewrite "When a Man's Not Working" as a "reading play," then brought him back in November wanting further modifications so he could buy it.

In December 1906, Fort wrote in his journal, "Have not been paid for one story since May. Have two dollars left. Watson's has cheated me out of $155. Dreiser has sent back two articles he told me he would buy, one even advertised to appear in his next number."

Matthew Wallace, receiving desperate requests for money in Albany, knew that Fort's bitterness toward his father only exacerbated the problem. Raymond, the favored son, was working in the family business in Albany. Charles was ignored.

I know considerable of your private life, and the family. It is sad, but more so, to know the intense feeling you harbor. You have cause, and it is human to be bitter, I confess, but Charley, don't cultivate that hatred. Endeavor to live it down (if it will down).

Anna took work in a Manhattan hotel laundry to support the couple. It was hard work, involving long hours each day and evenings; she was required to live in dormitories in the hotel for days at a time. Fort was left home to complete the novel that was now consuming him. This seemed to be the only hope, a substantial work capable of generating income. The pressure only added to his misery.

Late one afternoon, as Fort sat writing, his thoughts were distracted by financial worries. The couple was in desperate need of food. He heard a knock at his door, and opened it in the cold twilight to find a grocer's crate that contained "a bottle of milk, a loaf of bread, a can of beans and a few cans of other food." Fort asked his neighbors if they had ordered the food. They hadn't. Finally, he took in the crate of food. For many years he remembered this odd incident; he wondered if, in some strange way, his misery had brought the food to his door.

It was the troublesome property in Albany that triggered disaster. Early in 1906, Fort had taken out a $500 mortgage on the property, but was unable to make payments. "I owe $15 since July on the mortgage," he wrote in his journal.

A note written in Fort's hand was evidently handed to Annie at work:

> My dear Annie,
> We are busted. I must see you to talk about selling the house. Be on the corner of Eighth Avenue and Forty Sixth Street at half past eight, tonight.
> ["At half past eight," was then crossed out and Fort wrote the words, "right now."]
> Very truly yours,
> Charles Fort

Fort could only record his misery in his journal. "Everything is pawned. W [Wallace in Albany] led me to believe he would buy the house and now backs out. I am unable to write. I can do nothing else for a living. My mind is filled with pictures of myself cutting my throat or leaping out of the window, head first."

In December, 1906, Wallace had more bad news.

Your tenants do not pay until about the middle of the month and since I sent you our last money I have paid out some $15 for topping out chimney and carpenter work in connection with plumber, so therefore we are "busted" up here, also. However, to help you out, in your distress, and save a distinguished and useful life I enclose check for $20.

The following month, the situation was no better. "Great God! Can it be that we have pulled through till now?" Fort asked himself. "Smith lent us $11. Otherwise, dead." He fretted over his pawn receipts. "The two clocks! The misery of it!" In February, he held out hope that some of his rejected stories, now sent to *Collier's* and *Harper's*, might sell. "Only the good old hope without backing, because stories kept longer than usual." They didn't sell.

Can't go out without getting feet soaking, because poor shoes. Everything just as miserable and horrible as ever. Oh, hell! It's good for me! Nothing like it to develop this poor damn fool who thinks he's a genius.

More than likely, Fort had been trying to write several novels, one after another, overlapping, stealing bits of one to inspire another, in quick succession. He desperately needed a project that could be sold. In March 1907, the Forts were evicted—"dispossessed"—from the apartment on Eighth Avenue, and there's evidence that Charles wandered the streets, sleeping in parks, before scraping together the money to move downtown into a gritty little back building on the west side of Manhattan.

One day in his small room, Fort had another odd experience. He was helpless with despair—unsure of his writing and terrified of poverty. As he hovered over the small stove, feeding in bits of

Left:
Fort's childhood home, where he slammed the door, was on State Street in Albany; this is a modern photograph.

Right:
Charles Nelson Fort, Fort's father, was a wealthy businessman and a dandy; he was called "They" in Fort's autobiography.

Raymond, Clarence, and Charles Fort ("The Other Kid," "The Little Kid," and "We") shared a tumultuous childhood.

Charles Fort, age fifteen, shortly before he began writing for the Albany newspaper.

Charles Fort left school and became a newspaper reporter for the *Brooklyn World* when he was nineteen years old.

Young Anna Filing met Charles Fort in Albany, where she may have worked as a domestic servant.

Theodore Dreiser achieved success as a journalist and editor of pulp fiction before his career as a novelist.

Anna and Charles pose in a scratchy Coney Island portrait; he later wrote about a couple fondly guarding their cheap Coney Island tintypes.

During Fort's writing career, Anna worked as a domestic servant and in a laundry—the model for Fort's character Mrs. Birdwhistle.

Dreiser's deliberately artistic Greenwich Village apartment featured
an elaborate desk built from his brother Paul's piano.

Fort's apartment was on the top floor
of this Hell's Kitchen walk-up; here he
wrote *X, Y,* and *The Book of the Damned*;
this is a modern photo.

In a snapshot of Anna and Charles,
"Momma" looks stern as Charles fingers
a bit of paper—perhaps one of his notes.

Above:
Dreiser *(left)* and Horace Liveright.
Liveright was blackmailed into publishing
Fort's *The Book of the Damned.*

Right:
A formal portrait shows the mysterious,
publicity-shy author who bemused
readers of *The Book of the Damned.*

Anna and Charles in the early
twenties; with a successful book and
a small inheritance, he made plans to
leave New York.

Anna and Charles, on their passport.

Fort's last residence was the second floor of a quiet boarding house in the Bronx. Here he hosted De Casseres and Dreiser; this is a modern photo.

Alexander King's illustrations for *Lo!* captured the surreal nature of Fort's research and his ridicule of astronomers.

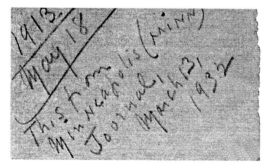

A typical Fort note, written on a rectangle of paper and cross-referenced in shoebox files.

Above:
A rare excursion for Charles Fort, visiting Dreiser at Mt. Kisco. The shy author left early to return to his wife in the Bronx.

Left:
Anna Fort with her two parrots; behind the open door, in carpet slippers and reading a newspaper, is her camera-shy husband.

Charles Fort grabbed a pencil and recorded that his final book, *Wild Talents*, had been delivered to Aaron Sussman.

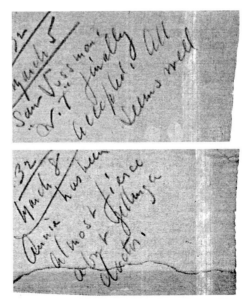

A Fort note written near the end of his life; Anna was "almost fierce" about his seeing a doctor.

Charles Fort at his Super-checker board; he created the game and was always in search of new players.

A newspaper portrait of Fort, near the end of his life.

The Fort family grave in Albany was constructed for his grandfather; it is guarded by a sculpted goddess, lost in thought.

Anna Fort on the roof of her Manhattan apartment with her pet parrot, after her husband's death.

coal and broken boxes that he had managed to pick up around the streets, he became aware of an unexpected golden color, which seemed to linger in a corner of the room. He later described it "a soft, golden yellow mist or glow." As Fort studied the manifestation, its mysterious, warm qualities "caused the mood that was enveloping him to disappear entirely."

EARLY IN 1907, while he was still working at *Broadway*, Dreiser was determined to have Fort writing for him again. But he'd lost track of Fort for more than six months. He'd sent letters but received no response. One morning, determined to find his old friend from *Smith's*, Dreiser took a day off and went to Fort's address. No one knew what had become of him. Dreiser questioned the local neighbors, saloonkeepers, and grocers.

> *Finally, after some hours of this, I ran across an old street sweeper who said that yes, he knew Fort. He believed that he had moved four or five blocks south. He thought his new address was in the middle of a given block and that if I asked around there I might find him. He believed that his wife was working somewhere in this neighborhood still. This came as a surprise because up to this time I never knew he had a wife.*

Dreiser took several hours "on one of the gloomiest days ever," going from house to house and searching for Fort in the working class neighborhood known as Hell's Kitchen.

> *Finally, one of the denizens of a particularly moldy cellar put her head out of the window and said, "Oh, yes, Mr. Fort. I believe*

he and his wife live across the street in that rear house." The second
floor of a rear tenement [was] as down in the heel a residence as
anyone could imagine. It was really not so far from suggesting the
world that he had written about in the story I was forced to refuse
for my magazine. I know, I said to myself, he has decided to make a
study of this region. Making my way in the dim gaslight, I went up
and knocked.

After a time I heard someone shuffling around inside and then
the door opened. And there he stood, but so changed in mood and ap-
pearance that I could scarcely believe it was the person I had
last seen.

Fort was just thirty-two years old, but looked older and wearier.
He was wearing shapeless trousers, a shirt open at the collar, and a
pair of old carpet slippers. The room, once a hall bedroom, had
been turned into a kitchen. Beyond a doorway were four walls of
peeling paint and an unmade bed. Fort squinted at Dreiser through
his glasses, noticing his prosperous appearance. "Oh, it's you. Come
in. Take the chair here."

I was so astonished and so, in a way, hurt that I wanted to do
something, put my arms around him or say that I was sorry, but I
didn't dare to. In order to get myself in hand what I did say was,
"For God's sake, what do you mean by leaving me and not answering
my letters or letting me come to see you?" He was so moved himself
that I saw tears come in his eyes. At this I stepped forward and put
my arms around him.

Dreiser offered his encouragement and listened to Fort's string
of hardships. Dreiser couldn't understand his friend's stubbornness.

"Why didn't you come to me? You know that I have been ready all of this time to do anything for you." Dreiser felt that Fort had reached a "temperamental block," turning his back on short stories but refusing to admit that he was without means. Dreiser realized that Fort's wife felt the importance of the book and had taken the job in the laundry to support him.

The manuscript of Fort's novel, partly completed, was sitting in the center of the kitchen table. It was titled *The Outcast Manufacturers.*

Dreiser returned about a week later. Annie was home from the laundry, preparing a late dinner. The rooms had been scrubbed clean and candles flickered in the window in expectation of their visitor. Dreiser noted her familiar way of saying "He don't like his dinner late. He likes it so that we can get through in time to go to a moving picture."

Fort sat, "bland and contemplative as a Chinese Hoti," as Annie hovered over him. Dreiser thought the relationship between the two of them odd. (Dreiser, who had a series of mistresses through his life, sometimes seemed mystified by stable relationships.) He felt that she played the part of the affectionate servant, perplexed by the person she was serving, but knowing that she was "part of something magnificent." Dreiser sensed a simple, humble charm: "This woman cannot think, she feels." Over dinner Annie spoke innocently of a tomcat that had been visiting the apartment, and the birds that perched outside the building each morning when she threw out some grain.

At some point in the conversation, Dreiser asked if Fort would be looking for a publisher, and Fort nodded. After years of false starts, Dreiser explained, his first novel, *Sister Carrie,* was about to be republished by B. W. Dodge and Company. Part of their arrangement was that Dreiser now owned an interest in the Dodge publishing company.

Over that simple tenement dinner with Theodore Dreiser in the spring of 1907, as Annie poured the coffee and chatted about the sparrows in the backyard, Charles Fort's luck was changing.

"To Work!" Cried
Mr. Birtwhistle

I cannot say that truth is stranger than fiction, because I have never had acquaintance with either.

With the B. W. Dodge edition of *Sister Carrie*, the success of Dreiser's book was assured. *Sister Carrie* had already earned an underground reputation in the United States and praise in England. Most critics now proclaimed its genius, and within days the initial printing of three thousand copies sold out. "Amid the thousands of anemic novels," noted the *New York Sun,* "here is a book written by a man." The *Los Angeles Times* thought it was "somber, powerful, fearlessly and even fearfully frank." Fort found a copy of the book in his mailbox, eagerly read it, and sent a note to its author on May 26, 1907. "Good luck on your book. I hope you'll make a barrelful, even if you are my traditional foe," he teased. "There are passions in it. Can't you get along without passions?" The banter about "passions" sounds like a response to Dreiser's pep talks on Fort's own manuscript. Dreiser was his best friend, but also a "traditional foe" as his potential publisher, editor, and competition.

In August, Fort realized how dependent he was on this friend. Dreiser was now the editor at Butterick Publications, in charge of their trio of successful magazines, the *Delineator*, the *Designer*, and *New Idea Woman's Magazine*. When Fort called downtown at the elegant Butterick offices, he was shocked to hear that the editor was in the hospital after an appendectomy. He tried his best to write an encouraging note. "I'd drop by and tell you my troubles to cheer you," he offered. "It's very hard." Dreiser recovered, and Fort completed the manuscript of *The Outcast Manufacturers*, delivering it early in December.

In his journal, Fort spilled all his concerns:

> *Dreiser has the book. It is good. Can it be that, next year, I shall look at this and say, "It was bad?" If so, how shall I ever live till next year? I can't see anything bad in it. Everything I have striven for is in it, wideness of character style, dramatic power, humor, plot, psychology. How can it be bad? Always I have thought my bad work good. I suspect nothing wrong with this book—except—is my style a species of vanity? No!*

Dreiser felt that the manuscript required a good amount of work. He sent it to readers at the *Delineator* for their advice, and then returned it to Fort for corrections. In May 1908, he reported that he was "surprised at how well you have taken out the unessential parts," but cautioned that the book still needed descriptive matter "to take away the extremely bald conversational progress." "The way you introduce the speakers from line to line is so abrupt that I am afraid it is going to be awfully trying to the average reader."

Although his letter was delicately worded, Dreiser was emphatic about more changes. He noted that Mrs. Dreiser, "a great admirer of your work," had also found it difficult. "You use very little of the art of luring your reader on. Don't you think it would be wise to correct this?" Dreiser noted that he'd now given the manuscript to a fourth reader at the magazine.

His comments must have sent Fort reeling. Despite his skepticism about *The Outcast Manufacturers*, Dreiser was determined to shepherd it through Dodge. He recalled his own terrible experience with *Sister Carrie* and Doubleday—the publisher that changed his mind. Dreiser was always convinced that it had been Mrs. Doubleday who had actually talked her husband out of his book. When he mentioned his own wife's criticisms of *The Outcast Manufacturers*, it was a virtual guarantee that he was going to see the book published—that he would rise above Mrs. Doubleday's perfidy.

Dreiser later wrote that he forced the book "on an unwilling publisher in the theory that, in due course, it would bestow undying luster on his name." *The Outcast Manufacturers* was published on March 31, 1909 in a pretty edition with a New York skyline embossed on the front cover. To celebrate, Fort was invited to the Dreisers' apartment for dinner. Fort's response suggested that Anna, still working at night, was not available for the social call. "It will be a pleasure to see Mrs. Dreiser," Fort wrote, and then joked about Dreiser's flashy wardrobe; "it will be an opportunity again to see Mr. Dreiser's waistcoat, which, down in the office the other day, I admired very much." Fort signed Dreiser's copy of the novel, "To his partner, from the author, Charles Fort."

THE OUTCAST MANUFACTURERS is a tenement story. Sim Rakes, a young man from the country, arrives at a dirty street in Manhattan, overlooking the Palisades. He's applying for work at the Universal Manufacturing Company, surprised to discover that it's

actually the front room of a ground-floor apartment. There he
meets Mr. Isaac Birtwhistle, a jolly moon-faced man, and his wife,
Delia, an efficient housekeeper who speaks with a tinge of an Irish
accent. Other employees are the gentle, slow Asbury Parker, who
sits at the typewriter replying to orders, and the gossipy Miss Guffy,
an Irish immigrant with a hunchback. Mrs. Birtwhistle's nieces, the
Dunphy girls, appear in between their jobs as domestic servants in
the homes of wealthy New Yorkers.

The company doesn't manufacture anything, but sends out cat-
alogs of assorted junk: tricks, novelties, a baby carriage, a coffee
grinder, or "The Great Ten-Cent Package." When an order is received, Universal Manufacturing retains several cents, and then for-
wards the rest of the money to the McGuire Supply Company, who
stores the merchandise and fills the order.

Birtwhistle is the grand, charming dreamer who imagines that
this is a going concern. He has no sense of money and a fondness
for leisure. "To work!" he shouts. But he quickly takes to the sofa,
playing with a kitten or lying idly on his back, "with thumbs and
forefingers, making rhomboids at the ceiling." When an enormous
order appears in the mail, Birtwhistle spends foolishly, raising his
own rent for a month to impress his landlord and taking his associates to Coney Island for a day of frivolity.

A month later, they're broke. Their landlord serves dispossession
papers, and a neighbor adroitly advises about the details of the law.
Miss Guffy, determined to help the company, appears miraculously
with the rent money, but it becomes apparent that she's just stolen
it from the desk of the landlord. The police arrive, and Guffy is
sent to jail. The Birtwhistles are evicted.

Mrs. Birtwhistle takes a job in a laundry. The rest of the group
are taken in by a neighbor, but with the apartment now jammed
with people, they are forced to leave, sleeping in Washington Square

Park. There Asbury Parker instructs them in how to keep warm by tying newspapers around their bodies.

They explore the docks, where they meet a sea captain who offers them quarters in his scow. Birtwhistle and Rakes go to the piers on the Hudson and accept a debilitating job, rolling logs onto the mud flats to form a platform. Although he's always disdained physical labor, Birtwhistle proves to be a good worker. The foreman discharges him, explaining that he's too powerful and is wearing out the rest of the crew.

Taking his paycheck, Birtwhistle buys a box of cheap toys, fluttering paper birds and jumping jacks, then carries them to a street market, determined to sell them all. But he fails as a salesman, intimidated by the other peddlers and bullied by the street urchins. He's surprised to meet his old landlord, who had been searching the city for him. Explaining that he's going to be running for a position in city government, the landlord has realized that it will make him look bad to have dispossessed poor tenants. He offers Birtwhistle his rooms once again.

At the end of the novel, the Universal Manufacturing Company is proudly back in business in the same tenement, with carpeting on the floor and a suite of new furniture. Birtwhistle is self-confident and happy again. He now operates a correspondence school on how to succeed in mail order.

DREISER WAS RIGHT. Long passages of dialogue are not "luring the reader" through the story, and the settings can seem oppressive. At the end of one chapter, when Birtwhistle happily marches out of the apartment to go to Coney Island, a reader expects to be treated to a new, fresh scene. But on the next page, Birtwhistle is back in the apartment, suffering the latest calamity. We are denied any moments but the most claustrophobic and chaotic. Miss Guffy, arrested by the police, never reappears and seems to be forgotten by her coworkers. Sim Rakes is introduced on the first page as the outsider; it seems as if his point of view should predominate through the novel. But Rakes soon becomes a secondary character and the story focuses on Mr. and Mrs. Birtwhistle.

In spite of its faults, the novel is refreshing and addictive. Fort tells the story in third person, pausing for his odd images and often reworking the descriptions through the narrative:

> The other Miss Dunphy came into the room, a straight-up-and-down young person, dressed in white. Had she stood very still, with her big, colorless, round face, she might possibly have been mistaken for an aquarium globe on a marble pedestal.

> . . . she flushed a little—flushes like goldfish in an aquarium, fluttering in her globe-like, colorless face—goldfish in a globe of milk, perhaps—or goldfish struggling in a globe of whitewash, have it.

> Round white lights in a mass of trees, like such perforations in darkness as would be seen by a bug in a pepper-box, looking up at the sky.

> Mrs. Tunnan, nose like a tiny model of a subway entrance; nostrils almost perpendicular and shaped like the soles of tiny feet; soles of the feet of a fairy, rest of him investigating within.

It's as if Fort is continually whispering into the reader's ear, constructing and adjusting each metaphor as the action proceeds. The Birtwhistles' indigence seems assured on the first page. Mr.

Birtwhistle bemoans their poverty, but as readers we see that they are very good at being poor. Their attitudes are perfectly suited to these hardships. Sometimes on the verge of argument, their problems dissolve into unexpected, warm laughter. One memorable scene occurs after the couple is dispossessed. Mrs. Birtwhistle is summoned from her job inside a hotel laundry, and the Birtwhistles, Rakes, and Parker pace up Fifth Avenue in the middle of the night—accompanied by the soft clicks of four pairs of worn-out shoes—coolly discussing their future finances. Science fiction author and Fort biographer Damon Knight noticed the comparison of this scene with Fort's aforementioned frantic note to Annie when she was working at a laundry: "We are busted. . . . Be on the corner right now." If Annie were the model for the efficient, loving Mrs. Birtwhistle, then her monologue on Fifth Avenue would be an account of Annie's travails:

> "We're not paid till the tenth, and then they hold back ten days' pay. Yes! Go down and try it! 'Tis easy to imagine. Work twelve hours a day without rest, all day long—we did get a few minutes off this afternoon, to go up and see the corpse of a millionaire, upstairs. He shot himself. But there's not a millionaire corpse every day. Far from it.
>
> "Easy, is it? Down forty feet below the sidewalk, standing all day on a little box, shaking linen, and if you step down, burn your feet on the steam pipes when your shoes is bad. It isn't the work, but the rotten people you meet. At dinner, all of them grabbing at a loaf of bread, tearing out the inside chunks and leaving the crust. Nothing for dinner but the heads and tails of herrings, the middles gone to the officers' tables. Or when you try to sleep, to be up at six in the morning, and the late watch comes in, laughing and carrying on, and won't let you sleep because they don't have to report till eleven the next day.

"Or some beast you sleep with! She comes in late, soused. She comes into bed with you in silk waist, hat and shoes. "Woman, get up; your hatpins is sticking me!" She says, "I'll have to sleep with all me clothes on; I must be up for mass at six in the morning."

They pause in front of an illuminated window on Fifth Avenue.

A man was sitting by a table with a lamp on it. A woman was fiercely shaking her fist at him. "She's giving it to him—wait!" laughed Mrs. Birtwhistle.

"We don't want to stand here all night, do we?" asked Mr. Birtwhistle.

"Just wait! Let's watch them!" said fascinated Mrs. Birtwhistle.

Man looking up, and his hands moving in weak, apologetic gestures. Woman stamping and pounding her fists upon the table, then pointing at him and shaking a fierce forefinger at him, throwing arms wide to express scorn and contempt for him, and then again shaking her fist at him.

"Oh, I'm homesick! I'm as homesick as I can be!" wept Mrs. Birtwhistle.

If Anna had inspired Delia Birtwhistle, Fort must have seen himself as Isaac: unrealistic, and strangely inefficient at crucial moments. Even Birtwhistle's loose trousers and carpet slippers match Dreiser's description of Fort padding around his tenement apartment. The character longs for anyone to say "I believe in you." We can suspect where fact and fiction overlap. The description of rolling logs onto the mud flats is remarkably gritty and distinct; the lecture on dispossession shows the typical gossipy details shared by tenement neighbors when the Forts were evicted; the meticulous lesson about how to use newspapers while sleeping in the park sounds painfully true. In this case, it's interesting how Fort imagined Birtwhistle's fate. Thinking himself unsuitable for manual labor, Birtwhistle proves to be surprisingly resilient, just as Fort had surprised himself at fisticuffs or in odd jobs on a cattle ship or in a hotel kitchen. Down and out, Birtwhistle attempts to make money selling cheap paper novelties in Paddy's Market. It seems to a reader that this will be the enterprise that redeems him, calling upon his personal charm and salesmanship. Instead, he fails miserably and is saved by politics, not ability, when his landlord unexpectedly invites him back. Similarly, Fort tried his hand at inventing cheap little gadgets, but was too much the idealist to be a good salesman. After his failed writing career, he was saved by the magical reappearance of Theodore Dreiser at his kitchen table.

Some reviews noticed the author's fondness for his characters. The *Springfield* (Massachusetts) *Union* titled its review "A Chronicle of Deadbeats," critical that the "author rambles along at will, getting nowhere except that he show an intimate knowledge of the life of the shiftless and thriftless." The *Louisville Courier-Journal* was annoyed by the repetitive words, calling the technique "an amateurish way of attempting to make sentences impressive," but concluded that "so vivid are some of the pictures that they command attention." Several reviewers thought the prose "jerky," or "choppy," and the *Atlanta Georgian* was sure that Fort felt that complete sentences were obsolete. The *New York Times* wrote that "the dialogue is unusually clever," but claimed there were barely five pages of description in the entire book. The novel was "realistic in the last degree, though not concerned with matters where realism is sometimes called immorality."

To a modern reader, Fort's realism is hardly immoral, and his stylistic conceits can be compelling. Damon Knight later complimented the book on its comic fantasy and continual tricks of perspective. "Fort has put his characters into a shoebox stage and made them seem like tiny engaging puppets, dressed in scraps, with faces the size of buttons." Author and editor Anthony Boucher felt that it "deserves attention which it has never received as a purely realistic genre novel well ahead of its time—objective, unromanticized and observed with acute eyes and ears closer to those of Ring Lardner or Sinclair Lewis than the average novelist of 1909." Theodore Dreiser, similarly, felt that Fort never received proper credit for the work:

> It is better than Tales of Mean Streets or New Grub Street. What keeps this book from its proper rank in great letters is that it had almost no connection with the tastes of its age. Fort was never concerned with sex, romance, reform, or gentility. A little more sex and a little more gentility and this book might have been popular. As it is, a G. K. Chesterton, an Anatole France, a Laurence Stern would like it—but who else?

The Outcast Manufacturers didn't earn a second printing, and Fort couldn't have profited more than a hundred dollars from the work. For example, notes show that he received $22.40 for 1910 royalties. Harper's magazine rejected a serialized version of the novel, but Pearson's accepted it, and Dreiser suggested the necessary cuts for the magazine. Unfortunately, only five chapters appeared before the Pearson's editors tired of the story.

Fort found some satisfaction in an article in the Albany Argus—his old newspaper—titled "Albany Author of Remarkable Novel." The Argus noted that he was the son of grocer Charles N. Fort, with "extensive business in this part of the state." The article complimented the book: "the same jerky, lightning-like delineation that is something new in contemporary fiction." Fort had responded to the newspaper's inquiries with a long account of his travels. Significantly, he never mentioned his family, but his last paragraph indicated his years of poverty.

> [You asked for] snapshots? Ever since [my travels] I have lived nowhere but in the rear houses and back tenements, so I never have known anybody with a camera. No one has ever taken a snapshot of me.

Fort was pleased to think that his father, sitting at the dinner table, read praise for his novel. More than a few Albany readers must have wondered why the son of a wealthy businessman had been living in back tenements.

Anna and Charles Fort moved their few possessions to a small apartment at 428 West Fortieth Street. Dreiser was fascinated to be shown Fort's boxes of metaphors, tens of thousands of "little pieces of paper on which were written descriptive sentences," now lining a shelf of their apartment. He remembered one slip in particular, a comparison of a night market to a torchlight parade. In fact, Fort used this in *The Outcast Manufacturers*:

> Paddy's Market! Every Saturday, though not fully epileptic with writhing and squirming, groan and convulsion. Wagons and stands, each wagon and each stand with a torch, or with several torches, so that, from a distance, Paddy's Market looks like a torchlight parade going up one side of the avenue and down the other side—a night parade of flagellants shrieking with self-inflicted torture.

Then, heard in the market itself, confused lamentation degenerates into distinct and mercantile cries—flagellants scourging themselves only with their arms, beating their breasts only to keep warm—to rid themselves not of sin, but of cauliflowers and beets.

"It was amazing," Dreiser recalled, "the force or beauty of these sentences." Dreiser was excited by the collection of boxes and offered: "Here, I'll buy these from you. They are better than any thesaurus, a new help to letters." Fort politely refused Dreiser's offer.

Planning his next novel, Fort tried strange experiments to visualize elements of the story. Again, he had little confidence in his talent, but was searching for a system that would guarantee success.

I covered sheets of paper with scrawls, to see what I could visualize out of them; tacked a sheet of wrapping paper to a ceiling and smudged it with a candle flame; made what I called a "visualizing curtain," which was a white window shade covered with scrawls and smudges; went on into three dimensions with boards veneered with clay. It was my theory that, with a visualizing device, I could make imaginary characters perform for me more vividly than in my mind, and that I could write a novel about their doings.

Fort toiled at the kitchen table, obsessed with novel writing. "I thought that, except in the writing of novels, which probably looked like the offspring of kangaroos, not an incentive could there be to go on living." He later estimated that he wrote 3.5 million words over the next few years, "though that's only an estimate." Even accounting for rewrites, it's a staggering figure, the equivalent of several thousand words each day. One of Fort's journal entries contains a reference to a "Bayonne story" that he was writing, but none of these manuscripts survive.

Fort's experiments also produced magazine stories that proved to be less commercial and more stylistic than his novel. In July 1909, Dreiser sent an exasperated letter from the *Delineator* offices:

> My dear Fort,
> Read these criticisms.
> "I get nothing from these; they are like kaleidoscopic pictures, as they are doubtless intended, but with no raison d'etre so far as I can see." Mr. Towne
> "These don't register and they lack the humor of The Outcast Manufacturers. They are impressionistic sketches, too vague to tell a story." Mrs. Kinkaid
> "Impossible." Mr. Harrison
> Now you see what I mean. The chance of doing anything on this basis is nil, and yet right at your door lies the opportunity to do magnificent, really spectacular work, but you insist on destroying this opportunity by stringing together a long litany of similes. You may eventually bring the public to accept this theory of writing; for magazine purposes I can't see it, and I believe now that it is quite hopeless to make you see it.
> Very truly yours,
> Theodore Dreiser

Always the little boy from Albany seeking approval, Fort was stung by the sharp rejection. He realized that he had become overconfident, both in his abilities and in his friendship with Dreiser. Despite his inscription in *The Outcast Manufacturers*, Dreiser was not his "partner"; Dreiser was a popular editor and author who had written an important novel, *Sister Carrie*.

In his boyhood, when Charles Fort was slapped, he retaliated as a martyr, punishing himself and his father at the same time—as when he dripped blood into the stairwell. Now he stoically responded by burning his collection of notes. "They were not what I wanted," he reported years later, "and I finally destroyed them. For that, Theodore Dreiser will never forgive me."

X Exists!

One does not apologize for the gods and at the same time feel quite utterly prostrate before them.

In the spring of 1908, Henry Louis Mencken sauntered into Dreiser's lush office of fumed oak furniture and thick carpets at the *Delineator*. The two men had corresponded for over a year, Dreiser commissioning articles from this clever young Baltimore journalist and inquiring about the publication of Mencken's new book. Mencken was a ruddy, blue-eyed twenty-seven-year-old sporting a bright silk tie and yellow leather shoes. Dreiser recalled his first impression:

> *More than anything else, he reminded me of a spoiled and petted and possibly over-financed brewer's son or wholesale grocer's son who was out for a lark. With the sang-froid of a Caesar or a Napoleon he made himself comfortable in a large and impressive chair, which was designed primarily to reduce the over-confidence of the average beginner.*

The mention of a "wholesale grocer's son" is interesting: Fort was the wholesale grocer's son whom Dreiser had mistaken for a wealthy dilettante three years earlier. Dreiser always felt that the important turns in his life had been signaled by meeting specific men. Now Mencken took on Arthur Henry's role and became a catalyst for Dreiser's work: his literary cheerleader, defender, sometime editor, and brutal critic. H. L. Mencken became, to Dreiser, what Dreiser had been to Fort. As a friend, the Baltimore writer enthusiastically supported Dreiser's serious literary efforts, bolstered his cynical and skeptical views of society, and encouraged his scientific and sociological interests.

But as their friendship developed, Mencken—always sharply opinionated—grew critical of the other half of Dreiser's character: the superstitious, Ouija-board-consulting, lapsed Catholic, a sucker for mysticism and fringe philosophies, always prizing his own ability to think artistically and avoid societal constraints. Mencken felt that it was exactly this sort of bohemian mush that was limiting Dreiser's success.

In 1910, Dreiser was facing a new boss at Butterick, and he found the work there uncomfortable. When his staff became aware that Dreiser had started an affair with the daughter of a coworker, it was pointed out to the editor that he should politely resign. He returned to two unfinished novels.

THE FOLLOWING YEAR the wholesale grocer Charles Nelson Fort was diagnosed with cerebral meningitis. His wife, Blanche, was going blind. Charles Hoy Fort wrote a perfunctory letter to his father, formally wishing him well. In March 1912, he received a response.

Charles (H.) Fort

Dear Sir,

Observe the style of address—vide the parenthesis (H.) I had been more cordial had you not set the pace for me but your CNFort was too cold. I will endeavor to answer your letter seriatim et brevitum—how does that hit you?

Paragraph number one rehearses my recovery. I regret to write that I am not better but worse. I fear that my case is incurable. . . .

Presumably, Charles Nelson Fort still considered his son too much of a Hoy, and the Latin phrase was intended to tweak the high-school dropout and supposed novelist. This was the father's last, tender last communication to his son. Two months later, Fort received a note from a family friend in Albany:

I'm writing for your father and mother. Mr. Fort is very bad, he has had quite a long serious spell for the last two weeks. He says this morning he feels as though he could never write again as his letter would be unintelligible to you. There is nothing present to ask of you but to stand loyal in the future, as you have in the past. There is no letter that gives [your mother] more pleasure than the ones received from you. Though you are not her son by blood, you are by Heaven, which sometimes binds closer.

On his deathbed, Charles Nelson Fort kept a portrait of his first wife, the boys' mother, Agnes, under his pillow. On June 27, 1912, Raymond wrote with the news that their father had died that morning. "Funeral 2 o'clock Saturday." The letter reached Charles at 330 Riverside Drive, a fashionable apartment building where Fort may have taken work as a custodian. There is no record that he returned for his father's funeral.

Not surprisingly, Charles Nelson Fort's will had been constructed as a final punishment to his wayward sons. The full estate went to his widow, Blanche. Upon her death, almost a year later in 1913, it passed to Raymond—the son who followed his father's footsteps into business. In settling the securities, Charles received a thousand dollar bond with U.S. Steel. "The old man left everything to Ray," Anna told a friend many years later, "who was always a fast, good-for-nothing." According to the provisions of the will, if Raymond had died, the estate would have passed to his children. Only if Raymond had had no children would Charles Nelson Fort's money have ever been inherited by Charles and Clarence, his oldest and youngest sons.

When he left the Berkshire Industrial Farm at age thirteen, Clarence returned to his family in Albany. He then served in the U.S. Army during the Spanish-American War before returning to his home town, living in a cheap apartment and working in a metal foundry. He never married. One afternoon, a month after his father's death, Clarence had been drinking and decided to visit Raymond, looking for money. "I have just had the pleasure of meeting Clarence and being called every vile name that immortal man could invent, but I held my temper," Raymond wrote to Charles. "He was very drunk." Clarence then went to Matthew Wallace's office, complaining that the properties from his grandfather's estate had earned so little money. He exploded with a long string of profanity and threatened to take the brothers's finances from Wallace, mumbling about seeking Charles's advice, and storming out the door.

When Clarence was sober, nothing came of his outburst. Charles's and Clarence's financial hardships seemed assured.

. . .

ANNA FORT RECALLED several odd occurrences in their apartment after Charles Nelson Fort's death. One morning, the old man seemed to be rapping at the door—his son recognized the distinctive knock. At the same time, they heard the father's voice calling through the door, "Charlie, Charlie." A bamboo stick alongside the bed seemed to vibrate and rattle with a distinct tattoo. Anna said, "If I understood telegraphy, I could get some message." The rapping continued for months, finally climaxed by a mysterious clatter in the kitchen—Anna and Charles rushed into the room to find a pile of pots and pans in the middle of the floor.

Fort never spoke of the ghostly annoyances.

AROUND THE TIME of his father's death, Fort dramatically changed the focus of his writing. For years he had been struggling with fiction, confessing his insecurities in his notebook:

See now that I am not a short story writer. All that was only developmental for novel writing. In the first place, short stories never attracted me.

[In the next entry:] I now see no such thing. The trouble with me is similar to that preceding my tenement stories. It was then impossible for me to get into them, away from the mere plot I was studying. Now I am impelled to wider field than such restriction, and I can't think how, to save me.

I am now occupied with style. Figures. Now know the value of a figure lies in making a vivid picture; and to do this all that is

required is the right word. Years ago, I read of Stevenson's delight and
search for the "master word." I might have been advised then; but
value of such a tip could not be until I was ready for it.

What is the novel's reason for being? To entertain? Then the form
of a novel cannot express entertainingness, but be the instrument
itself. Therefore the form of a novel should all be subservient to
its climax.

Troubles. Distracted. Reading the above, I return that philosophy
is the reason for being. Climax is the form's reason for being. Well,
then, it seems that there is light, right here upon my troubles. I have
been trying to start my new book. Impossible! Then it seems that I
must round out my ten years with a final study of philosophy.

Many years later, Fort recorded his limitations as a story writer.
"I was a realist, but knew few people; had few experiences for my
material. I very much made up for this by knowing where to go to
get material." As he found it difficult to focus on his stories, the
regular trips to the library—and his latest studies—became more
obsessive:

One day, when I was down, worst I ever have been, I was study-
ing the infinitesimal calculus. Every morning, I'd try to write some-
thing that would bring in some money; every morning, by ten o'clock,
I was back studying transcendental functions and things. It's utterly
past my power to do things I feel I ought to do.

The library research began as a way to find material for his
stories, but by 1912 it was the research, not the stories, that took
priority. Fort was thirty-nine years old, and about to begin a new
sort of education.

My first interests had been scientific—realism sent me back. Then for eight years I studied all of the arts and sciences I had ever heard of and I invented half a dozen arts and sciences. Then came to me a plan of collecting notes upon all subjects of human research upon all known phenomena, and then to try and find the widest possible diversity of data—law or formula, something that could be generalized.

I collected notes upon principles and phenomena of astronomy, sociology, psychology, deep sea diving, navigation, surveying, volcanoes, religion, sexes, earthworms—that is, always seeking similarities in widest seeming differences.

Fort began visiting the library every day, his pockets stuffed with blank paper slips. He furiously scribbled as he paged through technical books and periodicals. The little cardboard boxes in his apartment that once contained his collection of metaphors now started to fill up again. As before, the slips allowed him to categorize and rearrange his interests. He assembled his slips according to relationships: "Harmony," "Equilibrium," "Catalysts," "Saturation," "Supply and Demand." Gradually, he was drawn to apparent anomalies—strange phenomena that defied neat classification. He started to discover them everywhere, prying them out of established journals and histories. After years of collecting—idly arranging and rearranging objects, phrases, or information—he now began to notice patterns. Odd patterns.

To Charles Fort, these oddities were the proof of what he had suspected all along: the world was a very strange place.

Fort soon had 1,300 general subjects and 40,000 individual notes. "They were 1300 hell hounds gibing," Fort reported, "with 1300 voices, at my attempt to find finality."

> *All the time I was reading and studying to cast off this terribly*
> *hard-earned realization, to reach the metaphysician's realization of*
> *maturity. In the years 1912–1913, the metaphysician was almost*
> *all in me. I see all this as travail, of emerging as more or less of a*
> *metaphysician from a story writer.*

FORT KEPT a little ritual. When his library card expired at the Lenox Library at Seventieth Street on the East Side of New York, he wrote to Theodore Dreiser to have it renewed. As a well-known editor and author, Dreiser could sign an application giving Fort access to all the stacks. In 1910, just after Dreiser left the *Delineator*, Fort sent his application, explaining that he was currently in a "mathematical framework," and that he needed good quality technical books.

In May 1914, Fort's application for another library card, at the new public library on Forty-second Street, reached Dreiser at his new Manhattan apartment in Greenwich Village. Fort was now living at 341 West Forty-third Street, another tenement back building on the edge of Longacre Square. Dreiser wrote back, amused by his friend's continuing obsession.

> *Either you have fourteen novels and nine plays concealed some-*
> *where or you are compiling an Encyclopedia Fortiana. Which is it? You*
> *are a library mole, burrowing underground. You are a troglodyte,*
> *rejoicing in unheralded caves. Well, consume more data to your own*
> *confusion. Eat libraries and suffer inevitable encyclopediac apoplexy.*

Fort wasn't interested in writing novels, plays, or encyclopedias. It was a full year later before he reported the results of his research.

On May 1, 1915, Fort sent a four-page letter to "My dear Dreiser," with an astonishing revelation.

> *I don't know whether you are now a dealer in loud noises or not, but, if you are still in the publishing or editorial calamity, I have produced some vibrations that you might like to turn loose.*

Charles Fort had discovered X.

X WAS NOT ONLY the title of Fort's book; it was his name for an outside motivating source that influenced all of society. In his text, Fort suggested this controlling force resided on the planet Mars. Today this sounds like science fiction, but Percival Lowell's published observations of Mars, from 1906 and 1909, were prominent in the news. Thanks to Lowell's maps of Martian canals, it was generally assumed that Mars held intelligent life. By assigning Martians particular powers or motives, Fort's speculation was particularly topical.

According to Dreiser's recollection of the book, X communicated through rays that could create all things: "you, me, all animals, plants, the earth and its fullness, its beauty and variety and strangeness, its joy and sorrow and terror as well as the ecstasy of this thing we call life." Fort likened the rays to photography, similar to how light or shadow affects chemicals and creates pictures. In this case, earth was the sensitive film.

Fort explained the nature of his theory:

> *If, in acting upon us, X could only make use of what we should naturally do anyway—we should, if stimulated to action*

by X, *think that we were but following what we call our own
free wills.*

Then, in the search for X, *we should look not for strange, seemingly supernatural phenomena, but for things that we should have
done anyway, but in a lesser degree, historical events which have
heretofore been accounted for by reason, but have in them somewhere
a vague mystery or an atmosphere of the unaccountable, despite all
the assurances of their own infallibility that our historians have
given us.*

I shall try to show that X *exists; that this influence is, and must
be, evil to an appalling degree to us at present, evil which at least
equals anything ever conceived of in medieval demonology.*

The evidence of *X*, which Fort found in "vague mysteries," was
an important part of the book. Dreiser wrote that Fort's "interwo-
ven comments on the history of man" included:

> . . . *strange, arresting explanations and deductions from a thou-
> sand sources that I had never contemplated as sources—newspaper
> clippings, published but ignored data of the most amazing kind from
> the world's scientific journals. The great Chinese wall leaves China
> and goes for miles under the sea. The Sphinx evidently stood for some
> length of time under salt water. There was a vessel-like mechanism
> with great wheels of fire that passed before the eyes of shipmasters in
> various parts of the Pacific. There were recorded footprints of an
> immense giant in some northern snowfield. Here and there and ev-
> erywhere were rains of blood. . . .*

Fort's letter to Dreiser about *X* included a number of puzzling
statements. The finished text was nearly a hundred thousand words,

but Fort seemed uninterested in book publishing, thinking that it might make a better series in a magazine. He boasted of the quality of his argument: "as logical and carefully worked out as if I believed every word of it myself."

> So there it is. I've given up fiction, you see—or in a way I haven't. I am convinced that everything is fiction; so here I am in the same old line.

There's little question that Fort took X seriously, and the doubts he expressed were his modest way of kidding his efforts. "The whole thing is becoming so reasonable that it humiliates me," he wrote to Dreiser. "I thought at first I had got hold of the unbelievable."

It took Fort an additional two months to complete the manuscript, include some new notes and finish the typing. At the end of June 1915, he wrote to Dreiser that he wasn't sure of his new address in Greenwich Village, but found his old address in *Who's Who*. Fort teased Dreiser about the *Who's Who* entry:

> I'm not a "who." I'm only a "which." If you're not laying cornerstones, or doing some of the other things that you "whos" do, about which I am rather vague, I'll drop in next Tuesday night, and have X along.

Dreiser had none of Fort's doubts and found X stunning. "My general feeling is that it is a remarkable book," he wrote to the author. He was unconcerned with the science. "Slightly worked over, it should sell a hundred thousand. Congratulations." Dreiser later recorded his impression of the manuscript:

> *It was so strange, so forceful and so beautiful that I thought that whether this was science, or apocryphal and discarded, it was certainly one of the greatest books I have ever read in my life.*

Dreiser quickly invited Fort to a welcoming party for poet Edgar Lee Masters at the Greenwich Village apartment. His partnership with Dodge publishing had dissolved years before, but Dreiser was trying to lure several publishers to his party, playing matchmaker for Masters's *Spoon River Anthology* and, now, Fort's *X*.

Forgetting his shyness and still stunned by Dreiser's assessment— a hundred thousand copies!—Fort accepted. It was a typically bohemian Village literary soiree, a collection of about two dozen people: authors, musicians, producers, actresses, and even a few socialists. Dreiser introduced Fort to his new secretary, his latest mistress, Kirah Markham. Without enough chairs, the guests sprawled on the pine floor and avoided the clusters of burning candles; Masters read from his *Spoon River Anthology* and another guest picked out a tune on the ukelele. It's hard to imagine Fort in this atmosphere— a man who rarely left his tenement apartment and, indeed, seldom left his oilcloth-covered kitchen table. A photographer from the *New York World* recorded the event.

Fort, naturally, was too introverted to make contact with any publisher that evening. But late that night he returned to Forty-third Street and boyishly reported on the party to Anna. For the moment, it was enough to once again have the solicitous attention of his friend Dreiser, and be a part of his warm, glowing success— punchbowls, poets, and intellectual discussions. He was humbled by Dreiser's interest, writing: "I think it's the most extraordinary thing I ever heard of, the way you're taking up *X*." Days after the party, when Dreiser reported that he was leaving on a "joy ride" back to his childhood homes in Indiana, Fort joked, "Can't think why anybody should go to Indiana. Thought everybody came away from Indiana." But he admitted that he had seen his photo in the *World.* "I'm taking a joy ride, too, in a literary sense."

IT'S EASY TO RECOGNIZE that *X* contained a formal, mysterious version of the same philosophy permeating *The Outcast Manufacturers.* According to Fort, we have no free will but are controlled by a powerful, outside force that *simulates* free will. It was echoed in his own powerlessness, the inability "to do things I feel I ought to do," that Fort felt in his everyday life. What was significant was Fort's expression that this force—the equivalent of a godlike, all-creating power—was evil and dangerous. The ending of the book promised little hope: "Our goal is the nothingness of a Nirvana-like state of mechanistic unconsciousness, in which there is neither happiness nor unhappiness." For much of Fort's life, the inescapable force—denying him happiness or free will, corrupting his finances—was not from Mars but rather seemed to be emanating from Albany.

Much of *X* may have been inspired by conversations with Dreiser, and accidentally—or deliberately—arranged to complement his beliefs. Fort had perfectly addressed Dreiser's interests, stirring together science and speculation into an astonishing metaphysical stew. Theodore Dreiser always loved mysticism, but he couldn't abide the judgmental quality of organized religion. *X* contained bits of Herbert Spencer's Social Darwinism and Ernst Haeckel's views on monism. Both authors were heroes of Dreiser, and the characters in his novels give evidence of the forces and struggles borrowed from their philosophies.

In *X*, Fort went one better by proposing orthogenetic evolution in place of Darwinism or Spencerism. Orthogenesis insists that evolution is never random or scattered, but proceeds along a predetermined path, cosmically or chemically implanted in every organism. In Fort's book, his discussion of orthogenesis—at the time, an increasingly fashionable approach to evolution—allowed him to introduce *X* as a guiding force through all of nature. Dreiser was fascinated with the notion, which hinted at a grand organizing principle behind the mechanics of life: a seemingly mysterious and artistic vision, godlike but not confused with theology. "From a biologic point of view—autogenetic orthogenesis—I am in complete agreement with most of your deductions," he wrote Fort.

ACCORDING TO DREISER, *X* had a profound influence on him. "I thought to myself, well, here at last is something new, a new mind and a new approach." Several weeks after reading the manuscript, he was awakened in the middle of the night by a dream "which seemed in no indefinite way to confirm [*X*]." Dreiser wrote out an interpretation of that dream, using Fort's thesis "as the backbone of the action."

It was a fifteen-page, one-act reading play called *The Dream*, first published in 1917 in a periodical called *Seven Arts*.

Three men walk along a street in New York late one night: George Syphers, a professor of chemistry, argues the nature of life with a professor of philosophy and a professor of physics. Syphers efficiently states Fort's premise in *X*:

The whole thing may have been originated, somehow, somewhere else, worked out beforehand, as it were, in the brain of something or somebody and is now being orthogenetically or chemically directed from somewhere; being thrown on a screen, as it were, like a moving-picture, and we mere dot pictures, mere cell-built-up pictures, like the movies, only we are telegraphed or teleautographed from somewhere else.

Syphers returns to his rooms, imagining that a fully equipped laboratory would allow him to test his theories. "Life is really a dream," he tells himself. "We are all an emanation, a shadow, a moving picture cast on a screen of ether. I'm sure of it."

As Syphers falls asleep in his bed, he dreams that he is isolated in a field, trapped in a fierce war. A score of soldiers hunt him down and surround him, drawing their guns as he cowers in the corner. He speculates that he is in the middle of a nightmare; he defies the soldiers to "do your worst" and prove the nature of his fantasy. They fire. Syphers is shot, and feels sure he is dying; he contemplates which state is the real dream, and the soldiers ridicule him. "You may be waking into another state, but you'll be dead to this one!" As the soldiers fade from view, Syphers discovers himself waking in his bed once again. "Am I dying, or waking up? Which is it? Are there various worlds, one within another?"

The sound of gunfire resolves into furious knocking at his door. He pulls on his clothes and opens the door to find a telegram delivery boy. The telegram announces that Syphers has just inherited $300,000 from a deceased uncle—he now has the money to build his laboratory.

Dreiser showed the play to Fort, who may have been puzzled by it all, for *The Dream* was, according to Dreiser, "nothing like [Fort's] book in action, and less so in effectiveness." The debt to *X* is little more than a burst of dialogue that sets up the action. Author Keith Newlin has pointed out that Dreiser's play also indicates his interest in Freud's dream theory: the battle with the soldiers is clearly intended to represent his verbal battle with his colleagues. The closest tie to Fort may not be the underlying philosophy, but the final plot twist. As we'll see, when Fort's uncle Frank died in 1916 (shortly before Dreiser wrote *The Dream*) the inheritance allowed Fort the freedom to research in the library, pursuing his metaphysical books. In this way, Syphers is a "loquacious, fiery" embodiment of Fort himself, a professor frustrated by his lofty thoughts. Just before he falls asleep, as Syphers wonders about the mysterious orthogenetic force, it's easy to imagine Fort's voice:

> *The curious thing is, why should any dominant force outside this seeming life wish to create it—the smallness, the pettiness, the suffering? I must write a book about that.*

As HE STUDIED the totality of *X*, Theodore Dreiser, previously Fort's patron saint, became his first disciple. "When I sensed the imaginative power of such a concept, I was in a worshipping state of mind. True or false, marvelous."

A Battle Is About to Be Fought

Almost do we now conceive of a difficulty of the future as being not how to reach the planets, but how to dodge them.

Four months after completing the manuscript of *X*, in October 1915, Fort was preparing the outline of his next book, *Y*. In a breathless summary to Dreiser, he explained that it started where *X* had ended. He proposed a theory of "complementaries," that every phenomenon has a complementary phenomenon. Similarly, *X* has a complementary force, called *Y*, and this is acting upon the earth.

> *We now have one of those dynamic crystal situations that you sometimes speak of. There are two complementary civilizations, orthogenetically isolated that they may reach high individual development first. Y, for reasons we'll go into, is far ahead of us.*

Fort proposed that Kaspar Hauser, a strange boy who stumbled into Nuremberg one day in 1828, was actually an envoy from *Y*.

Hauser exhibited odd traits like supernatural senses, but could barely communicate and did not recall any family. After making his home in Nuremberg, he was killed under puzzling circumstances— stabbed as he walked in the middle of a snowy park; no other footprints in the snow, no murder weapon.

"Y-land" existed in a sort of depression or basin at the top of the earth, according to Fort. Drawing upon other accounts, he would document blond Eskimos, warm climates near the North Pole, and Perry's peculiar explorations. John C. Symmes's early nineteenth-century theory of a hollow earth was, according to Fort, "worthless," but Symmes had amassed a great deal of interesting data. "Then comes our own evidence," Fort explained to Dreiser; "I have had time only to start collecting this, but already have some." Fort made assumptions based on the rotation of the earth and the way that heavy metals separated: Y was a land with a mountain of gold but no iron, and their civilization was based on an "iron standard."

The climax of the book would mix Fort's peculiar scientific theories with a thrilling treasure hunt.

> *Final overcoming of the physical barriers of the arctic by adventurous aeronauts. Frenzy—final giving up all attempt to amass fortunes, merging of the two races, no other forces then interfering, so adjustment to X—Nirvana, Kismet, Amen.*

DREISER HAD ALREADY sent on the manuscript of X to several associates for their professional opinions. When he read Fort's summary of Y, he was heartened by the author's enthusiasm and sent an unqualified endorsement.

Fairest Fort,

My impression is that you are out-Verning Verne. Talk about scientific imagination! I wonder you don't put this second book in the form of a romance. If you did it would create a sensation. Done as a scientific dream, it may and it may not. But interesting is no name for it.

My compliments. You are one of the most remarkable literary figures I have ever known. I wish you luck and success. Hope to hear sure tomorrow as to X.

After years of struggling, Fort wasn't used to reading these sorts of comments, and blushed at the compliments. He responded the same day:

Such things have a most encouraging effect—positively a vivifying effect. The kindest and best people in the world are pessimists.

May the neo-gods preserve us from the smirking fools or rascals that we call optimists.

Thanks for the letter. It felt electric.

Unfortunately, X was proving to be a more difficult sale than Dreiser had suspected. Part of the problem was Dreiser's perception of X as a book of science. He had sent the manuscript to Waldemar Kaempffert, the editor of *Popular Science Monthly,* for his impression. Fort was surprised to hear this, reminding Dreiser that a chapter of X had managed to ridicule Kaempffert's views on gravitation "a little, not much." When Kaempffert's criticism arrived, he expectedly sniffed at the preposterous science in X.

A vast amount of reading has been done which has not been correctly applied. When a man says that there is no such thing as objective

reality and then utilizes scientific experiments on objective realities
to prove a point, surely something must be wrong.

Fort shrugged it off, joking to Dreiser, "Oh, Waldemar, you discourage me. How can I be bright and intelligent if you're part of the general mind in which I'm a unit? Speak to me, Waldemar! Tell me." Fort cautiously warned his friend, "Don't send X to Professor Lowell." He was another scientist who had received a drubbing in the book.

FOR SEVERAL MONTHS in 1915, Dreiser was convinced that he was about to become a part of the motion picture industry. He was hired by a New York firm, Mirror Films, as a scenario director. He wrote to Fort and Mencken, asking for ideas for stories. Fort confessed that he was now completely obsessed by work on *Y*: "Something's got me! I have no mind of my own." He responded with a five-page proposal to dramatize *X*.

The film would cut between odd discoveries—layers of salt inside the chambers of the Egyptian pyramids, walls on the planet Mars, the end of the Wall of China leading beneath the ocean—and Fort himself, "seen in my studio, thinking of these data, and wondering what they mean."

> For the drama we have the conflict of two opposing forces:
> One is the tendency of all phenomena toward the goal of the whole;
> The other is the tendency of each individual phenomenon to develop for its own sake.
> Scenes of human activity. Poor and rich, all suffering. What for?

Scenes of marching troops.

Evolving life. Sphinxes build the pyramids. They know not why.

Onwardness of life. Modern factory scenes, strikes, all our miseries due to individual versus the whole.

The action moves toward a climactic battle.

Then there's a war.

The battleground is in Egypt.

A battle is about to be fought near the pyramids. Camp scenes, soldiers revolting against war, some of them fearful because an officer has overheard them. He feels the same way.

Opposing armies and the pyramids. The battle can't begin. Here and there ranks are deserted, strange call of the pyramids. Soldiers are climbing them. They don't know why. Strange attraction felt by others. Soldiers climbing the pyramids. Others cheering. They are generating force.

At last mankind has learned what it is for.

Vast final scene, dancing, hosts. . . .

Curtain.

Fort suspected that his idea was impractical, requiring "a million dollars or so." The proposal is curiously prescient. It reads like a paranormal version of D. W. Griffith's *Intolerance,* the innovative epic film that combined several historical stories as it built to a climax—gathering pace and meaning by cutting between the parallel plot lines. *Intolerance* was first premiered in New York almost a year after Fort's proposal, in September 1916.

Months later, Fort tried again with a simpler story, a scenario for a comedy called *Spectators Interfere,* that he had once submitted to Edison Films. Unfortunately, this outline has been lost. "Swear to me that I needn't write love stories," Fort wrote to Dreiser. "If lovers there must be, let someone else put the damn things in." Funding fell through, and the Mirror Films project never materialized.

THEODORE DREISER's fifth novel, *The "Genius,"* was published at the end of 1915 to mixed reviews. Even his friend H. L. Mencken had found it unevenly written and repetitive when he was asked to read the manuscript the previous year. He thought the book was "as shapeless as a Philadelphia pie-woman." But Mencken also realized that *The "Genius"* was overtly sexual and sordid—Mencken, of course, wasn't offended by this sort of thing, but was convinced that, after his previous difficulties with *Sister Carrie,* Dreiser was inviting unnecessary condemnation.

He was right. John Sumner at the New York Society for the Suppression of Vice banned *The "Genius,"* citing seventy-five lewdnesses and seventeen profanities. John Lane, Dreiser's publisher, was threatened by Sumner and postal inspectors, and recalled copies at bookstores. Fort was busy revising *Y,* and consoled his friend by feigning jealousy.

> *High priest of Evil,*
>
> *Damn it all! Speak to me! Tell me! What shall I do to be lewd?*
>
> *How may I part with the innocence of my ratiocinations? Must I bargain with you, or, if I but touch the hem of your garment, can you, out of the abundance of your lasciviousness, bestow impurity upon me? Decompose the mists of my ignorance, and tell me how sexuality can be indecent.*
>
> *Taint me with your leprosy, and I will confide to you my lunacy.*

But with the sales of the book suspended and future projects called into question, Dreiser wasn't laughing. He solicited Mencken's help to fight the ban. Despite publishing a poor review of the book, Mencken agreed, as he was happy to decry the "Puritans" who controlled American culture. Through the Authors League of America, he drafted a careful declaration and then petitioned top authors to endorse it.

Dreiser sent a copy of the protest to Fort, asking him to join the effort. On September 21, 1916, Fort responded:

> My dear St. Theodore,
> Or you will be, if you can only stimulate them to persecute you enough.
> I signed and forwarded the protest with pleasure. Now I hope some day to call upon you to express indignation with the outrageous way I shall be treated.
> Did you get my ground for future martyrdom, entitled Y, which I sent you several weeks ago?
> Saint Charles

But Fort was exactly the sort of fringe writer that Mencken was hoping to avoid. When the preliminary list appeared, Mencken was disgusted by some of the names that had been solicited by Dreiser.

> I note that, despite our talk of last week, you have inserted the names of four or five tenth-rate Greenwich geniuses, and left out such men as [Winston] Churchill and [George] Ade. Just what satisfaction you get out of this course I'll be damned if I can see. All these jitney geniuses are playing you for a sucker. They can't advance your reputation an inch, but you make a very fine (and willing) stalking horse for them.

Mencken stage-managed the protest as a delicate political operation. He wanted to cherry-pick endorsements of blue-ribbon authors, and was particularly critical of radicals or socialists who might serve as a lightning rod for Dreiser's critics. Dreiser snapped in response, "Your letter seems to me to be curiously animated by something which does not appear on the surface. Have I tried to supervise your private life or comment on any of your friends or deeds? What's eating you, anyhow?"

But he ultimately trusted his fate to Mencken's aggressive plan. The final protest, "We, the undersigned, American writers observe with deep regret the efforts now being made to destroy the work of Theodore Dreiser . . . ," was signed by 130 authors. The list included Mencken, of course, along with David Belasco, Irvin S. Cobb, Walter Lippmann, Jack London, Ezra Pound, Ida M. Tarbell, Booth Tarkington, and even, from England, H. G. Wells. Charles Fort, presumably one of the "jitney geniuses," did not make it onto the list. The petition effectively thwarted Dreiser's censors, and the publicity surrounding The "Genius" helped to make it one of his most successful novels.

On May 28, 1916, as mentioned previously, Fort's uncle Frank A. Fort died unexpectedly. He was Peter V. Fort's youngest child, just five years older than Charles, and had been living on fashionable West End Avenue in Manhattan.

Provisions in Peter V. Fort's will dictated that payments from the estate to Frank Fort now passed to the three grandsons: Charles, Raymond, and Clarence. There was a delay in settling the arrangements—"The executors of my grandfather's estate don't like me," Fort reported—but Charles and Anna, who were used to a frugal existence, calculated the inheritance and realized that, with a little careful planning, Anna could stop working and they could be financially independent. Based on the will, Fort received a loan from an Albany bank for five hundred dollars. The couple bought some furniture for $180: two rugs, a sofa, two chairs, a new set of dishes. They took a lease on a nice apartment one block from their tenement flat—the top floor of a five-story walk-up at 445 West Forty-third Street, with several rooms and a bathroom.

A self-proclaimed pessimist, Fort grumbled to Dreiser about his good fortune:

> *My wife, from the best and most helpful woman in the world, has become a snob. She insists that now I must always have a clean shirt on. My dear Dreiser, pity me; I must have my shoes blackened. But I must leave rear houses.*
>
> *For twenty years, I have lived with strange orthogenetic gods, who are not snobs, who brood over stables and dumps and rear houses. But now Amorpha, who, being feminine, scorns dumps and rear houses, has in the past overlooked me, will, in three or four rooms and a bath, have me at her mercy. The matter of a bathroom is breaking my heart. My wife insists, but she's playing right into Amorpha's hands.*
>
> *Then I shall lose my literary soul. Pray for me. Have masses said for the repose of my aspirations. It may be that, by means of surreptitious old shirts, I can hide from my wife and rub around on the floor when she's not looking. Or maybe I'll go into that bathroom and only splash around the water, and make a noise, but not really get into it.*

The death of an aunt brought another inheritance; Dreiser recalled that this was a considerable amount of money.

Unfortunately, Clarence Fort, "the little kid," did not live long
to enjoy the income. His health was poor, and his drinking made
him argumentative. "It's a shame, but he won't listen to me or anyone else," Raymond reported to Charles in a letter. On January 14,
1917, Clarence died in Albany of pneumonia. He was just thirty-
eight years old. His inheritance was divided between Raymond and
Charles, as well as "a few thousand dollars," according to Raymond's calculations.

AS THE MONTHS DRAGGED ON, Dreiser reported his failures
with X. Fort responded: "Brace up. This is only the beginning. The
gods have appointed me in this life, which is hell, to punish you for
something awful that you did once, perhaps in Jupiter or Neptune."
Repeating his mistake, Dreiser had sent the book to *Scientific American*, which "denounced the manuscript as nonsense, no base in
verified fact." He also recommended it to Knopf, Macmillan, Harper's, Scribner's, and John Lane. Dreiser wrote dejectedly that they
all "decided that it was nothing that they could publish, not in their
field, no line to sell. Not this, not that."

By the end of 1916, publisher Carl Brandt was considering the
manuscripts of *X* and *Y*, but seemed to be dragging his feet, doubting the contents, asking for a list of other publishers who had
turned down the books. "Strange, orthogenetic gods have deserted
me," Fort grumbled to Dreiser. He thought he might never write
again.

When Brandt kept the manuscripts for over six months, Fort
suspected the worst. Despite the intense efforts of America's great
novelist—a full year of Dreiser's unqualified promises, endorse-

ments and efforts—both books surely were doomed. Fort described himself as a "lost soul." "You have done all that can be done in this matter," he wrote to Dreiser. "What would you do if you had the kind of brains I have? I suspect that strange orthogenetic gods are mixed up in all this." Dejectedly, he asked Dreiser to renew his library card again. Like the thirteen-year-old boy from Albany, he sulked about his prospects.

> *I think I'm going to take up a study of occult things. I may find out something. It will take me ten or fifteen years, I suppose. I'll let you know in 1925 or 1930.*

Fort's passions with X and Y became a source of his disappointment; as we'll see, he later destroyed both manuscripts, so it's now impossible to judge the contents of the books. Descriptions sound like a bewildering mix of philosophy, history, science, and science fiction. Surely this mixture had delighted Dreiser, but also frustrated the publishers: "not this, not that."

Author Damon Knight later speculated that the excesses of X and Y were fashionable "excesses of belief." Fort had written his book according to the models of the day, and felt obliged to explain his oddities by constructing a complete theory:

> *In rejecting conventional systems, Fort felt obliged to set up his own unconventional ones and defend them. He did this, I think, because he knew of no other way to write an unorthodox book. He had yet to invent his own way.*

Had they been published, X might well have been remembered as "rays from Mars," and Y as "the race at the North Pole," both joining the ranks of the great "crank" books: Delia Bacon finding coded messages in Shakespeare; Charles Piazzi Smyth measuring the pyramids; Ignatius Donnelly describing the culture of Atlantis.

CHARLES AND ANNA invited Dreiser to Thanksgiving dinner in 1917. He brought his current mistress, Estelle Kubitz, the sister of Mencken's mistress. On the way to the Forts' new apartment, Dreiser showed Kubitz the old, ratty tenement where he had discovered Fort writing a decade earlier. The new apartment was "charming," Dreiser recorded. "Not two but five or six rooms. Good if not too artistic furniture. A plentiful sideboard. Beer and whiskey for the asking." He noticed that Anna had a new dress.

At the Fort apartment, Dreiser and Estelle Kubitz met Charles and Betty Bizozer, a young couple who lived around the corner on Seventh Avenue. Bizozer was Italian, born to a French father. He worked as a typist, but over dinner explained that he had constructed a universal language, similar to Esperanto. Bizozer had not yet named his innovative language. Fort listened quietly and suggested he call it "Bunk." The couples discussed politics, the war, and American Puritanism, a subject now gnawing at Dreiser.

Anna and Charles served a beautiful golden turkey, and Fort proudly introduced a peculiar new preserve he'd invented called "Topeacho," a mixture of tomatoes and peaches. Dreiser found it tasty but Kubitz avoided it, as the combination sounded so strange to her. Typical of Fort, a small, funny obsession like Topeacho was indicative of his larger philosophy. He later wrote of his boyhood adventures in his grandfather's grocery store; we can imagine him telling this story as he spooned out Topeacho.

> *In days of yore, when I was an especially bad young one, my punishment was having to go to the store, Saturdays, and work. I had to scrape off labels of other dealers' canned goods and paste on my parents' label.*
>
> *One time I had a pyramid of canned goods, containing a variety of fruits and vegetables. But I had used all except peach labels. I pasted the peach labels on peach cans, and then came to apricots. Well, aren't apricots peaches? And there are plums that are virtually apricots. I went on, either mischievously, or scientifically, pasting the peach labels on cans of plums, cherries, string beans, and succotash. I can't quite define my motive, because to this day it has not been decided whether I am a humorist or a scientist. I think that it was mischief, but, as we go along, there will come a more respectful recognition that also it was scientific procedure.*

The following month, Dreiser and Kubitz invited the Forts to Kubitz's uptown apartment for a holiday meal of steak and kidney pie, spinach with eggs, lettuce, beer, wine, coffee, and mince pie. Fort spoke warmly of tenement life and described his brushes with psychic experiences, including an episode when he had the strange sensation of colors in his apartment, "red and gold in a dark room." He also related a dream about a "snowy bird emerging from filth." Fort unveiled a jar of "To-pruno," his latest experiment with tomatoes and prunes, for everyone to sample.

Despite his year of hardships, Fort was in an expansive mood. Although he hadn't told Dreiser, he had already settled on his next project, and was researching at the library every day.

• • •

IN FACT, the strange "orthogenetic gods" had not deserted Charles Fort: rather, they had rewarded him with a comfortable inheritance that had seemingly dropped from the sky; they had filled his apartment with a growing array of notes; they had given him a taste for science, and an unusual understanding of something beyond science.

After toiling away for months in silence, Fort wrote to Dreiser in July 1918. Dreiser opened the envelope and found three lines, adorned with three exclamation points.

> *Dreiser!*
> *I have discovered* Z!
> *Fort!*

One can imagine the knot that must have formed in Dreiser's stomach. But Z was not just another book.

It Is a Religion

I believe nothing of my own that I have ever written. I cannot accept that the products of minds are subject-matter for beliefs.

In May 1911, the New York Public Library had been re-opened in its new Beaux-Arts marble temple at Fifth Avenue and Forty-second Street. The city's Lenox and Astor collections were consolidated in the spectacular building, just four blocks from Fort's apartment. In fact, the smug, stolid carved lions that guard the front entrance on Fifth Avenue were quickly nicknamed "Leo Lenox" and "Leo Astor" by the public. It was only decades later, during the Depression, when they were given the names "Patience" and "Fortitude" by Mayor Fiorello La Guardia—to serve as inspirations for the patience and fortitude he was asking of New Yorkers.

Now diligently working on his next project, Charles Fort walked to the library every morning, five days a week. He trudged up the flank of white polished steps, took a seat at one of the wide oak desks in the reading room beneath the gilt and coffered ceiling, removed his coat, and slid it carefully over the back of his chair. He read meteorology, natural history, shipping reports, and science journals, squinting through his glasses as he turned page after page. With some regularity, he turned to the sheet of paper on the table and scratched a pencil note of some neglected phenomenon.

All of his notes were written on various grades of pulpy paper that were then ripped against a ruler into small rectangles. Some slips were torn from old correspondence; some were thin onionskin. Each piece was about one and a half by two and a half inches. Fort's handwriting was on a severe diagonal, lower left to upper right, tightly capturing the essence of each report with abbreviations. When he needed extra room for his pencil scrawl, a slip was torn long, then folded to match the dimensions of the other notes. An extremely elaborate note might require an entire sheet of paper, pleated and fixed with a paper clip so it ended up the same size. He managed to assemble forty thousand notes, by his own estimate, deliberately seeking information of the widest possible diversity: "astronomy, sociology, psychology, deep sea diving, navigation, surveying, volcanoes, religion, sexes, earthworms."

In this way the entire world could be reduced to a row of one and a half by two and a half inch scraps, then stored away in Fort's pigeonholes that edged the walls of his apartment. After lunch, he walked home from the library and sorted his precious phenomena by date, then cross-referenced them with a second set of slips organized in broad categories. In the afternoon, he sat at the table and wrote.

Anna made dinner. Fort liked rare roast beef, fricassee of chicken on toast, roast chicken, or pork chops, with vegetables and potatoes. Despite his boyhood obsession with cake, he no longer cared for sweet desserts. Anna cleared the dishes; then the couple walked the five flights down the stairs, strolled along Forty-third Street, turned the corner onto Seventh Avenue, and enjoyed a newsreel and a motion picture show. Anna remembered only one occasion where they saw a stage production—it was *Aïda* at the Opera House.

Back at their apartment, they might treat themselves to bits of rat-trap cheese, a sharp, crumbly white cheddar that was a specialty of dairies around Albany, and a glass of beer—their beer man made a delivery once a week.

It was a simple, pleasurable existence. As the world seemed to grow stranger and stranger, Charles Fort took satisfaction in telling himself that he knew all about its strangeness; he had it all neatly sorted and accessible in his cardboard boxes.

z WAS ONLY the simplest, most obvious working title for the new book. For his next project, he considered researching psychic phenomena—"things that have been called souls and spirits." He wrote to Dreiser of his intentions:

> Mine is a coarse and more cynical mind than those that have heretofore examined such phenomena, also it has some other qualities and a different attitude toward what is called the scientific method.

A "cynical" book about such phenomena implies a skeptical tone. But we don't know Fort's intention, as his skepticism was remarkably fluid and even-handed: he could be equally skeptical of the occult, the scientific method, philosophy, analysis, great thinkers, and even his own judgments.

When he first considered the subject, Fort conducted his own psychic experiments as he walked to the library on Forty-second

Street. He would attempt to predict what was in a store window on the block ahead. "Turkey tracks in red snow," he once said to himself. When he looked into the window, he saw groups of black fountain pens, grouped in triangles like bird tracks, against a pink cardboard background. "I was a wizard," Fort marveled for one afternoon. Unfortunately, he admitted that his experiments "kept up about a month. Out of a thousand attempts, I can record only three seeming striking successes."

He may have first intended to research "souls and spirits," but Fort discovered handfuls of weird oddities within his thousands of notes. A year of compliments and criticisms on X and Y convinced him that his "evidence" in those books was stranger and more phenomenal than accounts of ghosts that rapped on tables or moaned in Victorian parlors. Fort had discovered that it wasn't merely houses that were haunted; our reality is haunted, out textbooks are haunted, our sciences and understandings are haunted. He later explained his process:

> I wrote a book [presumably Fort was referring to X] that expressed very little of what I was trying to do. I cut it down from 500 or 600 pages to ninety pages. Then I put it away. It was not what I wanted. But the force of the 40,000 notes had been modified by this book. Nevertheless, the power, or the hypnosis of them, orthodox notes, all of them, orthodox materialism. Tyndall says this, Darwin says that, authoritativeness, positiveness, chemists and astronomers and geologists have proved this or that, nevertheless, monism and revolt were making me write that not even are twice two four, except arbitrarily and conventionally. The oneness of allness. One cosmic flow called disorder, unreality, inequilibrium, ugliness, discord, inconsistency; the other called order, realness, equilibrium, beauty, harmony, justice, truth.

Fort no longer wanted algebraic placeholders. With the failure of X and Y, he deliberately picked a title that emphasized the essence of the text, the memorable but ignored facts that were strangely invisible to scientists but were now clogging the pigeonholes stacked in his living room. He called his new book *The Book of the Damned.*

Fort was energized by the project, delighted by the magical way his little slips of paper could be marshaled to produce his latest book. There was also something liberating about his new tone. His breakthrough seems to have been a daring agnosticism that teased his readers and gave a mysterious, haunting quality to his accounts. The previous formula for "crank" books had been to doggedly gather observations and assign them to a grand theory: X continually postulated a race on Mars; Y tied its facts together by speculating on a continent concealed at the North Pole. In contrast, long stretches of *The Book of the Damned* seemed content to be damnable, and nothing but damnable. Instead of assembling his data to support a theory, he treated these oddities like his characters in *The Outcast Manufacturers*—releasing them in front of his audience and then stepping back to watch them perform; whispering suggestions in the reader's ear, playing the master of ceremonies with an occasional wry comment or observation.

At the end of July, in a celebratory mood, the Forts invited Dreiser and Kubitz to dinner at their apartment. "You shall have Topeacho," he promised Dreiser, who had found Fort's concoction tasty. "Stringbean for Mrs. Kubitz," Fort offered, as Dreiser's mistress continued to express her doubts about the weird preserve.

Fort's enthusiasm was contagious, and Dreiser listened attentively to Fort's plan for the new book. "You're a great old chap," Fort wrote him after their dinner. "I have invented a new dish in your honor . . . jelly with live tadpoles in it. Mrs. K., maybe I'll buy you a beer sometime."

The Book of the Damned benefited from an amazing confluence of forces at the beginning of 1919—those weird coincidences worthy of Fort's books. For the first time in his life, Dreiser was in a unique position to guarantee Charles Fort's success.

EARLY THAT YEAR, Fort wrote to Dreiser, acknowledging the strange turn of events:

> *My dear Dreiser,*
>
> *I'm very much astonished to learn that you've been talking about me behind my back. I have just received a note from Boni & Liveright telling me that you've been saying things about me.*
>
> *But, like most atheists, I'm a good Christian. I not only forgive you, but I have honored you. I have invented something. I have named it after you.*
>
> *It's a meatless cocktail.*
>
> *You take a glass of beer, and put a live goldfish in it—instead of a cherry or olive or such things that occur to a commonplace mind.*
>
> *You gulp.*
>
> *The sensation of enclosing a squirm is delightfully revolting. I think it's immoral. I have named it the Dreiser cocktail.*

Dreiser's controversial novels had made headlines and forged an admirable reputation, but he was continually mistrustful of his publishers, fearing they were not properly advertising his books or were cheating him out of royalties. According to Mencken, his friend Dreiser "had rows with anyone who ever published him, and on his side at least, those rows were often extraordinarily bitter and raucous."

In 1917, when he was between publishers, Dreiser was approached by Horace Liveright, a flamboyant thirty-two-year-old New York publisher. Liveright was tall and gregarious, a natural salesman with a sharp profile and wavy brown hair. He had teamed up with bookseller Albert Boni and, under the imprint of Boni & Liveright, produced the prestigious Modern Library series, and also signed new books by authors John Reed, Eugene O'Neill, and Upton Sinclair.

Liveright knew Dreiser's reputation, but gambled that the author would be a coup for Boni & Liveright. He offered Dreiser a 25 percent royalty, more than twice the going rate, and promised to reissue Dreiser's previous books—because of the controversies, many had a spotty publishing history.

Soon, Dreiser was complaining about Boni & Liveright's sales of his old novels. In their letters, Mencken and Dreiser, anti-Semites, exchanged suspicions about Boni and Liveright, two of the few Jews in the publishing field. Liveright remained optimistic about Dreiser, tempted by his promise of another big new novel, *The Bulwark*. Dreiser drew advances on the book but dragged his heels on the novel. Instead, he submitted a number of smaller books that generated little interest, including a play based on a sex crime, *The Hand of the Potter*, and an erratic collection of essays, *Hey Rub-a-Dub-Dub: A Book of the Mystery and Terror and Wonder of Life.*

Fort sent the completed manuscript to Dreiser in the spring of 1919.

> *Dreiser,*
> *I send you, this afternoon, by express,* The Book of the Damned.

It is a religion.
Our beer man comes Tuesdays.
Fort

Dreiser wrote back his congratulations:

I have just finished The Book of the Damned. *Wonderful,*
colorful, inspiring. Like a peak or open tower window commanding
vast realms. My hat is off. All of your time has been admirably spent.
This book will be published and I offer my services to that extent as
a tribute.

And then a postscript: "Yet *X* and *Y* should be published as they
are." Dreiser pledged his loyalty to *The Book of the Damned*, but continued, "believing that *X* was even more wonderful." *X*, after all, had
put together bits of Dreiser's favorite philosophy, and as a novelist
and an aspiring mystic, he was never daunted by its audacious conclusions.

Dreiser's confidence that the new book "will be published"
was not an idle compliment. He resolved that he would not "waste
time with scientific publications or their editors or just any
publisher."

*Rather, I took it—*The Book of the Damned—*direct to my*
personal publisher, Horace Liveright, and, laying the book on the
table, told him to publish it. And when, after a week or so, he an-
nounced, "But I can't do it. We'll lose money," I said, "If you don't
publish it, you'll lose me." So the book was published.

In fact, Fort's book was one of several hoops through which
Liveright was expected to jump. Liveright's tendency was to keep

jumping, having invested time and money in Dreiser's imminent novel, *The Bulwark*. For example, Dreiser's old mentor from the newspaper days, John Maxwell, had been toiling away on a massive book—a projected five volumes—in which he was determined to prove that Shapespeare's works were actually written by Robert Cecil, the first Earl of Salisbury. In addition to Fort's new book, Dreiser delivered Maxwell's manuscript to Liveright, insisting that he publish it.

Maxwell and Fort were two of the typical "jitney geniuses" that, according to Mencken, had distracted Dreiser and kept him from pursuing his own projects. Liveright, with his eye on *The Bulwark*, may have agreed. If he was merely humoring Dreiser by considering these books, it's interesting that he positively rejected Maxwell's book. Liveright had tried it out on a Columbia professor, who found the Shakespeare research dubious.

As for Fort, Dreiser's memory might be right—"We'll lose money"—but Liveright quickly adopted the project and gave it his full attention. Edward L. Bernays, then the publicist for Boni & Liveright, remembered that Horace Liveright spoke of Fort's book with "equal enthusiasm" as he did the books of his leading authors.

By April 1919, the Liveright contract in place, Fort wrote his official thanks to Dreiser:

> *As a humbler discoverer to a greater discoverer. I offer you my congratulations.*
>
> *Charles Fort has discovered Monstrator and Azuria and Melanicus and the Super-Sargasso Sea.*

These were his tongue-in-cheek inventions in *The Book of the Damned* to explain the phenomena:

But Theodore Dreiser has discovered Charles Fort.

And then the usual invitation for a drink:

Relatively insignificant Charles Fort's beer man comes Tuesdays.
Charles Fort

AT THE SAME TIME, Dreiser was contemplating a hybrid book-magazine dedicated to good fiction, *The American Quarterly*, and had secured another promise from Liveright to publish it. He wrote to Mencken and Fort of his plans, soliciting one of Fort's old stories, "And Now the Old Scow May Slant As It Pleases." Fort sent the manuscript, urging Dreiser to "keep [it] or do with [it] as you see fit." He felt there were a great many crudities, including "local color dragged in by the ears and other parts." But Dreiser's *American Quarterly* never materialized.

Just days after receiving Fort's "Old Scow" manuscript, on May 11, 1919, Dreiser was knocked down by a car as he crossed Columbus Circle in New York. He suffered cuts, scrapes, and two broken ribs. Fort wrote an urgent note to his friend.

We were very much shocked to hear about you. It's an achievement on your part. I've read your stuff for a good many years now without sprinkling holy water around me. This time you gave me a shock. I've heard over the telephone that you're all right.

Charles Fort avoided using a phone; it was a sign of his distress that he phoned Estelle Kubitz's apartment to inquire about Dreiser.

As Dreiser recovered, his mind turned to metaphysics, including Fort's curious speculations. He considered writing about the subject, and suggested that he could boost Fort's upcoming book by furthering Fort's theories.

Fort was wary. Uncharacteristically optimistic about *The Book of the Damned*, he may have doubted whether Dreiser's overwrought philosophical obsessions could complement his own—which had been constructed with a light, humorous touch. Fort wrote a long, cheery letter that was artfully discouraging.

> *I do think that intellectual species are bound by pretty hard and fast lines in the public mind. Mark Twain, for instance, felt that he had to publish his historical novel,* Joan of Arc, *anonymously. To have Dreiser come out with meteorological or anthropological opinions would be as confusing to popular narrownesses as to have had Darwin come out as a dramatic critic.*
>
> *You're a boneless sardine and I'm a greasy Dutchman. Or, in other words, we get along very harmoniously so long as we don't see each other. Or, to use up some more words, I think there is a strong gravitation between us, or our minds, and that there has been for so many years that, if this book should come out without some kind of expression of association with you, the thing would be accursed— quite as Nature might react against a rain of oxygen uncombined with hydrogen.*
>
> *. . . it is obvious that Dreiser has secret hopes of being a swami someday. Or, to use up some more words, he's so glib and detailed, up on roofs, attributing morals of the harem to great innocent souls, because the imaginings are polished by familiarity to him.*

In order to remove all doubt, Fort outlined the main philosophy of his book, the idea of "intermediate existence" between the pos-

itive and negative, and that all things aspire to positiveness or
realness:

> Here is the aspect that you can point out and spread yourself
> upon. You can fly with this. If I were you, I'd take up this one
> subject. Something like this:
>
> Here is a book that seems to answer the everlasting question,
> "What is the good of it all?" If religions come, and religions go, and
> if sciences rise by displacing superstitions, only to be found out later
> as delusions, what's the good of a false, frail thing if it will be pushed
> out of the way by something that will, in turn, be derided?

Fort believed that the striving toward "positiveness" was its own
goal. He offered Dreiser the example of an early Christian in the
time of Nero.

> There's nothing to him but the quasi-soul of a hack poet or a
> swineherd. There's nothing to him to mark a self or a soul: nose
> of one parent, eyes of the other, even his laugh is like his grand-
> mother's. His flesh and his bones are only shifted matter. He's noth-
> ing but an expression of relations. Whatever it may have been,
> relation of some kind, sex-relation, perhaps, something had led him
> into Christianity.
>
> Now he stands condemned to the lions. They've given him a final
> push and left him in the arena. Shouting and creaking, a famished,
> lumbering thing, looking to the right and snarling to the left, but
> making straight for him.
>
> The good of it all.
>
> That it's functioning.
>
> The Christian, with his face in the dirt, turns erect. He casts

wide his arms and looks up to the heavens. The lion may spring or not, and be damned to him. The Christian shouts to the rabble, "I believe in the Lord Jesus Christ absolutely!" Something goes up from that arena. It is now in the Positive Absolute.

So this is the new Dominant, and so it is functioning.

And then the waning of it.

Because it comes into power, because it no longer offers material for positiveness. It has beaten down all opposition. Because then to say what that early Christian had said would be mouthing common-places.

As Fort's disciple, Dreiser's enthusiasm was sincere, but he must have been disappointed to receive specific instructions—notes on the approved sermon—rather than Fort's broad encouragement for his efforts. Six months later, when *The Book of the Damned* was published, Dreiser offered only a simple endorsement on the dust jacket.

Boni & Liveright was publishing Dreiser's play, *The Hand of the Potter*, under duress. It was one of Dreiser's most troubled works. When it was first written in 1916, he had sent the manuscript to Mencken, who condemned it as a badly written play and an immoral subject—a young man who sexually molests and murders an adolescent girl. Mencken pointed out that "I have no patience with impossibilities."

I say the subject is forbidden on the stage, and I mean it. It is all very well enough to talk about artistic freedom, but it must be plain

that there must be a limit in the theatre, as in books. You and I, if
we are lucky, visit the bowel pot daily; as for me, I often have to leave
a high-class social gathering to go out and piss; you, at least, have
been known to roll a working girl on the couch. But such things,
however natural, however interesting, are not for the stage.

Mencken was enraged to read the play just after he had mounted his campaign defending the author's controversial book *The "Genius."* It seemed as if Dreiser were addicted to such troublesome subjects. "Think how the moral reviewers will fall upon it and bellow, 'I told you so.' Really, the enterprise is quite insane."

Broadway producer Arthur Hopkins optioned *The Hand of the Potter* but failed to mount a production. Dreiser foisted the manuscript on the hapless Liveright, who tried to avoid its publication, but finally yielded to Dreiser's test of loyalty.

Dreiser was still revising the play as the galleys were set in type, incurring additional expenses for Boni & Liveright. The exasperated publishers finally issued the book in September 1919.

Dreiser sent a copy on to Fort, who was anxiously awaiting the publication of his own Boni & Liveright book.

> *My dear Dreiser,*
> *That's malice.*
> *Out of that envelope, I could feel a chuckle coming from you:*
> *"Here's a sample of what Fort's going to get very soon now!"*
> *As I see it, there's only one trouble with your latest enormity:*
> *You have gone the limit.*
> *Therefore you have no repression.*

Even Fort, diplomatic and indebted to Dreiser, doubted *The Hand of the Potter.*

But must there not, in all art, be something held back?

I am not convinced that every subject is a "proper" subject for fiction. I am not convinced that urinals and cases of syphilis are "proper" subjects for paintings. I'm not sure that the faint sounds of squirming maggots are fitly interpretable in musical compositions.

He finally worked his way around to an arch compliment, that a play is more scientific, more suitable for such subjects.

I am convinced that such subjects are "proper" subjects of scientific examinations.

I think that you have not worked out as much as you will, nor recognized enough that you are a scientist, and that your attitude always has been scientific.

I like to read your stuff.

It makes me feel so saintly—relatively.

Fort

WHEN HIS CARTON of books finally arrived at the apartment on Forty-third Street, Charles Fort sliced open the cardboard and pulled out a bright copy that still smelled sweetly of ink. Admiring the volume's heft as he turned it over between his pudgy fingers, Fort peeled back the paper cover to examine the neat red fabric binding. He signed the first copy of *The Book of the Damned* to his wife on January 7, 1920. Now that it was done, now that Annie had listened to his prose and Charles had proofread all the pages, there was not much else to say: "To Annie Fort from Charles Fort."

The book had been officially published on December 1, 1919, but most copies didn't make it onto the bookshelves before

January—which meant that *The Book of the Damned* was there to welcome in the New Year.

The 1920s were ready—questioning their heroes, celebrating
their rascals, trembling with doubts, and aching to be scared. *The
Book of the Damned* was the book they were waiting for.

Children Cry for It

I think this is a vice we're writing. I recommend it to those who have hankered for a new sin.

In the spring of 1919, as Charles Fort had been sending off copies of his new incendiary manuscript to Liveright and Dreiser, anonymous terrorists were mailing bombs across America.

There were thirty-six of them, each carefully packed with enough dynamite to kill a man and nicely wrapped in authentic Gimbel Brothers paper. They began to arrive in mailboxes at the end of April. When the box addressed to Georgia Senator Thomas Hardwick was opened by his maid, it blew away her hands and burned the senator and his wife.

A postal worker in New York read a newspaper story about Hardwick's bomb and realized that he'd just seen a stack of similar Gimbel boxes; they'd been relegated to a shelf for insufficient postage. He dashed back to the post office and located the packages, matching them with the newspaper account. They were all addressed to politicians and businessmen like John D. Rockefeller, J. P. Mor-

gan, Attorney General Mitchell Palmer, Secretary of Labor William
B. Wilson, Seattle Mayor Ole Hanson, and Supreme Court Justice
Oliver Wendell Holmes.

America's first Red Scare sent shock waves around the country.
It was apparent that the bombs were intended to arrive on May 1,
May Day, and the Bureau of Investigation identified the source
as anarchists or Bolsheviks who had intended to bring down the
government.

In June, a second installment of bombs arrived, hand-delivered
to the front doors of American mayors and judges. One even went
to a church. A package carried to Attorney General Palmer's door
in Washington, D.C., damaged the brickwork and shattered
windows, but by exploding in the hands of its anonymous terror-
ist, it scattered his bloody body parts along R Street. Alice Roosevelt Longworth arrived that morning to visit her cousins Franklin
and Eleanor Roosevelt, who lived nearby. "A leg lay in the path
to the house next to theirs, another leg farther up the street. A
head was on the roof of yet another house." Fluttering amid the
carnage were copies of a flier titled "Plain Words," printed on
pink paper:

> *There will have to be bloodshed; we will not dodge; there will have
> to be murder; we will kill.*
> —*The Anarchist Fighters*

The terrorists achieved a sickening climax a year later, on September 16, 1920. One hundred pounds of dynamite and five hundred pounds of steel shrapnel were exploded in front of the J. P.
Morgan offices on Wall Street. Four hundred people were injured.
Thirty-eight were killed.

. . .

IT WAS EXACTLY WHAT America had tried to avoid, what the public feared most. When the Great War raged through Europe, President Woodrow Wilson, the egghead, former president of Princeton University and governor of New Jersey, pledged peace and neutrality. He was reelected in 1916 with the slogan "He Kept Us Out of War." But shortly after being sworn in for his second term, he raged against the German submarines, insisted on freedom of the seas, and sent American troops to Europe.

For many Americans, the victory in "Mr. Wilson's War" was bittersweet. Wilson had effectively knocked down the walls of neutrality, and Europe's problems seemed to follow our boys back to our shores. First came the Spanish influenza, then a crippling wave of inflation blamed on the war industries. Wilson pledged his loyalty and our future troops to Europe, detailing his Fourteen Points at Versailles and outlining his plan for the League of Nations. Months later, America was rewarded with European-style socialists taunting politicians, striking against American industry, and finally delivering bombs to elected officials.

Attorney General Mitchell Palmer—working with his twenty-four-year-old assistant, J. Edgar Hoover—organized a series of dramatic raids against labor unions and Socialist organizations. Working without arrest warrants, Palmer rounded up ten thousand suspected Communists or anarchists on November 7, 1919. In January 1920, another six thousand were collected and held without trial; four thousand individuals were jailed in a single night. Many were later released. Almost two hundred fifty were deported to Russia. The Palmer raids were conducted with a daring disregard

for civil rights. Palmer cited the Espionage Act of 1917 and the
Sedition Act of 1918 to justify the arrests.

Palmer continued his campaign, terrifying America by solemnly
warning that a major revolution was being planned for May 1, 1920.
On that day, New York placed eleven thousand police officers on
twenty-four-hour duty; Chicago garrisoned two Army companies to
protect the streets. When May Day passed quietly, Palmer's insights
and tactics came into question. With his unsuccessful run for the
Democratic presidential nomination later that year, the public suspected that his intense Red Scare had been a political ploy. But
there's no question that the Palmer Raids were a product of America's shifting focus. No longer was the country interested in intellectual, global, liberal pursuits. They'd had enough of that.

The 1920 presidential election proved it. A photogenic matinee
idol of a man, Republican candidate Warren G. Harding was a
former newspaperman, bandleader, lieutenant governor, and senator. Harding was one of the most unqualified men ever to aspire to
the office, but in the political climate of 1920, his incuriousness
was part of his attraction. He conducted most of his campaign
from the front porch of his Ohio home, sipping lemonade and
fielding reporters' questions. In an early speech, he promised very
little:

> America's present need is not heroics, but healing; not nostrums,
> but normalcy; not revolution, but restoration; not agitation, but
> adjustment; not surgery, but serenity; not the dramatic, but the dis-
> passionate, not submergence in internationality, but sustainment in
> triumphant nationality. . . .

Harding became famous for coining that word "normalcy";
most English speakers would have used "normality." A political

rival, William McAdoo, marveled at Harding's nonsensical speeches, comparing them to "an army of pompous phrases moving across the landscape in search of an idea." Mencken wrote that Harding's prose "reminds me of stale bean soup, of college yells, of dogs barking idiotically through endless nights."

Harding's political cronies had carefully steered him into the nomination. He thanked them by awarding them positions in the government. They reciprocated by stuffing money into their pockets. Warren G. Harding presided over a hopelessly graft-filled administration that climaxed with the Teapot Dome scandal. The escalating headlines were finally cut short with Harding's fatal heart attack in 1923.

TODAY WE REMEMBER the twenties for its free spirits and loose morals. But most of all, it was a decade of topsy-turvy priorities. Flagpole sitters, dance marathon winners, goldfish swallowers, and hoodlums became popular heroes. Harding's gray conservatism continued with the famously grim Calvin Coolidge, as well as other manifestations—notably Prohibition.

A former street thug from Brooklyn named Alphonse Capone was elevated to the head of Chicago's mob. In spite of murder, bootlegging, extortion, and bribery, he was a hero for boldly taking on Prohibition. Capone was admired in the same way crooked politicians were necessary: he knew how to get things done. America seemed to have a sense of national pride in producing a scoundrel of such swaggering prominence.

With Prohibition came Isolationism and Fundamentalism. The theory of evolution was hauled into court in Ohio, and the grand William Jennings Bryan, former presidential candidate, was forced to testify about his favorite Bible stories. Aimee Semple McPherson and Billy Sunday attracted millions with their evangelical road shows. Spiritualism—talking to ghosts in a dark room—enjoyed a popular revival.

"The inferior man's reasons for hating knowledge are not hard to discern," wrote H. L. Mencken.

> *He hates it because it is complex. Thus his search is always for short cuts. All superstitions are such short cuts. The cosmologies that educated men toy with are all inordinately complex. But the cosmology of Genesis is so simple that even a yokel can grasp it. So he accepts it with loud hosannas, and has one more excuse for hating his betters.*

MENCKEN WAS CAPABLE of coining his own words too. He feared that America was becoming a "boobocracy," and when he read *The Book of the Damned,* he found it full of the ignorant superstition he abhorred. He was already suspicious of Dreiser's causes; now he wrote to his friend in disbelief:

> *Dear Dreiser,*
> *I have just read Fort's* Book of the Damned *and note your remarks upon the slip cover. If they are authentic, what is the notion that you gather from this book? Is it that Fort seriously maintains that there is an Upper Sargasso Sea somewhere in the air, and that all of the meteors, blood, frogs and other things he lists, dropped out of it? The thing leaves me puzzled.*

Although the publisher's blurb on the dust jacket mentioned that Fort was capable of "sardonic humor," Mencken was uncharacteristically tone deaf. Dreiser responded in defense of Fort's talents:

> *I consider Fort one of the most fascinating personalities I have ever known. He is a great thinker and a man of deep and cynical humor. He is so far above any literary craftsman working in the country—your own excellent self excluded—that measurements are futile.*

Many critics were unable to calculate his sense of humor. Even Edward Bernays, advertising the Boni & Liveright books, admitted to being puzzled by Fort, who gave no hint of his intentions. "I do not know to this day whether Fort took himself seriously or wrote tongue in cheek."

The simple answer is that he did both: he was a writer of humor, and he thought he'd discovered chinks in the armor of science and holes in our concept of the world.

Ben Hecht, then reviewing books for the *Chicago Daily News,* understood perfectly.

> *Charles Fort is an inspired clown who, to the accompaniment of a gigantic snare drum, has bounded into the arena of science and let fly at the pontifical sets of wisdom with a slapstick and bladder. He has plucked the false whiskers off the planets. He has reinvented a god. He has exposed the immemorial hoax that bears the name of sanity. In the light of all reason he stands—a gibbering idiot thumbing his nose at the awful presence of world intelligence.*
>
> *Is it true? Has science, by a process of maniacal exclusion of*

telltale data, foisted an algebraic Mother Goose upon the world in the name of astronomy? Laughter—the immemorial laughter of to- day's sanity—answers.

Early in 1920, Booth Tarkington, who had just received the Nobel Prize for his novel *The Magnificent Ambersons*, found himself bedridden, recovering from influenza. He sent to a bookstore for any volumes about crimes and criminology. Mistaking the title, *The Book of the Damned*, for a book about criminals, the bookstore sent over Fort's new title. Tarkington found himself reading "all night when I certainly should have slept." He later wrote an endorsement in *The Bookman* and recalled being spellbound by Fort's oddities.

> *Here indeed was a "brush dipped in earthquake and eclipse" though the wildest and mundane earthquakes are but earthquakes in teapots compared to what goes on in the visions conjured up before us by Mr. Charles Fort. For he deals in nightmare, not on the planetary, but on the constellational scale, and the imagination of one who stag- gers along after him is frequently left gasping and flaccid.*

WRITERS MARTIN GARDNER and Ian Kidd have analyzed Charles Fort's monistic philosophy, a search to identify continuity through all things: "That all things are one, that all phenomena are governed by the same laws; that whatever is true, or what we call true, of planets, plants and magnets, is what we call true of human beings." Fort's likely inspiration was the biologist Ernst Haeckel, a hero of Dreiser's. Haeckel's monism is evident in Dreiser's novels and must have been a subject of conversation with Fort. Kidd points out that Fort's own theory must have preceded his collection of data, because Fort wrote "I had a theory. Because of the theory, I took hundreds of notes a day." But Fort further defined his philosophy by noting that all things seek to become real, or positive, by defining themselves as separate from other things; or damning those other things and excluding them. His prose artfully elevates these damned phenomena to places of honor in his continuous philosophy.

> *The notion of things dropping in upon this earth is as unsettling and as unwelcome to Science as tin horns blowing in upon a musician's relatively symmetric composition; flies alighting upon a painter's attempted harmony and tracking colors one into another; a suffragist getting up and making a political speech at a prayer meeting.*

This becomes Fort's philosophy of Intermediatism. Everything is part of a hyphenated existence, between positive-negative, or animal-vegetable, or even yellow-red.

> *I should say that our existence is like a bridge, like the Brooklyn Bridge, upon which multitudes of bugs are seeking a fundamental— coming to a girder that seems firm and final—but the girder is built upon supports. A support then seems final. But it is built upon underlying structures. Nothing final can be found in all the bridge, because the bridge itself is not a final thing in itself, but is a relationship between Manhattan and Brooklyn. If our existence is a relationship between the Positive Absolute and the Negative Absolute, the quest for finality in it is hopeless. Everything in it must be relative, if the "whole" is not a whole, but is, itself, a relation.*

The continuity, the gradual state of positive to negative, explains Fort's skepticism of scientific knowledge: "That nothing ever has been proved. Because there is nothing to prove." Fort believed that the continuity of all things meant that attempts at scientific definitions—animal, plant, atom, or planet—were completely arbitrary, or pointless.

Despite Fort's claim that "everything in it must be relative," his bridge also happens to be a very good analogy of the scientific method. The ends of the bridge start on the solid foundations of Brooklyn or Manhattan, over land, and are then carefully built, by stretching cables, toward the water. A bridge, like scientific knowledge, is not speculative at its foundations, just at its extremes.

Fort understood this, even if he could comically understate it in his book:

> In continuity, it is impossible to distinguish phenomena at their merging points, so we look for them at their extremes. Impossible to distinguish between animal and vegetable in some infusoria—but hippopotamus and violets. For all practical purposes they're distinguishable enough. No one but a Barnum or a Bailey would send one a bunch of hippopotami as a token of regard.

EDWARD BERNAYS's assignment to advertise *The Book of the Damned* called for some ingenuity, for the newspapers of 1920 were already reporting stories every bit as strange as Fort's phenomena. Marconi had noticed radio signals that, he speculated, originated from Mars. Professor Lowell had already diagrammed straight canals that he believed he saw on the planet. Newspaper readers were being told that Mars was inhabited and that the Martians were trying to contact us.

"The book received much publicity," Bernays later wrote, "as we tied it in with news coverage of scientific events." The advertisements for Boni & Liveright quoted the most enthusiastic reviews and breathlessly reported: "Marconi says that strange interruptions in the wireless service 'may have originated outside the earth.'"

The wry humor of Fort's book came from his collections of weird phenomena and his attempt to reconcile them with science. His basic skepticism, agnosticism, and humor tempered his comments, but his willingness to believe anything, or believe nothing, could addle most readers. Fort teased established scientists and accepted theories with these damned facts, asking why his own outrageous theories ("Genesistrine," the floating junkyard) were not any more reasonable.

"Science Mocked," the *New York Tribune* titled its book review, endorsing the book:

> In the middle ages, science disposed of disturbing facts by declaring that they did not exist and showing that Aristotle had no record of them. Mr. Fort's phenomena cannot be disposed of so easily. Unless his book is smothered by a conspiracy of silence, it should provoke an extremely lively series of scientific controversies.

Questioning science, or even worse, stopping to laugh at it, broke an established taboo and off-footed many commentators, who were surprised at Fort's conclusions. Fort wrote:

> They're so hairy and attractive, these scientists of the 19th century. We feel the zeal of a Sitting Bull when we think of their scalps. Though every one who scalps is, in the oneness of allness, himself likely to be scalped, there is such a discourtesy to an enemy as the wearing of wigs.

Several reviewers quoted Fort's neat dismissal of Darwinism:

The fittest survive.
What is meant by the fittest?
Not the strongest, not the cleverest—
Weakness and stupidity everywhere survive.
There is no way of determining fitness except in that a thing does
survive.
"Fitness," then, is only another name for "survival."
Darwinism:
That survivors survive.

Except that Darwin was cleverer than this. "Survival of the fittest" is Herbert Spencer's phrase to define Darwinism. Spencer's Social Darwinism was an important influence on Theodore Dreiser, who found Spencer's philosophy both captivating and terrifying. By taking jabs at Spencer, Fort was playing to his audience: his best friend. Fort's grand first-person plural, a tone borrowed from his childhood autobiography, *Many Parts,* appeared through sections of *The Book of the Damned* as the author makes trenchant, self-deprecating observations. Much of the dense philosophical posturing is made palatable by Fort's unexpected jokes or weird analogies.

This is worthy of a place in the museum we're writing. . . .
So it's a book we're writing, or it's a procession, or it's a museum,
with a Chamber of Horrors rather over-emphasized. . . .
According to our religion. . . .
Our opponents hold out for mundane origin of all black
rains. . . .

Considering that he was a new writer on these subjects—with materials gathered at the New York Public Library and a manuscript composed on his kitchen table—the suggestion of opponents should have surprised a few readers. More than likely, this was a bold *en garde*, imagining Waldemar Kaempffert, *Scientific American*, and the host of publishers that had scoffed at X and Y.

In the end, Fort's transgression was being critical of science and poking fun at scientists—who had been elevated to a modern priestcraft for the sophisticated twenties. Even Mencken was stunned by this crime and thought Fort guilty by association. Fundamentalists were critical of science; only ignorant people sneered at the discoveries of scientists.

In retrospect we see that Fort was right. Alongside Fort's reviews, the newspapers of 1920 included long, authoritative articles quoting Marconi and Lowell, discussing the achievements of the Martians. Every once in a while, scientists deserve to be laughed at.

IN JUNE 1920, Fort wrote to Dreiser of his success:

> *Been interviewed half a dozen times, got disciples, page and more in magazine section of the Sunday* World, *favorable criticism in* Popular Astronomy; *Booth Tarkington in a frenzy over it, and an editor in Camden, New Jersey, going to organize a worldwide society to look for more phenomena. Children cry for it and the more devout say it will cure rheumatism.*

But, Fort admitted with some embarrassment, "*Catholic World* says that your book is awful and that mine is a good book." Dreiser had just published *Hey Rub-a-Dub-Dub*, a collection of essays, including his X-inspired play, *The Dream*.

As usual, it was Dreiser's morality that had come into question. *Catholic World* criticized the essays denying God, espousing monism, and questioning Christian marriage. "Mr. Dreiser has no saving sense of humor, hence this awful book," the review concluded.

As for *The Book of the Damned*, the same publication sniffed at Fort's "sensational" title and a "staccato style that soon produces the wearying effect of a series of explosions." But *Catholic World* was fascinated by the book: "[The] compilation represents research of a particularly difficult kind." Writing to Dreiser, Fort dismissed the praise: "I do not think I deserve this." Oddly, *Catholic World* could overlook Fort's own monism or godless cosmology, and would appreciate any book willing to take a swing at Darwinism and detail manna falling from the skies.

Fort ended his note with the usual promise of a drink: "Annie saved a bottle of brandy, expecting you to drop in, until past human endurance." Prohibition was changing even his hospitality.

Fort was beginning to appreciate the delicate position of his new philosophy, and marvel at the unexpected friends who were willing to pledge allegiance as "Forteans."

No prophet actually selects his devotees.

The London Triangle

If we could stop to sing, instead of everlastingly noting vol. this and p. that, we could have the material of sagas.

he *Book of the Damned* enjoyed a second printing in 1920, and sales were respectable if not spectacular. But Dreiser was still worried about X and Y, nagging his friend about the manuscripts. In June 1920, he wrote to Fort from Los Angeles, where he was renting a house with his latest mistress, a much younger second cousin named Helen Patges Richardson. Richardson was attempting to find acting work in motion pictures. Dreiser congratulated Fort on the "stir" caused by *The Book of the Damned.*

> *If you are wise you will publish X, just as a great piece of writing. And Y also. And you ought to gather up those short stories. If I were a publisher, I would have done it for you.*

"As a great piece of writing" is evidence that Dreiser understood Fort's hesitation with X: the book's elaborate theory would now

look ridiculous next to the agnosticism of *The Book of the Damned*.
Dreiser's own spotty sales and the long-delayed novel meant that
he'd lost his equity with Liveright and couldn't push X and Y. In a
letter to Mencken, Dreiser confessed his concerns:

> *I have read X and Y and they are marvelous. I have the sicken-*
> *ing feeling that in some bitter mood [Fort] will some day destroy*
> *them, and they are so wonderful to me that it would be like destroy-*
> *ing Karnak.*

Dreiser was right about Fort's mood shifts, and his dismissive
attitude about old work. Anna was equally to blame. "One day he
went away in a temper," Anna recalled years later, "and told me that
he was never coming back. So I threw away all his old junk." The
"junk" consisted of his stack of magazines with his short stories.
The next morning, when Fort returned, contrite, he noticed that
the magazines were gone. "I threw them all away," Anna reported.
Fort shrugged.

SHORTLY AFTER *The Book of the Damned* was published, on one of
his regular trips to the New York Public Library, Fort went to the
circulation desk and asked for a copy of the book. He took it with
obvious pride—standing beneath the gilded ceiling, surrounded by
the reverent, hushed whispers that had accompanied his years of
patient research. The book's presence at that very library was a sign
of his success. But as he squinted through his glasses, the Dewey
decimal marks, scratched in white ink on the spine, seemed odd to
him. Fort leaned over the desk and asked the librarian about the

classification. Author Edmund Pearson, who had worked as a librarian there, later told the story of Fort's visit.

> *The librarian, not aware that he was speaking to the author of the book, said that these marks indicated the class of "Eccentric Literature"—perhaps he may have said, "Books by Cranks." There was an instant explosion, scolding, and entreaty by the author, who demanded that his book should be classed with those on—well, I cannot imagine what. In the end, I think he got part of his desire, but not all. The stubborn librarians would not endorse his amusing treatise as orthodox science.*

Pearson didn't understand. Fort never wanted to be part of "orthodox science," nor would he have anticipated a place of honor next to Newton or Darwin. But his book had criticized science and gathered together neglected research. It was a particular insult to find the words "crank" or "eccentric" coded into the classification, branded into the binding, at his very own New York Public Library.

Fort voiced his displeasure in an interview in the *New York Tribune*, and then typically, shyly, felt all the worse for losing his temper and calling attention to himself. Like the Albany schoolboy, Fort sulked; imagined himself the martyr; readjusted his collection; executed the paper soldiers that had betrayed him; plotted to run away.

Theodore Dreiser was still in Los Angeles when he opened Fort's letter, dated November 7, 1920.

"I am going to drop out," Fort reported.

> *Forces are moving me. I've cut ties with Albany and published in the* Tribune *my dissatisfactions with the New York Public Library,*

so that I can't very comfortably go back there, and have burned all my notes, 40,000 of them.

Those precious notes had been Fort's organizing principle through *X, Y,* and *The Book of the Damned*—the boxes of phenomena that had been meticulously pried from scientific journals.

Fort had always been afraid of being possessed by his collections, and later wrote of his obsession:

> *My miserliness for notes. . . . Oh, but how we also, at times, hate what we love most! I've often been on the verge of burning the thousands of treasures that are dearer to me than anything else in the world. I abuse them sometimes, make them up into bundles to burn or throw away, and then don't. It's one of the complexities of idolatry.*

With his notes finally burned, Dreiser realized that mysterious, perhaps disastrous, forces were indeed moving Fort.

> *Forces are moving me to London. Annie and I sail on the 27th. I hope you'll always write to me, once a year, c/o Mssrs. Brown, Shipley & Co., 123 Pall Mall, London, SW. I have burned and destroyed and cut, but have kept some letters—and may strange, orthogenetic gods destroy me if I ever forget all that was done for me by Theodore Dreiser!*

Drieser wrote back:

> *First of all, I hope you have not destroyed X and Y. Next, I'm sorry America is going to lose you. Not permanently, I hope. You loom very large on the horizon. Lastly, I hope to do more to speed your fame.*

Fort had often ended his letters to Dreiser with a reminder about his beer man's deliveries, or the promise of a bottle of brandy. Dreiser added a friendly, Prohibition-inspired plea:

> *For God's sake, send me a bottle of scotch from England. I'll pay you in cash.*

With the properties in Albany finally sold, Fort's inheritance and the royalties from his book meant financial security. Annie and Charles could live where they wished—if they lived frugally—and Fort could continue research and writing at his leisure. Anna had been born in England; Fort had fond memories of London during his travels.

Fort was not quitting. He was upping the ante. He and Annie arrived in London on December 4, 1920, and took a small, furnished flat at 15 Marchmont Street near Russell Square. Fort planned it carefully so he was a short walk from the famous repository of literature, history, and scientific knowledge, the reading room of the British Museum.

ANNA FORT later recalled their time in London. Her "Charlie" lived by the clock. He was up for breakfast at eight. He would then "knock around the rooms" and she would serve lunch at twelve. Around two, he went off to the British Museum, where he read every afternoon.

The magnificent round reading room, topped with a metal filigree dome, had been built in 1857 in the court behind the British Museum. Fort was in good company; the reading room had been used by Marx, Lenin, Kipling, Shaw, and Wilde during their own

researches. The collection offered unprecedented access to published materials, and Fort was soon making his "grand tours" of
the collection.

Sitting at one of the wide desks, he surrounded himself with
stacks of bound scientific journals and periodicals, meticulously
sweeping through separate categories. He made his notes on rectangles of torn paper that could be rearranged or sorted. At five, he'd
gather his notes, close the books, nod politely to the staff, and
saunter back to his rooms.

Then Charles and Anna would have their supper and walk to a
movie in Leicester Square—four or five times a week—or over to
Hyde Park. Fort met literary people, amateur philosophers, or zeal-
ots attracted to the Speaker's Corner. "An orator shouts, 'What we
want is no king and no law!'" Fort remembered a chaotic speech.
"'How we'll get it will be not with ballots, but with bullets!'" After
the talks, Anna recalled, "They bunched off in groups." Fort would
find a friendly argument as Anna wandered around the park. At
nine, when she returned for him, he stopped his discussion, and the
two of them walked back to their flat. "The men used to make fun
of him going home," she recalled, "but he'd had enough of it by
that time. He liked solitude. He was a hermit."

Early in 1921, Charles Fort sent a happy letter back to
Dreiser.

> *Do you want to break my heart? Send you a bottle of scotch?*
> *How? Tell me and I'll send you a million bottles of scotch.*

Fort sent his new London address, and admitted that he had
been suffering from "metaphysical dissatisfactions" and "in a horrible state, revolting against writing."

We just had another fight. Annie said if she'd had her voice cul-
tivated she'd be a [Nellie] Melba. I said that one damn genius in
the family is too damn much.

But he and Annie had resolved to make the best of it, and settled
down with two bottles of Bass Ale. Fort's penmanship grew especially sloppy, the ink bleeding through the page, as he continued to
describe their carefree evening on Marchmont Street.

I said, we'll have another, and we did. And we began to sing,
"Oh, Elsie, kind and true," and I haven't been so happy in years and
years, and there were four black bottles on the table.

We sang "Juanita," and there's a dip in it when I bring in the
bass in a way that moves me more than the profoundest of meta-
physical discoveries ever could. And there were six big black bottles
on the table.

And we sang "On the Banks of the Wabash," and I almost cried
because it made me think of the dear, horrible, delightful, humble days
of our greatest poverty, when we always had two or three pots of beer
a night, and sang and scrapped and were happy. And there were eight
or nine black bottles on the table.

"On the Banks of the Wabash" triggered a memory.

Annie said, "You must write to Mr. Dreiser." And I'm an athe-
ist, but I said, "God bless him, I will." And she got paper for me,
and ink for me, and all is well, except that I don't know how to send
you the million bottles of scotch and am waiting for you to tell
me how.

. . .

FORT WROTE a teasing letter to his brother Raymond in
Albany.

>*What do you know but that I've heard some talk about taking my
>stuff seriously. Somebody may organize an expedition to the Moon,
>to find out what there is in these things I'm writing about, and I'll
>have to go along—how can I get out of going?*
>
>*England seems some distance, but I have an awful suspicion that
>I'll be up in the moon next Christmas. Of course I'll take Annie
>with me.*

According to Anna, during their walks Charles would stand
on the street in London, staring up at the night sky, pointing
out constellations or planets. He explained the history behind
them, the ancient mysteries, or the recent discoveries. "Then up in
our rooms he would throw open the windows and stand gazing at
the stars," she later told Dreiser. "That was his delight for a long,
long time."

AFTER SIX MONTHS, the Forts returned to New York on the
Finland, arriving on June 13, 1921. He wrote leisurely through the
autumn, sifting the phenomena into his new manuscript, and intriguing Liveright with the information that he was hard at work
on another book. In December the couple left for London—now
taking a flat just down the road from their previous rooms, at 39
Marchmont Street, Flat A, over a greengrocer.

Once again, they settled down to their routine. Anna took care of the meals and household chores. The new apartment was leased with a maid service, but Fort didn't want anyone else cleaning the rooms, so Anna took on this job as well.

Fort was particular about his food. "He did not like delicatessen stuff," Anna recalled. Once, when she brought back some meat from the deli, Fort complained: "It's a damned shame, that's what it is, for you to bring in old, cheap stuff to me." Anna coolly went back to the deli and got a copy of the bill to show him that she'd paid a dollar a pound for the meat, a princely sum. Fort apologized.

One afternoon, the couple went grocery shopping. He bought a pungent Limburger cheese, one of his favorites, and put the bundle in his pocket. Later, when they approached the vegetable stand, he realized his error. He was fond of the young girl who sold vegetables, and enjoyed innocently flirting with her. But that day—conscious of the smell—he stood across the street and directed Anna to buy the vegetables. She teased him mercilessly for that.

Every afternoon, he took on loftier pursuits. He had focused on astronomical phenomena, suspecting that there were unexpected connections between the planets, earthquakes, meteors, and explosions in the sky. His work in the British Museum was unearthing hundreds of correlations.

They returned to New York in June 1922 aboard the *Olympic* and took an apartment at 105 West Fortieth Street. J. David Stern, the editor of the Camden, New Jersey, *Daily Courier,* had been an admirer of *The Book of the Damned* and anxiously inquired about the author's next book. Fort sent Stern a copy of his new manuscript, titled *Chaos.* But Fort still wasn't satisfied with it, and hesitated delivering it to Boni & Liveright. He spent months rearranging the material, pulling out various accounts of phenomena and substituting others from his files. Late that year, the completed manuscript had been titled *New Lands.* Fort sent a note to Dreiser in January 1923, informing him, "We've put over another one."

> *We may have to take ourselves somewhat seriously? That would be a damn shame, wouldn't it?*

He proudly reported that Liveright accepted the book for publication later that year. The Forts had moved to an apartment at 1962 Seventh Avenue, "top floor, of course," but Anna was "in despair; she hasn't any Topeacho for you." Dreiser arranged to visit them, but joked that "the absence of Topeacho is fatal," signing the note, "Simon, surnamed Peter."

NEW LANDS was a deliberately contrary title. The book was not about lands at all. It was about oddities in the skies. Fort's opening sentences explained the title.

> *Lands in the sky—*
> *That they are nearby—*
> *That they do not move.*

Fort compared his planetary discoveries with the discoveries of new continents, although he admitted that his theories were merely "suggestions and gropings and stimuli."

> *Islands of space and the rivers and oceans of an extra-geography.*
> *A scientific priestcraft. "Thou shalt not!" is crystallized in its frozen textbooks.*

I have data upon data upon data of new lands that are not far away.

The first section of the book is a fulsome criticism of astronomy. Fort was outraged that it had been portrayed in absolute mathematical terms—predictions that are carefully calculated, then checked and double-checked. Fort filled his pages with examples of ridiculous predictions that were hailed and then discovered to be wildly off, of planets that weren't where they were supposed to be, of comets that never came back, of infighting between astronomers and astonishing miscalculations of physical phenomena. He makes the case that it has been a very messy science indeed. "It will be one of our most lasting impressions of astronomers: they explain and explain and explain."

Then Fort hints at the frights he's discovered in the sky.

That our existence, a thing within our solar system, or supposed solar system, is a stricken thing that is mewling through space, shocking able-minded, healthy systems with the sores of its sun, its ghastly moons, its civilizations that are all broken out with sciences; a celestial leper, holding out doddering expanses into which charitable systems drop golden comets? If it be the leprous thing that our findings seem to indicate, there is no encouragement for us to go on. We cannot discover; we can only betray new symptoms. If I be part of such a stricken thing, I know of nothing but sickness and sores and rags to reason with: my data will be pustules; my interpretations will be inflammations.

Fort ridiculed proofs of the shape of the earth, the speed of light, triangulation, and spectroscopic observations. He doubted Kepler and noted how Newton had used his mathematics to predict

planetary motion as well as the Old Testament's Prophecies of Dan-
iel. He also wondered—with the same troublemaking attitude
that accompanied the theories of *The Book of the Damned*—whether
the world is really round and, if it isn't stationary, whether the
moon and stars aren't really much closer than we suspect, and
whether there isn't a shell surrounding the earth, "in which the stars
are openings, admitting light from an existence external to the
shell."

The second part of the book consisted of Fort's masterful
collection of oddities: seemingly random, seemingly jumbled, but
carefully organized as in a horror story, to gradually surprise and
terrify.

Unexpected stars in the sky, objects crossing the sun, organic
matter dropping from the heavens. . . . Then mysterious forms of
people that some have interpreted as angels or phantom soldiers.
Mysterious lights or forms seen on the moon. A city identified.
Architectural structures. Mysterious explosions or flashes seen in
the sky, which Fort ties to the periodic adjacency of Earth to the
planets Mars and Venus. Mirages of strange cities on the horizon,
some recognizable and some not.

> *March 16, 1890, that at 4 o'clock, in the afternoon of March*
> *12th, in the sky of Ashland, Ohio, was seen a representation of a*
> *large, unknown city. Observers thought they recognized Sandusky,*
> *sixty miles away. "The more superstitious declared that it was a*
> *vision of the New Jerusalem." May have been a revelation of heaven,*
> *and for all I know heaven may resemble Sandusky, and those of us*
> *who have no desire to go to Sandusky may ponder that point.*

Stones fall from the sky, and alternately stones unexpectedly
shoot up from fields into cloudless skies. Mysterious missilelike

objects fall and injure people, or lightning strikes them dead on a cloudless day.

And then mysterious objects in the sky, years before any terrestrial airships. Dozens of strange vessels, "shaped like a Mexican cigar," or "cone shaped, 180 feet long, with large fins on either side," or "a round luminous object," or "with short wings, casually inclining sideways." Fort reported Lowell and Tesla's discoveries of a regular pattern of radio waves that seemed to be emanating from Mars.

NEW LANDS may have incorporated some of the earlier research from X and Y. For example, the accounts of unpredictable comets and speculations about a race of sphinxes in ancient Egypt or Kaspar Hauser had been elements of these earlier books. But not surprisingly, Fort's new research, which filled the pages, showed a tilt to England, something he admitted with his characteristic bombast:

> *Char me the trunk of a redwood tree. Give me pages of white chalk cliffs to write upon. Magnify me thousands of times, and replace my trifling immodesties with a titanic megalomania. Then I might write largely enough for our subjects. Because of accessibility and abundance of data, our accounts deal very well with the relatively insignificant phenomena of Great Britain.*

Providing an important inspiration to later paranormal authors, Fort identified a distinct area:

> *There is a triangular region in England, three points of which appear so often in our data that the region should be specially known*

to us, and I know it myself as the London Triangle. It is pointed in
the north by Worcester and Hereford, in the south by Reading, Berk-
shire, and in the east by Colchester, Essex. The line between Colches-
ter and Reading runs through London.

One of the most intriguing sections is Fort's reinterpretation of
his cosmology, which gives him a chance to definitely renounce
the Fundamentalists:

> *That the geo-system is an incubating organism, of which this*
> *earth is the nucleus. . . . That there is one integrating organism and*
> *that we have heard its pulse.*
>
> *In a technical sense we give up the doctrine of evolution. Ours is*
> *an expression upon super-embryonic development, in one enclosed*
> *system. Ours is an expression upon design underlying and manifest-*
> *ing in all things within this one system, with a Final Designer left*
> *out, because we know of no designing force that is not itself the*
> *product of remoter design. I point out that this expression of ours is*
> *not meant for aid and comfort to the reactionaries of the type of*
> *Col. W. J. Bryan, for instance. It is not altogether anti-Darwinian.*
> *The concept of development replaces the concept of evolution. In Dar-*
> *winism, there is no place for the influence of the future upon the*
> *present.*

In other words, Fort was still describing orthogenetic evolution on a grand, cosmic level, but carefully distinguishing it from
theology.

In an inspired and memorable flight, Fort noted how "art, science, religion, invention" could be "out of accord with established
environment," and yet "its unfitness made it survive for future
usefulness."

Also, there are data for the acceptance of all things, in wider being, held back as well as protected and prepared for, and not permitted to develop before comes scheduled time. Langley's flying machine makes me think of something of the kind—that this machine was premature, that it appeared a little before the era of aviation upon this earth, and that therefore Langley could not fly. But this machine was capable of flying, because, some years later, Curtiss did fly in it. Then one thinks that the Wright Brothers were successful, because they did synchronize with a scheduled time.

One of the greatest secrets that have eventually been found out was, for ages, blabbed by all the pots and kettles in the world—but the secret of the steam engine could not, to the lowliest of intellects, or to the supposititiously highest of intellects, more than adumbratively reveal itself until came the time for its coordination with the other phenomena and the requirements of the Industrial Age.

Nowadays, with less hero-worship than formerly, historians tell us that, to English and French fisherman, the coast of Newfoundland was well known long before the year 1492. Nevertheless, to the world in general, it was not, or according to our acceptances, could not be, known.

ANNA AND CHARLES had returned to London in May 1923, many months before *New Lands* was published by Boni & Liveright on October 8, 1923. Unfortunately, it generated only a fraction of the interest of *The Book of the Damned* and received the usual reviews.

The *Boston Transcript* claimed that it was "an amazingly interesting book." But the *New York Times* sniffed:

*The pages at hand champion—and most vigorously!—the cause
of certain astronomical hypotheses which are not recognized according
to the accepted theories of that science. Hence, possibly, the vigor.*

*New Lands has a double purpose. It scourges, abuses and flays
astronomy and astronomers for clinging to their data that cause them
to disregard Mr. Fort's theories, which are then built up upon the
foundation of their own data.*

In tone, it was the most serious of his books, but Fort's organization allowed readers to infer the worst. By ridiculing the faults of
astronomers and assembling his alternate theories in the first chapters, *New Lands* suggested a classic piece of crank literature—questioning the shape of the earth or the distance to the moon. It wasn't
until the twelfth chapter that Fort's famous lists of phenomena
began to addle his audience.

Fort was resigned to the mixed reviews and unconcerned with
book sales. He was contentedly busy in London, trudging back and
forth to the British Museum, obsessively filling his pockets with
notes, when *New Lands* happened to find an important new convert.
He was a young part-time actor, reporter, and bookstore clerk
named Tiffany Ellsworth Thayer. With *New Lands,* Thayer had just
discovered his gospel.

That Frog Would Be God

I do not know how to find out anything new without being offensive.

T iffany Ellsworth Thayer was born in 1902 in Freeport, Illinois, the son of actors Sybil Madeline Farrar and Elmer Ellsworth Thayer. His parents were divorced when he was five. When he was fifteen, the boy quit school and became an actor, touring in the Civil War play *The Coward*. He also worked as a reporter, settling in Chicago during the same time Ben Hecht was writing for the *Chicago Daily News*.

Somehow he'd missed *The Book of the Damned*, which was published when he was seventeen years old, touring as an actor. But when he found *New Lands*, he quickly devoured it—a book directed at the featherbrained establishment had an obvious appeal for the disaffected young man. He wrote a letter to the author, in care of Boni & Liveright, which worked its way to Fort at his desk in London. Thayer complimented him on the book and asked about Hecht's assessment of *The Book of the Damned*, that "five out of six persons who read this book will go mad." Fort was amused by Thayer's note, but he couldn't bring himself to use the name "Tiffany." He called him Ellsworth, and sent a letter in return:

> *Ben Hecht is pretty good sometimes, but I do not think much of him as an alienist. According to my own researches, five out of every five persons are crazy in the first place.*

ANNA MADE FRIENDS with the neighbors, including a couple named the St. Clairs, who shared many happy evenings at the Forts' table, sampling bits of strong British cheese, talking philosophy with Charles and neighborhood gossip with Anna. Another neighbor, an actress, was appearing in the popular American musical *Rose Marie*, newly imported to the West End. She painted such a gorgeous picture of the production, the costumes and songs, that Anna was beguiled and Charles was tempted to buy two tickets. "It was beautiful," Anna later recalled.

But *Rose Marie* was enough culture for Fort, who returned to his nightly routine of newsreels and silent moving pictures, or strolls through Hyde Park. His days were still spent at the British Museum, where he was amassing boxes of new notes. Like Tiffany Thayer, a number of readers contacted Fort, and many alerted him to some strange phenomenon that—they were convinced—should be part of his canon. Fort began to conduct quiet investigations by sending out letters, asking for additional information or questioning witnesses.

San Francisco resident Miriam Allen deFord and her husband, writer Maynard Shipley, read *The Book of the Damned* and contacted

Fort. His response came from London, instigating a correspondence that spanned many years. When newspapers ran accounts of stones falling from the sky in Chico, California, Miriam deFord went to investigate and watched one rock fall from a cloudless sky and bounce gently at her feet. She reported her discoveries. "The questions Fort asked me and the care he took in getting details straight taught me something of his obstinate search for verification," she later recalled.

For years Fort exchanged letters with John T. Reid of Lovelock, Nevada. Reid had sent accounts of fossils he had discovered. Fort responded by doubting the fossil record, pointing out accounts of footprints of a cow in rocks, a stick embedded in sandstone, and a nail found in a lump of quartz. "I think that space has been put upon a rack by the astronomers, and time upon a rack by the geologists, and that the stretching that they've done is quite outrageous, though humorous." Fort offered accounts of falls of living things, especially frogs, and argued that the whirlwind theory was illogical. "I have not heard of one fall, in this period, of dust, or pebbles, or leaves, such things as a whirlwind would be more like to carry, than frogs and fishes."

Writer Edmond Hamilton sent a newspaper account of a Princeton geology professor who had inexplicably found small living frogs in a puddle of water in the hot Arizona desert. He had written to the professor, suggesting the Fortean notion that the frogs had fallen from the sky, and received the response that this was "absolutely impossible." When Fort read this report, he laughed.

Like you, I noticed the learned gentleman's use of the word, "absolutely." If he could apply that word to anything, say a frog, that Frog would be God.

Nevertheless—with the absoluteness left out—he may be right.
It seems that those Arizona frogs were adults. There may have been
showers of adult frogs, but in my records, of about 80 instances, all
showering frogs were little ones.

On July 27, 1924, the *Philadelphia Public Ledger* published a letter
from Fort.

In the Public Ledger, *July 23, 1886, it is said that upon the*
morning of the 19th of July, at Hobdys Mills, Pennsylvania, after
a severe rainstorm, the ground was found to be covered with bright
red lizards; roads and fields scarlet with them. They were an inch
and a half long; row of small black spots on each side. It seems that
all were alive. In two hours all had crawled out of sight.

If anybody can send information to me at my present address, it
may be that we can have data upon a fall from the sky of living
creatures unknown upon this earth. If living things can come to this
earth from other worlds, we have the material for visions such as have
not excited imaginations upon this earth since the year 1492.

On August 24, 1924, the *New York Times* ran Fort's letter suggesting that objects from other planets had been falling to earth.

I point out that if upon this earth there has been considerable
interest in the idea of firing projectiles to the moon, or to other plan-
ets, there may be in other worlds some such enterprising notions
relative to this earth.

He listed dozens of sources for these falls, noting an 1883 *New
York Times* article about a long sword, covered with mysterious hiero-

glyphs, that reportedly had fallen out of the sky in Ulster County, New York.

Fort wrote that "It seems that in my notes I have not the full story," urging anyone who knew about the mysterious sword to contact him at his London address.

Fort followed with additional letters to the *New York Times*. He enthusiastically reported receiving data and clippings from readers: "There is considerable interest in this subject." Fort cited examples of mysterious meteors. Again, he asked to "hear from anybody who is interested in this investigation. We may be able to take it up and unearth more data in the United States."

Fort's letters gave a hint about his new areas of research. He speculated about planets being much closer than we suspect, and that explosions on other planets may be the source of dust and debris from the sky.

On June 6, 1925, *T.P.'s Weekly*, a British publication, offered another letter with a bold assertion from Fort: "There are recorded indications that this earth has, from time to time, been visited by explorers from other worlds." He offered several chilling accounts of luminous objects in the skies over Japan, or a "torpedo shaped object" over Burlington, Vermont.

In early 1926, Fort read of a fall of fish in the Toronto *Daily Star*. Residents of the town of Dundas, Ontario, were astonished to observe small fish falling with rain from the sky. He wrote to the editor of the newspaper, comparing the fish fall with the falls of other living objects. The editor researched the story and reported that the mystery had been solved. A resident admitted abandoning a fishing trip in the rain, and tipping his pail of minnows into a ditch, where they were discovered.

A September 5, 1926, letter to the *Times*, titled "Have Martians

Visited Us?" contained some of Fort's wildest notions, including a
theme from his manuscript *X*:

> *Why have they not landed, say in Central Park, and had a big
> time of it—monstrous parade down Broadway, historic turn-out,
> eruptions of confetti from skyscrapers?*
>
> *I can think of reasons, and one of them is that for ages Martians
> may have been in communication with this earth and have, in some occult
> way, been in control of its inhabitants, or have been exploiting them.
> They have not disclosed themselves except in openly patrolling the sky.*

He then continued with numerous accounts of mysterious lights
and airships in the sky. Fort suggested that, in a few weeks, when
the planet Mars was again in opposition, there may be a new wave
of sightings. "If anybody should see anything or hear of anything
that seems to be worth investigating, I should be glad if he will let
me know."

Fort tried subscribing to a clipping bureau to search newspapers
and supply him with articles about oddities. But the bureau was
confused about the subjects and only managed to supply articles
about spiritualism—which didn't interest him. He had better luck
with his readers. "They're a pretty good lot. Lately I've been gathering data by means of letters to newspapers, and I've been hearing
from cranks and wild men," he wrote to a fan. "Getting them from
the U.S., Canada, South Africa and Australia."

Letters received by Fort were tightly folded to the accepted one-
and-a-half by two-and-a-half inch size, fixed with a paper clip, labeled with the category of phenomenon, and filed with the rest of
his tiny paper notes. Once again, Fort had tens of thousands, collected in shoe boxes that were stacked around the London flat, all
in expectation of unleashing his next book of surprises.

. . .

ANYTHING ODD, any curiosity that temporarily captured Charles Fort's attention, was worthy of his notes. His landlord in London had an energetic puppy that patrolled the flats on Marchmont. "He had frenzies," Fort wrote. "Once he tore down the landlord's curtains. He bit holes into a book of mine, and chewed the landlord's slippers."

The landlord took the dog about ten miles away and abandoned him, "probably leaping upon somebody, writhing joy for anybody who would notice him."

Two weeks later, Fort was looking out the front window of the flat when he saw the dog sniffing along the opposite side of the street. He passed the house, continued smelling, then returned, crossed the street and sat in front of the house, waiting expectantly. The landlord took him in again and rewarded him with a bone.

Fort took notes of pictures falling off the walls—in his rooms, in the landlady's room, or at the upstairs tenants.

March 11: I was reading last night, in the kitchen, when I heard a thump. Sometimes I am not easily startled, and I looked around in a leisurely manner, seeing that a picture had fallen, glass not breaking, having fallen upon a pile of magazines in the corner.

Morning of the 12th: Find that one of the brass rings, on the back of the picture frame, to which the cord was attached, had been broken in two places—metal bright at the fractures.

Annie reminded me that, in tenant's room, two pictures had fallen recently.

March 18: I found a second picture on the floor, in the same corner. It had fallen from a place about three feet above a bureau, upon which are piled my boxes of notes. It seems clear that the picture did not ordinarily fall, or it would have hit the notes and there would have been a heartbreaking mess of notes all over the floor. I did not want to alarm Annie, and start a ghost-scare centering around me.

April 18: Annie took a picture down to wash the glass. The picture seemed to fall from the wall into her hands. Annie said, "Another picture cord rotten," then, "No, the nail came out." But the cord had not broken and the nail was in the wall. "I don't understand how that picture came down."

October 22: Yesterday, I was in the front room, thinking casually of the pictures that fell from the walls. This evening, my eyes bad. Unable to read. Was sitting, staring at the kitchen wall, fiddling with a piece of string. Anything to pass away time. I was staring right at a picture above corner of bureau, where the notes are. It fell. It hit boxes of notes, dropped to floor, frame at a corner broken, glass broken.

Over a year later Annie was in the flat, listening to a friend give a tiresome description of a motion picture. Suddenly, she heard a crash in the next room, and found that a large picture had fallen. "I have not strongly enough emphasized Annie's state of mind," Fort wrote. "The long account of a movie had annoyed her almost beyond endurance and her hope for an interruption was keen." Fort filed this note, with the others, under Letter E, for "experiments," in shoebox number 27, vowing to look for connections in similar phenomena.

When Fort wrote about these phenomena years later, he speculated about a kind of witchcraft. "I looked at a picture, and it fell from a wall."

The diabolical thought of usefulness rises in my mind. If ever I can make up my mind to declare myself the enemy of all mankind, then shall I turn altruist and devote my life to being of use, and of benefit to my fellow-beings.

Do unto others as you would that others should do unto you, and you may make the litter of their circumstances that you have made of your own. The good Samaritan binds up wounds with poison ivy. If I give anybody a coin, I hand him good and evil, just as truly as I hand him head and tail. Whoever discovered the uses of coal was a benefactor of all mankind, and most damnably something else. Automobiles, and their seeming indispensable services—but automobiles and crime and a million exasperations. There are persons who think they see clear advantages in the use of a telephone. And then the telephone rings.

FORT WAS SKEPTICAL of spiritualist mysteries—"the spiritualist has arbitrarily taken over strange occurrences as manifestations of the departed," and rather than investigating, "stuffs the maws of his emotions." He also ruled out biblical miracles for the simple reason that they fell outside of his research. "I have drawn a deadline for data at the year 1800. I take for a principle that our concern is not in marvels. It is in repetitions, or sometimes in the commonplace."

I incline to the acceptance of many stories of miracles, but think that these miracles would have occurred if this earth had been inhabited by atheists.

It wasn't surprising that Fort's contrary constructions—"an atheist, of zeal, may be thought of as religious"—confused readers. In a letter to Edmond Hamilton, Fort admitted the difficulty of criticizing science:

*It is quite as you say—poor old Theology hammered all around,
but Science the great Immune. And as far as I know, mine are about
the only books of impoliteness to scientific dogmas written by one who
has not the theological bias. Every now and then I get a letter from
somebody who thinks I am some kind of Fundamentalist, simply
because I don't take in, without questioning, everything that the scientists tell us. But I think I made it plain in the books that I am not
out to restore Moses.*

JUST PAST THE CENTER-POINT of the decade, July 1925,
marked a climactic battle between science and Fundamentalism.
The world gathered in a small courtroom in Dayton, Ohio, to
watch John T. Scopes, an assistant coach and substitute high school
teacher, tried for teaching Darwin's theory of evolution. The press
quickly dubbed it "The Monkey Trial."

H. L. Mencken was there in the front row, covering the trial for
the *Baltimore Sun*. He was ready for a showdown and was prepared
for high comedy; he'd arrived in town with handbills that parodied
evangelists, planning to distribute them and ridicule the naive yokels
of Dayton. Instead, he found a charming little city and sincere
citizens. Anticipating "the worst buffooneries to come," Mencken
identified only "a sort of mystical confidence that God will somehow come to the rescue, to reward His old and faithful partisans as
they deserve."

As the expectant press demanded, the trial degenerated into a
circus. On the seventh day, the leading attorneys had maneuvered
themselves into a remarkable situation: prosecution attorney William Jennings Bryan took the stand, as defense attorney Clarence

Darrow questioned him about the validity of the stories in the Bible. The line of questioning was done without the jury present, and later was ruled as irrelevant. But the damage was done. Journalists scrawled the testimony as the proud Fundamentalist Bryan smiled beneficently, held his chin high, and recited fairy tales. According to writer J. C. Furnas, Darrow took Bryan apart "like a dollar watch."

Darrow: You claim that everything in the Bible should be literally interpreted?

Bryan: I believe everything in the Bible should be accepted as it is given there.

Darrow: But when you read that the whale swallowed Jonah— how do you literally interpret that?

Bryan: When I read that a big fish swallowed Jonah—it does not say whale—I believe in a God who can make a whale and can make a man and make both what He pleases.

Darrow: You don't know whether it was the ordinary run of fish, or made for that purpose?

Bryan: You may guess; you evolutionists guess. . . . The Bible doesn't say, so I am not prepared to say.

Darrow: But do you believe He made them, that He made such a fish and that it was big enough to swallow Jonah?

Bryan: Yes, sir. Let me add: One miracle is just as easy to believe as another.

Darrow: Just as hard?

Bryan: It is hard to believe for you, but easy for me. A miracle is a thing performed beyond what man can perform. When you get within the realm of miracles; and it is just as easy to believe the miracle of Jonah as any other miracle in the Bible.

Darrow: Perfectly easy to believe that Jonah swallowed the whale?

Bryan: If the Bible said so; the Bible doesn't make as extreme statements as evolutionists do. . . .

Darrow went on from there: Joshua making the sun stand still, Eve being created from Adam's rib, the flood and Noah's ark. It might have been funny, but not to Mencken. "Let no one mistake it for comedy, farcical though it may be in all its details. It serves notice on the country that Neanderthal man is organizing in these forlorn backwaters of the land, led by a fanatic, rid of sense and devoid of conscience."

That summer, Fort was studying astronomical journals at the British Museum; had he been following the trial, he would have kept laughing. His perfect agnosticism was the antidote to the gnashing of teeth in Dayton. "Witchcraft always has a hard time, until it becomes established and changes its name," Fort wrote. "We hear much of the conflict between science and religion, but our conflict is with both of these. Science and religion always have agreed in opposing and suppressing the various witchcrafts. Now that religion is inglorious, one of the most fantastic transferences of worships is that of glorifying science, as a beneficent being."

The Scopes Trial was actually agnosticism on trial. But agnosticism is a giant shrug. "I am a pragmatist, myself," Fort wrote. "I see no meaning in pragmatism as a philosophy. Nobody wants a philosophy of description, but does want a philosophy of guidance." True agnostics like Fort rely on extremes—the devout or the atheists—to define the argument and wage the battles. "The simplest strategy seems to be never bother to fight a thing," he explained. "Set its own parts fighting one another."

Fort had his own ways to ridicule evolution:

An intelligence from somewhere else, not well-acquainted with human beings, but knowing of the picture galleries of this earth, might, in Darwinian terms, just as logically explain the origin of those pictures. Canvasses that were daubed on, without purpose, appeared; and that the daubs that more clearly represented something recognizable were protected, and that still higher approximations had a still better chance, and that so appeared, finally, highly realistic pictures, though the painters had been purposeless and with no consciousness of what they were doing.

And he offered an equal jibe to those who read their Bible:

No matter what sometimes my opinions may be, I am not now writing that God is an idiot. Maybe he, or it, drools comets and gibbers earthquakes, but the scale would have to be considered at least super-idiocy.

The theologians have recognized that the ideal is the imitation of God. When I see myself, and cats and dogs losing irregularities of conduct and approaching the irreproachable with advancing age, I see that what is ennobling us is senility. The ideal state is meekness or humility, or the semi-invalid state of the old. Year after year I am becoming nobler and nobler. If I can live to be decrepit enough, I shall be a saint.

The World Has Cut
Me Out—I Have
Cut Myself Out

Confusions. Showers of frogs and blizzards of snails; gushes of periwinkles down from the sky.

Theodore Dreiser announced a new novel, *An American Tragedy*. Dreiser had abandoned work on *The Bulwark*, but publisher Horace Liveright's years of patience were about to be rewarded when the eagerly awaited novel would be published at the end of 1925.

Fort was in the middle of his research in London, exchanging letters with correspondents, clipping articles, copying notes at the library. In June 1925, he wrote his congratulations to Dreiser.

> *Old Top!*
>
> *I wish you success with your latest. I mention the matter to Annie and she holds up a glass of beer, expressing herself quite intelligibly. I do the same. Later, I shall mention the matter again, and she will hold up another glass of beer.*
>
> *I shall mention the matter some more times during the evening,*

and there will be holdups. It isn't everybody who could interrupt our vices like that.

Hoping to put together a trip to London, Dreiser responded that he would call at Marchmont Street. He then returned to a favorite theme. "Why not publish *X* as written? It is a great book."

Dreiser had just completed his greatest book. *An American Tragedy* was a massive novel; the original manuscript may have been nearly one million words before being cut down by his editor. Liveright published it in two volumes, totaling 840 pages. Dreiser was braced for the worst, but critics generally greeted the book with praise, and Dreiser's famous story of the social-climbing Clyde Griffiths, who is caught in a love triangle and arranges the death of his pregnant sweetheart, became a best seller. Typically, one dissenting voice was H. L. Mencken, Dreiser's unpredictable friend, who panned the book in the March 1926 issue of his publication, the *American Mercury*.

Whatever else this vasty double-header may reveal about its author, it at least shows brilliantly that he is wholly devoid of what may be called literary tact. What was needed was a book full of all the sound and solid Dreiser merits, and agreeably free from the familiar Dreiser defects. Well, how did Dreiser meet the challenge? He met it, characteristically, by throwing out the present shapeless and forbidding monster—a heaping cartload of raw materials for a novel, with rubbish of all sorts intermixed—a vast, sloppy chaotic thing of 385,000 words—at least 250,000 of them unnecessary!

Dreiser had even more difficulties with Liveright. Their relationship had grown caustic—Dreiser had deliberately kept the manuscript for *An American Tragedy* out of his hands for as long as possible.

Together they planned a Broadway play based on the novel, and Liveright expected money for the film rights as well. During a now-famous lunch at the Ritz hotel, Dreiser and Liveright discussed the deal with Hollywood producer Jesse Lasky. The conversation disintegrated into an argument over Liveright's percentage. Dreiser picked up a cup of coffee, throwing it into Liveright's face and storming from the hotel.

BENJAMIN DE CASSERES, a New York journalist and poet, had admired *The Book of the Damned* and *New Lands;* his letters worked their way to Marchmont Street. "Your satire, your imagination, your originality, your epigrammatic quality, simply carried me off my feet," he wrote to Fort.

De Casseres was a year older than Fort, and had also begun in newspapers; he was a proofreader and writer for the *Sun* and the *New York Herald,* and contributed reviews, editorials, and commentary for various newspapers and magazines. He was an early friend of Dreiser's, who in 1915 recommended him to Mencken as a contributor to Mencken's *Smart Set* magazine. At first, Mencken was leery; De Casseres was Jewish and a Greenwich Village socialist, one of the "red-ink boys" and unsuited to the *Smart Set.* But Mencken came to admire De Casseres's essays and poetry, and the two writers became friends.

Fort returned the compliment to De Casseres. "I have recollections of striking lines and images of yours. I'm very glad to have your good opinions of lines and things that I have let loose." He playfully wrote that he was organizing "an expedition of Neo-Puritans to set sail for another world," and offered De Casseres the position of chaplain. "I usually think of you and St. John together," he wrote. "I've been placed in that category, myself, but it's a mistake, I think. You and the saint are sophisticated." Fort's highest praise was to compare De Casseres with his earth-shaking data.

> *There are few deluges or hurricanes of the past 125 years that I haven't a record of. That's why I think so much of your work. Almost, if I knew the exact dates of your publications, I'd list them in my records of catastrophes.*

THEODORE DREISER and Helen Richardson finally arrived in London in October 1926, where he surprised Charles Fort at his flat. Fort was hard at work on his notes when the door suddenly opened and Dreiser stepped inside. Reunited once again, the friends were quickly laughing and reminiscing about their days in New York. Fort boasted of his recent discoveries at the British Museum. Dreiser insisted on taking Anna and Charles out to high tea. Fort was so delighted to see his old friend that he agreed, forgetting his usual shyness and dislike for restaurants. "Life itself, with all its component parts, came in through the door when Dreiser appeared," Fort later remembered to Helen.

But there was also bad news that must have seemed inevitable to Dreiser. Fort finally confessed that X and Y had been destroyed years earlier. Dreiser wasn't told the circumstance; most likely the manuscripts were burned with Fort's notes when he was dejected over the New York Public Library, and he and Anna first left for London.

• • •

FORT HAD ANTICIPATED returning to America as early as 1924, but as his manuscript grew, the Forts remained in London—Charles was hard at work on the new book, reading bits of it to Anna for her approval. He incorporated much of his London research, as well as data from the *Chaos* manuscript. In the spring of 1925 he mailed his stack of typed pages, titled *Skyward Ho!*, to Boni & Liveright. "Mr. Liveright wrote to me that B&L would probably not publish this new book," Fort reported to De Casseres.

> *And I implored him to be firm about that and not publish it, so that I should be discouraged from writing such things, and turn to love stories and be respected and make lots of money and be literary and drink tea, afternoons, with women. After all that, judging by the contrariness of all things, I suppose B&L will publish the book.*

Boni & Liveright thought that it would take about eight months to decide whether they would publish it. Despite Fort's joke, the lack of interest disappointed him. Finally they returned *Skyward Ho!*, respectfully declining it. *New Lands* had been a poor seller, and they considered this book to be more of the same.

Fort's eyesight was failing. His right eye was quite bad, and he blamed it on the intense years of reading and note-taking. Early in 1928, Anna and Charles packed up their belongings and returned to New York City.

They took an apartment at 112 West 124th Street, and Fort quietly resumed his research at the New York Public Library. His research had generated several manuscripts, which he was anxious to complete. A year later, although Fort was barely fifty-four years old, his eyesight was bad enough that he had to completely stop his library work. "I mourned not a bit for that," he reported.

For months he had avoided telling Dreiser that he was back in New York, waiting for good news—the sale of a book or a new bit of research—that would allow him to send a cheery letter. But the Wall Street crash, at the end of October 1929, eliminated any optimism and filled Fort with self-doubt. Black Thursday was the climax of the 1920s, the upside-down priorities of the decade finally spilling into the marketplace and shaking loose America's confidence.

He treated his depression as a scientific experiment. "For a month, at the end of each day, I set down a plus sign or a minus sign, indicating that, in my opinion, life had or had not been worth living that day." He was surprised to find that the pluses had won the game. "It is not dignified to be optimistic."

Fort wrote his concerns in a journal, taking careful stock of his manuscripts, his health, and his finances.

The Book of the Damned *expressed me as a metaphysician, but the data of it started a new self, or the interests that compose a self, that then expressed in* New Lands *and in* Skyward Ho! *collection of data. Also mixed in were the psychic phenomena in collections and writings. I cannot, and never have been able to, specialize. But when the story writer was almost extinct, there came the metaphysic-psychic-*Skyward Ho! *conflict.*

He complained that three manuscripts, "S.H." (presumably *Skyward Ho!*), "M and F," and "W.W." were "pretty nearly dead. I cannot get them published, though I have not tried W.W. . . . I have, I think, finally put them away." His abbreviations, "M and F" and "W.W.," refer to manuscripts that are otherwise unknown.

I think that I, too, am coming to an end. My general health is very good, but I am almost blind in the right eye and the left eye is going. I have gone over my papers, sorted them and packed away my notes, as if quite clearly understanding that my time is coming. I cannot stand living in blindness. I have made arrangements for Annie.

Fort was slightly more optimistic about his finances, even in the weeks after Black Thursday. He wrote that just after the crash, he'd sold $12,000 of bonds and invested $7,500 of it into speculative stocks.

THE JAZZ AGE had actually been very tentative about anything as revolutionary as jazz. It was deliberately daring and new, but it was also a fashion that Americans had affected. Despite its title, *The Jazz Singer*, America's first popular talking picture, was filled with Al Jolson melodies from Broadway. In the film, his jazz is confined to a "jazzy" version of Irving Berlin's popular ballad "Blue Skies," pounded out on a piano.

At the start of the twenties, jazz was the noisy, nasty sound that was heard at a city's most disreputable clubs. But it remained clear and crisp when transmitted across early crystal radio sets; it stood up to the static of the early Hollywood talkies; and it sounded right in speakeasies. It kept the customers drinking. One gangster said he liked jazz because "It's got guts and it don't make you slobber." Al Capone, America's favorite criminal, appreciated jazz for economic reasons, and tipped the jazz bands in his speakeasies lavishly. But he preferred mushy, popular, sentimental tunes.

"The business of America is business," according to Calvin

Coolidge. And Capone agreed. "My rackets are run on strictly American lines and they're going to stay that way." It was simply supply and demand. America could stand Prohibition so long as booze was available; America could be forgiven its excesses and irrationalities so long as the economy was strong. But it was only a matter of time; and when the stock market rolled over in 1929, it was not the end of the twenties, it was just *more* of the twenties.

Capone was an inveterate gambler, but he never put money into Wall Street. "It's a racket. Those stock market guys are crooked," he said.

Charles Fort's "existence of the hyphen" was a perfect analogy for the decade: "that our whole existence is an attempt by the relative to be the absolute." In his books, he described the continuity as "positive-negative," "real-unreal," or "soluble-insoluble." America preferred "progressive-conservative," "hero-villain," "moral-immoral," "genuine-bunk," all in unexpected combinations.

> *Our state of the hyphen is the state of the gamble. Out of science is fading certainty as ever it departed from theology. In its place we have adventure, the acceptance that there is no absolute poise between advantages and disadvantages.*
>
> *My own expression is that any state of being that can so survive its altruists and its egoists, its benefactors and its exploiters, its artists, gunmen, bankers, lawyers and doctors, would be almost immune to witchcraft, because it is itself a miracle.*

FORT AVOIDED social situations, and wouldn't frequent a speakeasy for his beer. With Prohibition still in force, Anna and Charles learned to make their own homebrew like millions of other Americans. Starting with canned yeast, Anna produced homemade beer. The carbonation wasn't consistent, but it was flavorful, and the Forts shared several glasses each evening. Anna bought two colorful pet parrots—caciques—named Peggy and Chief. The birds squawked and screeched in the Forts' apartment, clattering across the kitchen floor and gnawing at the legs of their furniture. Fort, ever the curmudgeon, complained about the birds but spent hours watching them, feeding them nuts, and playing with them.

He spent the rest of his time working on a game of his own invention, called Super-checkers, that he'd first worked out in London in 1927. It involved hundreds of checker pieces, tiny bits of cardboard on thumbtacks, arranged on a gigantic tablecloth of gingham.

At the end of 1928, Fort sent a letter to the *New York Sun*—addressed "To the What Do You Think Editor." He outlined the elements of his game. He used slightly less than 400 pieces on a game surface of 800 squares. Each player began by massing the pieces in a formation. Fort preferred two wedges, meeting at their points.

It is an interesting game and is far more military, or pseudo-military, than either chess or ordinary checkers.

Fort compared the mass movements to troop movements. One player would begin moving pieces—for example, about a hundred—until the second player told him to stop. Then the second player makes a similar number of moves. This might be repeated in flanking maneuvers. Fighting would then take place, one piece at a time, as in regular checkers. Then the players would go back to battle tactics: "concentrations, raids, ambuscades, feints and other strategies."

For more than a year I have been playing checkers with myself,
which is a matter of difficulty only when I try to surprise myself.

Fort wrote that the game could be played through in two evenings, and settled in a shorter time.

He recruited neighbors and landlords, anxious to teach them the
rules, but the procedure sounds chaotic and the rules seem almost
improvised. Fort was the only person who ever fully understood
how it was played or why it was so diverting. "Super-checkers is
going to be a great success," he wrote to a friend. "I have met four
more persons who consider it preposterous."

THE FORTS moved to the second-floor apartment in a three-story
clapboard house in the Bronx at 2051 Ryer Avenue, a quiet street
just off the Grand Concourse, paying sixty dollars a month for their
apartment. Vincent and Anna Lamura, an older Italian couple on
the top floor, owned the building. Michael and Anna Demperio,
the landlords' daughter and son-in-law, lived on the ground floor.

In an effort to find a new direction, Fort worked on several
manuscripts, distinct and different from the books of oddities. *A
Book About Caciques* was his own account of living with parrots. In it,
Fort contemplated his loneliness:

*Something has isolated me, and mostly it has been because I have
put in my time as a writer of treatments and subjects with which the
world would have nothing to do. In earlier times I often got drunk
about this, but I am not resentful now. The world has cut me out for
the very good reason that I have cut myself out. I am not misan-*

*thropic: I have considerable liking for people, so long as I can keep
away from them.*

His most intriguing experiment was a hybrid of his short fiction
and his research. "The Giant, the Insect and the Philanthropic-
Looking Old Gentleman" was a story about Charles Fort. He
started by explaining the nature of his research:

> *I have forty-eight thousand notes. I've been through everything:
> chemistry, meteorology, sociology, electricity, magnetism, architecture,
> music, psychology, astronomy, ethics—over to the library in the
> morning, out for dinner, pencil and pad with knife and fork in front
> of me; back to the library, home, to take more notes until bedtime.
> Notes piling up on the mantelpiece, and when about three thousand
> are there, I classify them.*
>
> *So I wore out my eyesight and pencils and breeches material and
> got my coat all shiny at the elbows, for a theory that I had never
> tested, because so to do would be rationality of the second degree,
> which isn't human.*

Fort explains that he sometimes took "promising books with
good indexes" to Riverside Drive, where he would sit on a bench in
the sunshine, taking notes. Then he introduces a fictional story: on
Riverside Drive he discovers a character named Albert Rapp, staring
nervously at a large house across the street. Fort's description of
Rapp recalls the vivid images from *The Outcast Manufacturers:*

> *Extraordinary nose; made me think of a gargoyle. Long and lean
> and poised recklessly over a heavy underlip—like a precarious gar-
> goyle over a window sill with a red blanket out airing on it. He was
> nervous and two white teeth appeared frequently and bit upon and*

drew in the lower lip—very much as if he were a dwelling of some
tall, tower-like kind, a little butler wearing white gloves, inside, you
know. Little butler constantly fearing the hovering gargoyle, and for-
ever drawing in the too conspicuous red blanket with his white-gloved
hands, and then putting it out for an airing again.

Rapp explains that he is the editor of a German newspaper that
had written a sensational exposé about Dr. Katz, a patent-medicine
manufacturer. Now Rapp was facing a libel suit from the Katz family, and so he sits outside the Katz house, trying to discern some
evidence that would help him.

In the story, he explains to Fort his theory: that Dr. Katz is actually in poor health. But his son-in-law has substituted a healthy "Dr.
Katz," to match the illustration on the front of the bottle. He pa-
rades this philanthropic-looking old man on the street and at the
patent-medicine factory every day, and has even matched the old
man's slight limp, long white beard, and the mole on his cheek. But
Rapp is unable to prove it.

Both Fort and Rapp realize that this falls under the category of
"counter-adjustment," a common phenomenon in biology. For each
adjustment is a counter-adjustment. Fort takes Rapp to his rooms
and opens boxes, spreading out thousands of his notes, locating an
account of an insect that can take on the appearance of a flower.

I can't think without my notes. I have lived with them, and for
them, for so long that, though I know where to find the information
they have, that information is not available to me in my own mind.
We looked through notes upon "Imitation." We were referring to "Sim-
ulating," to "Assimilation," to "Protective Coloration."
. . . and we found the answer soon enough. By its own multipli-
cation this phenomenon is kept in check. We found a hint of this in

the observations by Mr. Bates and Dr. Wallace, that mimicking species
are always much rarer than the mimicked.

Discussing it with Rapp, Fort remembers the story of the Cardiff Giant, a carved stone man that was exhibited in the nineteenth century. It was a famous hoax, created by a tobacconist named George Hull to prove the gullibility of his friends. He had a crude, ten-foot long stone man secretly carved, then buried on his property in Cardiff, New York. It was "discovered" a year later, in 1869, when he instructed workers to dig a well. Supposedly, the carving was a petrified man, proving the existence of giants in biblical times. The giant proved a popular exhibit, drawing crowds, and its popularity led to its downfall.

> *Multiplication was the undoing of the Cardiff Giant. Reproductions of it sprang up all over the country. P. T. Barnum, when he could not buy the original image, had one made and exhibited as the original, in New York City. That convinced the public; knowledge of how easily a replica could be made. So ended the career of the Cardiff Giant. It could not survive its own multiplicity.*

Several mornings later, as Fort watches from his park bench, the benign Dr. Katz, the philanthropic-looking old man with a long white beard, a slight limp, and black mole, steps down from his porch and into the sunshine, accompanied by his son-in-law. And then, from another doorway, a matching man—with the same beard, limp, and mole. "From behind a tree! Two more philanthropic-looking old gentlemen." And then yet another from down the street. As Katz and his son-in-law reel in confusion, Fort notices Mr. Rapp approaching them, "Mr. Rapp cleaning his fingernails with his penknife; general air of casualness about him."

There's no evidence that Fort tried to sell "The Giant, the Insect and the Philanthropic-Looking Old Gentleman," but it is his only adventure in the realm of "Fortean" fiction. Fort's famous hyphenated existence, "that all things are one," manifests itself in the story as well as the format: his fiction had merged seamlessly into his phenomena. The story gives a curious suggestion about Fort's meticulous research. At the beginning, he writes:

> *That all things are one, that all phenomena are governed by the same laws; that whatever is true, or what we call true of planets, plants and magnets, is what we call true of human beings. That if, among such widely dissimilar phenomena as the moon, the alimentary canal of an anteater, and glacial erosions, we can discover uniformities, there we have the associations of events commonly called laws, which may be equally in control of human affairs. That, with uniformities discovered, we can apply them to our own affairs, controlling, preventing, predicting, utilizing, as has been the way in chemistry, for instance; or as is done in all the old, established sciences.*

In other words, Fort aspires to an extremely scientific use for his notes. The fictional story envisions just how these disparate observations can be put to practical use. Had Fort pursued these stories, he might have generated a series of mysteries, successfully recreating himself as a latter-day Sherlock Holmes, puzzling out the problems and the solutions through his notes.

TIFFANY ELLSWORTH THAYER had moved to New York in 1926 to pursue an acting career, but ended up working as a copy-

writer and publicity man. He became the advertising manager for
the Literary Guild at the Paul Mathewson Agency. He also sold
short stories to pulp magazines, under the names Elmer Ellsworth,
Jr. and John Doe.

In 1930, Thayer's first novel, *Thirteen Men*, became a best seller
for a minor New York publisher, Claude Kendall. It's a gimmicky
book, written in jangling prose that Thayer intended as an imitation of Ben Hecht's streetwise snarl. Each of twelve chapters told
the life story of a juror, and the thirteenth chapter was the con-
fession of the killer on trial. Thayer must have delighted Fort with
the killer's advice to parents: "*The Book of the Damned*, by Charles
Fort. . . . By all means forbid [your child] this parade of pallid data
relating to rainfalls of butter and pork chops. It is too heady for
mere men."

Early in 1930, Thayer met his hero, Fort, at the Bronx
apartment.

> *His sight was failing in his last years and his glasses had to be
> thick-lensed. He was an anachronism in modern dress, incongruous
> in his Bronx flat. We sat with homebrew of his making, strong
> cheeses, coarse rye bread and "whiskied grapes" at a circular dining
> table, talking the night away. On the walls of the flat were framed
> specimens of giant spiders, butterflies, and weird creatures adept at
> concealment. There was also framed a photograph of a baseball beside
> a hailstone, both objects the same size, sent to Fort by a correspondent
> and, under glass, a specimen of some stuff that looked like dirty,
> shredded asbestos, which had fallen from the sky in quantities cover-
> ing several acres. In all other respects the domicile was quite com-
> monplace, the sort of home indicated on theatrical scene-plots by the
> phrase, "shabby-genteel."*

Thayer's enthusiasm was addictive, and soon Fort was discussing his rejected manuscript, *Skyward Ho!* Thayer realized that he could help. He took the manuscript to Claude Kendall.

LIKE DREISER many years before, Thayer was in a particular position to twist the arm of his publisher. Aaron Sussman, a young advertising man and designer, was a coworker with Thayer at the Mathewson agency. Sussman was also a partner in the publishing firm with Claude Kendall.

Thayer convinced Sussman that it would be a coup to publish Fort, and they both liked the new book. Claude Kendall agreed to publish it. But Sussman objected to the title, which he did not think was commercial. Fort's original title had been *Snoozers and Saps and Skyward Ho!*, and he had simplified it to *Skyward Ho!* But the two young men were convinced the book would be confused for something else and, Thayer explained to Fort, "Books on aviation are not selling. Most folks work out their air-mindedness at two cents a copy each evening in the newspapers."

Fort thought it should be called *God and the Fishmonger*, based on one of his recurring themes. Sussman doubted whether this would generate sales, and suggested *God Is an Idiot*, taken from a line in the text. It was a title designed to attract headlines for the publishing firm. Fort objected, "because that is a most dogmatic statement." Even the idea of adding a question mark, Fort thought, "is weak." "If *Skyward Ho!* won't do, I think *God and the Fishmonger* will do."

But Sussman wouldn't agree. Fort then thought *If the Time Has Come* would be effective, repeating one of his favorite themes. Or it could be simplified to *The Time Has Come!* But Fort worried, "this

has the sureness, or the pseudo-sureness, of the crank and quack."
He admitted, in exasperation,

> *Good God—or Godness—or whatever it is—the people down-*
> *stairs had a baby, and they simply named her Madeline, and there*
> *wasn't any argument. Still, I do admit that they're not trying to sell*
> *their brat.*

Finally, Tiffany Thayer had an idea.

> Lo! *was my suggestion because in the text, the astronomers are*
> *forever calculating and then pointing to the sky where they figure a*
> *new star or something should be and saying, "Lo!"—and there's*
> *nothing whatever to be seen where they point. Fort agreed to* Lo! *at*
> *first hearing.*

SEVENTEEN

A Welcoming Hand
to Little Frogs
and Periwinkles

I expect to end up holy, with the general expression that all stories
of miracles are not lies; or are not altogether lies.

Charles Fort didn't possess a phone; he confessed to having
a "phobia for a telephone" and having made fewer than
twenty calls in his life. When Aaron Sussman had business
with the author, he sent telegrams or took the subway to the Bronx
and knocked on his door. Sussman enjoyed his visits to the Fort
apartment. Anna Fort, Sussman thought, was "one of the most
innocent innocents, a bustling, militant little hostess," with an especially kind manner of speaking to guests—"she made you feel
honored and grateful that you had taken the time and trouble to
come and see her."

Fort worked in a small bedroom that was filled by his wooden
desk and stacked shoeboxes of notes. Sussman found Fort to be a
"very gentle man, inveterately polite, very tender towards Anna,
most solicitous and concerned." To Sussman, he was like a Sch-
weitzer or an Einstein, deliberately withdrawn from the rest of the

world, but interested in people and "delighted to see you, no matter how busy he was." Fort had a rich bass voice and a booming laugh that came easily.

Sussman was planning a pretty edition for *Lo!,* with a smooth brown linen binding, an elaborate dust jacket, a dozen illustrations by Alexander King, and an introduction by Tiffany Thayer.

As an advertising man, Thayer's prose was deliberately bombastic. He described the author with phrases like "his demonic skill at overturning all that is pompous, smug and satisfied," "the lone dissenter, the one small voice raised in defense of suspended judgments," and "willing to forswear all that life offers and to blind himself by grueling, nerve-racking, boresome and cruel daily toil over piles of newspapers."

Fort was flattered but surprised. When he read the first draft of the introduction, he wrote back.

> *My Dear Ellsworth,*
>
> *I am much interested in your character, "Charles Fort." If I read your intro, I'd read his book. I know a Charles Fort who, with his belly full of beer, damns his little parrot for chewing up the furniture. I know this person as a discoverer of cheeses to spread on crackers with his beer.*
>
> *I like the final sentence and the statement that if Charles Fort should ever become orthodox and established, he'd be the first to start tearing down Charles Fort.*

But Fort was not disinterested in how he was being portrayed. When he suggested that Thayer omit the part about his previous books selling poorly, Thayer agreed. Fort also didn't like the description of—his interpretation—a "half-blind codger." But Thayer left this in his introduction.

With good news about *Lo!*, Fort finally decided to write to Dreiser, who had recently returned to New York City with his mistress Helen.

> *Here is a phenomenon that you and I have been used to since about 1905. Mysterious disappearance of Charles Fort. And then he reappears with a new book. And where was he? Ah!*

Fort explained that his publisher was looking for some confirmation "that I am sober and industrious and well worth the price of admission," and coyly asked Dreiser for a quote. He gave his new address and noted that he and Anna went to the moving pictures every night, but back about nine-thirty. Just like old times, Dreiser was invited up for a drink. Fort boasted that Anna's homebrew was even better than Bass's.

Dreiser quickly responded:

> *Dear Fort. I'll even make it Darling Fort.*
>
> *Your publisher wants opinions of your writings. To think that should be necessary, or even seem so. You, the most fascinating literary figure since Poe. You, who for all I know may be the progenitor of an entirely new world viewpoint. You, whose books thrill and astound me as almost no other books have thrilled and astounded me. And you write so authoritatively and delightfully. Well, such is life.*
>
> *And yet the same old writing paper! Where in God's name do you get it? Have you a storage warehouse full of it? And the same typewriter. And the same habits, and in these changeful days the same wife. Now really!*
>
> *I see you have my house number. But if the mountain won't move, Mahomet will try and find 2051 Ryer Avenue. (Only where is that?)*

Dreiser's letter, like the activity surrounding *Lo!*, was a tonic. Fort had forgotten the restorative effect of Dreiser's praise. It made him confident. He even felt that his eyesight had stabilized.

> *You know, Dreiser, I have my conceits and I say agreeable things to myself, about myself, but they don't sound authoritative. You talk about thrills, but I got some from your letter. You make me feel that, after all, I haven't wasted a lifetime.*

As Sussman went over the final galleys with Fort, he came across a page in the first chapter that was one line short. The paragraph dealt with Fort's philosophy of continuity, and ended with the words "If there is an underlying oneness of all things, it does not matter where we begin, whether with stars, or laws of supply and demand, or frogs, or Napoleon Bonaparte." Fort had a pencil in his hand. He squinted at the paragraph, and quickly added a short sentence.

> *One measures a circle, beginning anywhere.*

WHEN DREISER hesitated about coming up to the Bronx, Fort offered: "If you're scared of the Bronx, let me come down to see you. I'm a hermit and I hate to go to dinner anywhere. Once I went somewhere and had afternoon tea. Once."

Fort arrived at Dreiser's studio one evening. Marguerite Tjader, Dreiser's secretary, was unimpressed by his appearance, a "low-set man, dark with a greasy complexion, scant black hair brushed over a round, dynamic head; his hands were fat and protruded from filthy shirt-cuffs." Still, she found him fascinating, "carefree and all-knowing." She'd been warned that he was antisocial, but observed that Dreiser responded to his devilment, and deftly engaged him in conversation. "He could get Fort talking, in a smooth and glee-ful manner."

On another occasion, Dreiser invited Fort to meet the actress Lillian Gish. This was the sort of social call that Fort usually avoided, but he made an exception for Gish. Fort was a particular fan of her movies, as well as Jack Holt films. Otherwise, Anna re-ported, moving pictures "bored him to death, since he saw them every day; he got so he scarcely looked at some of them."

Whatever his expectations, he was disappointed to meet Gish. When he returned to the Bronx, he told Anna that the actress was "just ordinary."

Dreiser also invited him to his country home in the village of Mt. Kisco, about forty miles north of New York City. He'd pur-chased the land in 1926 with profits from *An American Tragedy*. Over the next three years, Dreiser had a rustic fieldstone house, cabin, and studio built on the hillside. He called the residence Iroki. Fort was uncomfortable with the thought of leaving his desk in the Bronx. "It is not that I won't go to Mt. Kisco, or Java. It is that I can't." Helen tried a simpler invitation, asking the Forts to dinner at Dreiser's home in Manhattan. As expected, Fort dismissed her suggestion. "You always have your place full of human beings. I don't care much for human beings."

AT THE END OF 1930, as *Lo!* was being printed, Tiffany Thayer revealed his most audacious plan to publicize Fort's book. He would start a new organization, The Fortean Society.

The idea was not a new one. Shortly after the publication of *The*

Book of the Damned, newspaper editor J. David Stern suggested organizing a group devoted to Fort's phenomena, without success. Fort
later wrote:

> *The great trouble is that the majority of persons who are attracted
> are the ones that we do not want: Spiritualists, Fundamentalists,
> persons who are revolting against Science, not in the least because they
> are affronted by the myth-stuff of the sciences, but because scientists
> either oppose or do not encourage them.*

Thayer borrowed the term "Fortean" from Ben Hecht's 1920
review, and contacted a long list of celebrities interested in Fort's
work—including Stern, who was now publishing the Philadelphia *Record.* He proposed the idea to Fort and asked him to
accept the honorary presidency. Charles Fort promptly turned him
down.

> *If you want to start a Society of the Damned, or a Stellar Ex-
> ploration Club, I might overcome my dislike for all organizations and
> join in. But if you name it after me, I don't join.*

Fort wrote to De Casseres, warning him of the plot.

> *There was something rather awful, a while ago, but I can't help
> it if I stir up freaks. I knew nothing about it until I received sta-
> tionery headed "The Fortean Society." And yet, the organizer of this,
> Thayer, is a clever fellow. You will understand him when I note that
> he is only 29 years old. Oh, dear me, the one consolation that you
> and I, who are not 29 years old, have, is in thinking of those
> who are.*

Realizing that Dreiser had been roped in, Fort dashed off a letter to his old friend.

About Ellsworth—it is this. He is a good fellow who is trying to limelight me, because he first read me when he was about twenty years old, and thinks he owes me a lot for it.

Fort believed Thayer had gone to "much trouble for nothing," because such a group might be suitable for a place like Orange, New Jersey, but was not "New Yorkish." "As you know, I had nothing to do with the plan," he explained. "I wouldn't join it, any more than I'd be an Elk."

DREISER HAD his own idea. He was buying up copies of Fort's earlier books and sending them "where they would do the most good," to writers and friends. For example, one copy went to H. G. Wells in England. Dreiser hoped these endorsements, with the publicity surrounding Thayer's Fortean Society, would push the new book onto the best-seller list.

"I am not at all so indifferent. I read your letter with excitement," Fort responded.

Oh, how I'd like to be a bestseller, just to swipe mine enemies. I wish I could have success, just to make trouble. I wish I could really take scalps of scientists. If I could, I'd give you the pick of them.

Dreiser had overestimated Fort's commercial instincts. After he arranged a series of articles by Fort for *Cosmopolitan* magazine—

Dreiser was an old friend of the associate editor Will Lengel—Fort selected dense chunks of material from his books that, Dreiser gently advised, "may not exactly fit in with the intelligence of *Cosmopolitan* readers." Lengel passed on the series. Dreiser insisted that the project could be revived, but he would need to stage-manage it all, bargaining with Lengel and submitting material.

Fort, now bored by the complications and Dreiser's fussy involvement, let the project slip away.

ON JANUARY 26, 1931, a snowy evening in New York City, Charles Fort was lured out of his house by a string of telegrams. He followed his instructions, took the subway, and met Tiffany Thayer and Aaron Sussman at the Savoy Plaza Hotel on East Fifty-seventh Street. When he arrived, he was quickly ushered up to the suite of J. D. Stern. It was only then that he realized that he'd been tricked; he was at the inaugural dinner of the Fortean Society.

Also present were Theodore Dreiser, Ben Hecht, Burton Rascoe, J. Donald Adams, and Claude Kendall. A knot of reporters had also been invited; they interviewed the assembled literati and were given copies of *Lo!*, just off the presses.

After dinner, Tiffany Thayer stood up and outlined the goals of the new Fortean Society—to promote the works and thinking of Charles Fort, discourage dogmatism, and promote skepticism. Thayer also hoped to preserve Fort's notes and papers. He admitted to the guests that Fort himself had been opposed to the Society, suspecting that it would exploit him and his views. Fort registered his complaint with the name, Thayer reported; but once he had understood the broader aims, he pledged support of the Fortean Society.

Thayer noted that John Cowper Powys, Booth Tarkington, and Harry Elmer Barnes were founding members of the Fortean Society, although unable to attend that night. Harry Leon Wilson and Alexander Woollcott, both fans of Fort's books, had also agreed to be members.

Theodore Dreiser stood and recounted a number of stories about his old friend. He explained how he had blackmailed Horace Liveright into publishing *The Book of the Damned* by threatening to take his own books elsewhere. He proudly told the guests that he was in communication with H. G. Wells, who was already reading Fort's books and would soon send his comments.

Fort said very little. He listened to the speakers, chuckled to himself, and fingered a black cigar that someone had handed him when he walked into the suite. He was delighted to finally see a finished copy of *Lo!* and held it closely all evening. Although he had been tricked into attending, the literary fanfare was a special delight and gave Fort optimism about *Lo!* As always, Fort's shyness—his expertise at deflecting attention rather than attracting it—confused those who didn't know him.

Author H. Allen Smith, then a reporter and book reviewer for United Press International, was present for the gala dinner. He took note of references to Fort's contrary theories, the hyperbole about his work, and the grand goals for the Society. "Dreiser did most of the talking," Smith later noted. "Fort himself, somewhat fuddled by it all, sat and puffed quietly at a fat cigar when he wasn't off in a corner admiring the binding of his latest book."

FORT AND DE CASSERES had been trying to arrange a meeting for months, with the usual difficulties. "About five years ago I had lunch with somebody, and about seven years ago I had dinner with some people. I have a hermit's hatred of going anywhere," Charles Fort wrote to De Casseres, who was living in Greenwich Village. Fort promised that he was just five blocks east of the Jerome Avenue subway station in the Bronx, and home every evening "almost exactly at half past nine." "Have you heard of Super-checkers?" Fort teased. "We have a new cult. The Forteans are now very old fashioned. They're three months old, and that is long enough for any cult. We are the Neo-Forteans."

De Casseres's latest book was titled *Mencken and Shaw: The Anatomy of America's Voltaire and England's Other John Bull.* Although Benjamin De Casseres had always disagreed with Mencken politically, he compiled an obsequious list of compliments for the author, comparing him favorably to George Bernard Shaw. Mencken himself was slightly uncomfortable with the book. He wrote to De Casseres:

> *I am going on a diet of spinach and Glauber salts and, after three days of it, hope to be in a fit condition, mentally and spiritually, to read the book again with microscopic care. My wife read it last night and reports that it is a masterpiece.*

Exhibiting a thin skin, Mencken noticed a few remarks within the text that seemed to be criticism. When Fort read the book, he distinctly remembered Mencken's slap at *The Book of the Damned.* He wrote to De Casseres:

> *Your* Mencken and Shaw *is as timely as once upon a time* Mencken and Shaw *were. If you tickled Mencken, Mencken tickled me by considering your images "criticism." Smooth little ponds reflect judiciously, but torrents flash their own images.*

De Casseres's next project was an article about Fort. He sent bits of his text to Fort, and invited him down to his home on Nineteenth Street.

> *I shall be happy to drop in some afternoon. But please write your article about me first. I so revel in being called a satirist. After about five minutes talk with me it would dawn upon you that I am a Harold Bell Wright, and no Rabelais. Please write that I am a satirist, and when it is too late to recall the article, see me.*

Harold Bell Wright was a popular novelist of the first part of the twentieth century whose books were full of middle-American church values. Fort visited De Casseres on February 9, 1931. "I suppose I should teleport myself into your presence. Still, wouldn't that be a vulgar display of powers? I think I shall modestly ring the doorbell." He signed the note, "Very truly yours, Harold."

Lo! IS CHARLES FORT'S most accessible, most readable book on oddities. It perfectly captures his fascination for the world, his skepticism about science, and his wry sense of humor. The book seems to be a graceful, extended conversation with an eccentric genius—oddities are wrapped with colorful storytelling, and theories are posed with a stream-of-consciousness flair. *Lo!* also incorporates psychic phenomena, adding to the richness of Fort's stories and the weirdness of his accounts.

Fort begins with beguiling mixtures of phenomena: accounts of manna falling from the sky, streams of water falling from a clear sky, stones from the sky, frogs, worms, and periwinkles. He suggests that any of these manifestations, like the manna, are part of a larger system.

> *Once upon a time, a whole responded to the need of a part, and then kept on occasionally showering manna thousands of years after a special need for it had ceased. This looks like stupidity. It is in one of my moments of piety that I say this. Let a god change anything, and there will be reactions of evil as much as of good. Only stupidity can be divine.*
>
> *Once upon a time, showers of little frogs were manifestations of organic intelligence, in the choice of creatures that could survive in the greatest variety of circumstances. But if organic intelligence is like other intelligence, there is no understanding it, except as largely stupid, and if it keeps on sending little frogs to places where they're not wanted, we human phenomena cheer up. To keep on sending little frogs where there is no need for little frogs is like persistently, if not brutally, keeping right on teaching Latin and Greek, for instance.*

Fort suggests that the solution may be a "transportory force that I shall call teleportation."

The popular notion of teleportation actually had preceded Fort and was described in early science fiction, like in Edward Page Mitchell's 1877 story, *The Man Without a Body* (the device that transports people is called a "telepomp") and Arthur Conan Doyle's *The Disintegration Machine*. But the word "teleportation" was coined by Fort and first published in the pages of *Lo!* as a suggestion for these phenomena.

"I shall be accused of having assembled lies, yarns, hoaxes and superstitions," Fort continued. "To some degree, I think so, myself. To some degree I do not. I offer the data." He follows with accounts of bleeding statues, mysterious animals, sea monsters, lights in the skies from unknown airships, unexplained cattle mutilations, spontaneous human combustion. He recounts the disappearing passengers aboard the famous *Mary Celeste*, as well as similar mysteries of the sea. He analyzes the appearance and murder of Kaspar Hauser, the strange young man who wandered into Nuremberg in 1828. (The Hauser story had been an element of Fort's book *Y*.) He discusses frauds in science, famous impostors, and missing people.

When Fort turns his attention to science, it is with curiosity and puzzlement.

> *Sir Isaac Newton looked at the falling moon and explained all things in terms of attraction. It would be just as logical to look at the rising moon and explain all things in terms of repulsion. It would be more widely logical to cancel falls with rises, and explain that there is nothing.*
>
> *Newtonism is no longer satisfactory. There is too much that it cannot explain. Einsteinism has arisen. If Einsteinism is not satisfactory, there is room for other notions.*
>
> *It is my expression that he has functioned. Though [Einstein's] strokes were wobbles, he has shown with his palsies the insecurities of that in Science worshipfully regarded as the Most High.*

A quote from Professor Todd, "Astronomy may be styled a very aristocrat among the sciences," provides obvious inspiration for Fort. "The aristocratic is only a poise between the arriving and the departing," he argues. "The literature of the academic ends with the obituary. Professor Todd's self-congratulation is my accusation."

Decades earlier, Fort's earliest expression of monism had worked its way into his short story "A Radical Corpuscle." In *Lo!* it provided the guiding principle for his reports. "I can think of design and control and providence and purpose and preparation for future uses, if I can think not loosely of Nature, but of a Nature, as an organic whole. Every being, except for its dependence upon environment, is God to its parts."

Fort turns to accounts of droughts around the world, relieved unexpectedly with torrents of rain—deadly floods that washed away entire cities. "The people had prayed for rain. They got it."

Show me a starving man—I pay no attention. Show me the starving man—I can't be bothered. Show me the starving man, on the point of dying—I grab up groceries and I jump on him. I cram bread down his mouth and stuff his eyes and ears with potatoes. I rip open his lips to hammer down more food, and bung in his teeth, the better to stuff him. The explanation: it is the god-like in me.

When he returns to his accounts of natural phenomena, Fort finds odd links: meteorology, astronomy, geology all intermingled. The appearance of new stars or meteors in the sky often presaged lightning, falls of dust or meteors, earthquakes or volcanoes. Fort describes a world beyond our usual understanding: beautiful and terrifying.

August 31, 1886—"Just before the sun dropped behind the horizon, it was eclipsed by a mass of inky, black clouds." People noted this appearance. Meteors were seen. Luminous clouds appeared, and people watched them. There was no thought of danger. There was a glare. More meteors.

The city of Charleston, South Carolina, was smashed.

People running from their houses, telegraph poles falling around them, they were meshed in coils of wire. Street lamps and lights in houses waved above, like lights of a fishing fleet that had cast out nets. It was a catch of bodies.

The ground went on quaking. Down from the unknown came, perhaps, a volcanic discharge upon this quaking ground: "volcanic dust" at Wilmington, North Carolina.

September 5—a severe shock at Charleston, and a few minutes later came a brilliant meteor, which left a long train of fire. At the same time, two brilliant meteors were seen at Columbia, South Carolina.

A "strange cloud" appeared, upon the 8th of September, off the coast of South Carolina. The cloud hung, heavy, in the sky, and was thought to be from burning grass on one of the islands. September 10—that such was the explanation, but that no grass was known to be burning.

Meteors kept on coming to Charleston. They kept on arriving at this quaking part of this earth's surface, as if at a point on a stationary body. The most extraordinary display was upon the night of October 22nd. There was a severe quake, at Charleston, while these meteors were falling. About fifty appeared. An extraordinary meteor, at Charleston, night of the 28th, described in the News and Courier *as "a strange, celestial visitor."*

"It was only a coincidence."

FORT'S ACTUAL PHILOSOPHY was hidden somewhere behind his storyteller's indulgences—between the Punch-and-Judy-like smacks at science and the icy skepticism that made the pages of *Lo!* scintillate. Early in the book, he eloquently warned of his priorities. It was typical Fortean prose, tantalizing the reader and negating his 411 pages of text at the same time:

I believe nothing. I have shut myself away from the rocks and wisdom of ages, and from the so-called great teachers of all time, and perhaps because of that isolation I am given to bizarre hospitalities. I shut the front door upon Christ and Einstein, and at the back door hold out a welcoming hand to little frogs and periwinkles. I believe nothing of my own that I have ever written. I cannot accept that the products of minds are subject-matter for beliefs.

EIGHTEEN

Not a Bottle of Catsup
Can Fall Without
Being Noted

In comments upon my writings, my madness has been over-emphasized.

Benjamin De Casseres's article "The Fortean Fantasy" appeared in the March issue of the *Thinker*. Fort himself had struggled against stylish writing, and Dreiser and Mencken were famous advocates of plain, unvarnished prose. But De Casseres's lyric phrases complemented Fort's philosophy.

> *We do not know how strange this world is in which we are living, because familiarity, convention, routine and repetition have dulled the infantile emotions of surprise and wonder in us. The Kingdom of God (by which I mean the Kingdom of Eternal Amazement and Doubt) is still, as ever, the heritage of little children and poets.*
> *Charles Fort, anathema among all professional scientists and the mere machine-brained mathematicians, is of this kingdom. He is a*

celestial horselaugh in the house of Rigamarole. In the closed corpora-
tion of professors he is a Tyl Eulenspiegel perched on the window sill
hurling all sorts of whimsical questions at them and waving over
seventy-five thousand "facts" at them, facts taken from everywhere—
including their own publications—that do not "fit in" with their dead
reckonings. Charles Fort fights with a weapon, among his many
weapons, against which official science has no armor: ridicule.

Unlike Mencken or Dreiser, De Casseres could clearly appreciate
Fort's delicate mixture of humor and data. He believed that "science itself is going Fort-ward."

> *Fort is essentially scientific-minded. He is not a Plotinus, a*
> *Swedenborg or a Hegelian. I should say he is not, strictly speaking,*
> *even metaphysical. He nowhere announces spirit. Rather, with his*
> *feet firmly planted on the earth, he extends the boundaries thereof*
> *indefinitely and annexes the unseen by materializing it before*
> *our eyes.*
>
> *In the torrent of Fort's ideas, epigrams, satiric explosions and his*
> *data of curious happenings, there flashes a mind as profoundly and*
> *authentically an unaccountable variation from the American writing*
> *and thinking herd as Poe, Robinson Jeffers and Cabell, or as James*
> *Joyce in Europe.*
>
> *Every once in a while, a strange mind, an unattached mind, a*
> *trans-sensory mind, comes into the world to make us laugh, wonder*
> *or unhinge us. Such a mind is Charles Fort's.*

Gratified by the article, Fort thanked De Casseres with a typically shy shrug: "As one torrent to another, I splash you my
acknowledgments."

. . .

IN "THE FORTEAN FANATASY," Benjamin De Casseres had
picked an odd analogy for science:

> *Reason, experience, hard-boiled facts are the new Trinity. Every-*
> *thing in the universe, including ourselves, of course, is to be filed,*
> *carded, indexed, labeled and "explained." There is a neat pigeonhole of*
> *a theory for everything. When science changes its mind, when it reverses*
> *itself, it merely re-letters the pigeonholes and juggles the contents.*

When he wrote this, he had not yet visited Fort's Bronx apartment
and seen the author's collection of scrap-paper notes. Charles Fort
had become his own phenomenon. In the late 1920s, as he gave up
his library researches, he began recording his own life on his precious
rectangles of paper—reaching for a slip to scrawl a brief note about
his health problems, his concerns about the manuscripts, the scores
of Super-checkers, observations about the parrots or the falling pictures. "If I can think of this matter, and can reach a pencil without
having to get up from my chair—though sometimes I can scrawl a
little with the burnt end of a match—I shall probably make a note."
Like so many tiny leaves that had blown through the apartment, these
slips of paper were arranged in stacks on the table next to his chair,
sorted into boxes at his desk, rearranged and categorized.

> *Experiment: Returning home this morning with* Herald Tri-
> bune *in my pocket, and mind went to subject of the Depression. This*
> *a thought, "America will lead the recovery." I then argued that this*
> *not be so.*

Parrots: The Chief would hear Peggy and go pattering from the kitchen to look for her. Peggy died yesterday. The chief showed no signs of missing her. But this morning, when Annie opened the cage door, he went pattering directly to the front room, obviously looking for her. Virtually he had never left the kitchen except to go in response to a call from Peggy.

First game, 421 scored, 30 + 4 by a neat unexpected cross-board cut.

Been few games. Just had a smashing defeat. Notice that the winners were pluses of last time. Inertia.

Fort was anxious about *Lo!* When the first few reviews came in—the usual mixture—he fell into a depression. On February 20, 1931, just two weeks after *Lo!*'s publication date, he grabbed a small bit of paper and penciled his concerns:

T. Thayer silent. Because all reviews, only one has been favorable? Anyway, I know that Lo! *is a flop.*

Journalist H. Allen Smith spent an afternoon Fort's apartment. At the time, he admitted to being "book author crazy," going out of his way to interview writers. Fort was called "The Mad Genius of the Bronx," Smith remembered. "Fort invented a frightening game of Super-checker, moving the pieces by battalions. The day I called on him he tried to show me how to play this game, but I can't even understand ordinary checkers." The shy Fort, shuffling through his rooms, pointing to the shoeboxes of notes, or quietly explaining the nature of teleportation, failed to impress. "After I had looked into the matter of Charles Fort's great genius, then contemplated the men who trumpeted that genius, I had a change of heart about book authors," Smith concluded.

Remembering the author smiling through the dinner at the Savoy Hotel, Aaron Sussman miscalculated Fort's indulgence. He suggested that the author might sign copies of *Lo!* at the George Washington Hotel, and the announcement slipped into the *Herald Tribune*. Fort was horrified when he read it, writing to Sussman, "There will have to be a retraction."

Fort received an enthusiastic letter from author Margaret Deland, who had observed a jellylike rain in western Pennsylvania when she was a little girl. "Of course, I ought to have called the attention of my elders to this, but equally, of course, I did not, children not being confidential as to their discoveries," she wrote. "Afterwards, when I spoke of it, nobody believed me. Then I read the description of the same thing in *The Book of the Damned*."

Deland was looking forward to *Lo!* and "other queernesses that I observed in my somewhat silent youth."

But an envelope from Dreiser contained bad news.

> *I'm sending you a copy of this letter from H.G. Wells, and since you are the object of all this calumny, I wish you'd get up a reply which will effect in Mr. Wells a momentary pause, then send it to me. I shall have one or two things which I want to add, and besides, I want to get an additional rise out of him.*

The attached letter was perfectly clear.

> *Dear Dreiser,*
> *I'm having Fort's* Book of the Damned *sent back to you. Fort seems to be one of the most damnable bores who ever cut scraps from out of the way newspapers. I thought they were facts. And he writes like a drunkard.*
> *Lo! has been sent to me but has gone into my wastepaper basket.*

And what do you mean by forcing "orthodox science" to do this or
that? Science is a continuing exploration and how in the devil can it
have an orthodoxy? The next thing you'll be writing is the "dogmas
of science" like some blasted Roman Catholic priest on the defensive.
When you tell a Christian you don't believe some yarn he can't prove,
he always calls you "dogmatic." Scientific workers are first rate stuff
and very ill paid and it isn't for the likes of you and me to heave
Forts at them.

God dissolve (and forgive) your Fortean Society. Yours,
H. G. Wells

Dreiser felt that Fort's level of success had changed him. "He
was now comfortable, witty, ironic. All was flux and flow." At the
same time, Dreiser sensed an indifference, "an almost corrupting
sense of the unimportance of everything."

To have made such tireless researches was nice. To be sure a man
might achieve a wider and wider fame. To be sure all this constituted
an achievement. But as one grew old, the fevers for such labors were
not only reduced, but one lacked the powers to evoke them.

As he had many times before, Dreiser rushed to defend his
friend, responding to Wells with a full fusillade.

At best, your letter hands me a laugh.
In regard to Fort's work, I am still of the opinion that such a
body of ideas, notions, reports, hallucinations—anything you will—
gathered from whatever sources and arranged as strangely and imag-
inatively, is worth any mind's attention. I think it arresting just as
pure imagination, as Jules Verne's Twenty Thousand Leagues
under the Sea *or your own* The Island of Dr. Moreau *is*

arresting. You, the author of The War of the Worlds *to be so sniffish and snotty over* The Book of the Damned!

Dreiser pointed out that only about a thousand copies of *The Book of the Damned* were printed, and he had first felt the book had "fallen absolutely flat." But in subsequent years he met many people who had been captivated by it. "Over here where, as you know, all the world's morons dwell, it seems to grow in value. In England, if I can trust your reaction, it will never make any impression."

One detail in Dreiser's letter sounds like ammunition offered by Fort:

> *I am ready to meditate upon his curious explorations among, as you say, "items of newspapers." I notice, though, that a respectable body of his data seems to come from scientific papers, reports and letters written to the Royal Society in England and the American Academy of Science here, and related bodies elsewhere.*

Lo! WAS NOT a flop. Burton Rascoe, an old friend of Dreiser's, his first biographer and a charter member of the Fortean Society, reviewed it in the *New York Herald Tribune:* "In any mood your temperament dictates and whatever way you read it, it is a good book." Maynard Shipley, a science writer and long-time correspondent with Fort, wrote the review for the *New York Times.*

> *Fort, it is true, writes thrillers—non-fictional thrillers, but more melodramatic than any mystery novel yet published. He is rash. He ventures where angels fear to tread. Often his daring oversteps his knowledge. But his data, if not his conclusions, are thoroughly*

grounded and well documented and he is perhaps the enzyme orthodox science needs most. He is the enfant terrible of science, bringing the family skeletons to the dinner table when distinguished guests are present.

Shipley admitted that Fort's literary admirers "overdo themselves and harm their idol" by exaggerated, uncritical acceptance. He felt that Fort's service to scientific inquiry was "more or less stultified by his lack of comprehension of scientific method," particularly his understanding of astronomers. "They work unceasingly and fruitfully, if not in the ways Charles Fort would direct them to."

Discount, however, every one of Fort's hypotheses, and the solid body of his data remains—a life work in itself. There is no describing such a book as Lo! *Reading Fort is a ride on a comet. If the traveler returns to earth after the journey, he will find, after his first dizziness has worn off, a new and exhilarating emotion that will color and correct all his future reading of less heady scientific literature.*

Fort immediately wrote to Shipley, delighted with his review.

I note that you speak of my "daring." Yours is a higher type than mine. In writing one of my books, I risk nothing but the trouble of finding a publisher. This time, I had none, though an earlier version of Lo! *traveled around unavailingly three or four years.*

Something that you see in Lo! *is that it is a kind of non-fiction fiction. I have a theory that the moving pictures will pretty nearly drive out the novel, as they have very much reduced the importance of the stage. But there will arise writing that will retain the principles of dramatic structure of the novel, but not having human beings for its characters, will not be producible in the pictures and will survive independently. Maybe I am a pioneer in a new writing that, instead of old-fashioned heroes and villains, will have floods and bugs and stars and earthquakes for its characters and motifs.*

I am very much encouraged with your review, the spirit of which is—discount what you will, something remains, just the same.

"The book will not be a bestseller, but it is going well," Fort wrote to De Casseres, reporting that *Lo!* had quickly gone into its third printing and would be published in London. "It's quite satisfactory." Sales of *Lo!* inspired Horace Liveright to issue a third printing of *The Book of the Damned.* Claude Kendall and Aaron Sussman arranged to publish Fort's next book.

BIRDS ALWAYS FASCINATED FORT. A neighbor on Ryer Avenue kept pigeons, and they perched on Fort's windowsill. As he worked on his manuscript, he tried to tempt the birds inside, but they resisted, "stretched necks, fearing to enter." Fort offered them food, and eventually the birds entered through the open windows.

Pigeons on the backs of chairs. They inspected what I had for dinner. Other times they spent on the rug, in stately groups and processions, except every now and then, when they weren't so dignified. I could not shoo them out, because I had invited them in.

Fort complained about walking "four blocks—eight blocks counting both ways" to buy bird seed. Dreiser worried about his friend. He noticed that Fort was sedentary and his health was failing.

The most he got in the way of exercise was to go to the store for
Annie, or to walk to a movie and back. More than this and the oc-
casional visitors he had, and the books and newspapers he read, there
was nothing. He complained to me that his body felt heavy, that it
was hard for him to walk, that his great satisfaction was just to sit
and work on his notes.

Visiting a physician—like using a telephone—was an act of desperation for Fort. He didn't trust doctors. But Fort admitted to Dreiser that he had consulted with one and was now taking treatments. Although he didn't reveal his illness to Dreiser, he had probably been diagnosed with leukemia.

Dreiser urged him to make a complete change, to move south or west and enjoy a healthful new environment. Fort listened to the idea as if it were an impossibility, pointing out that he was now too fixed in his ways. But at the end of September 1931, Fort finally accepted Dreiser's long-standing invitation. He packed a small bag of clothes and joined Dreiser and Helen for a week at Iroki, the country home at Mount Kisco, New York. Anna stayed in the Bronx to look after their parrot.

Helen Richardson remembered Fort's long, fascinating conversations with Dreiser at Iroki. "They were men of strong intuition, the value of which they both suspected to be precious beyond measure." According to Dreiser:

Once he said rather movingly that he was so glad he had the trip
around the world before his father cut him off. When I inquired why
he didn't come out more, go to the theatre, visit friends of his own or
mine, his invariable reply was that his notes and his materials didn't
let him. There was always something that he had to verify, not because
he really needed to verify it, but because if he wasn't verifying it, he

*felt out of place. He said that the best place for him was his little
room in his apartment.*

At Iroki, Fort was barely an hour outside of Manhattan, but he
was uncomfortable about being so far away from his apartment, his
wife, and his desk full of notes. After a week in the country, Fort
announced that he had to return to his apartment. "That for one
thing he did not like the country and for another that he could not
leave his wife alone—that they were used to their routine and that
worrying over it would do him more harm than good." Dreiser
protested, but Fort was firm. He packed his bag and returned to
the Bronx. "Following that, all later invitations were ignored."

Helen had taken snapshots of the men on the lawn at Iroki,
looking like two uncomfortable city boys forced into the sunshine.
When she sent the photos to Fort, he responded, "It's some kind
of trick of double exposure. Everybody knows I'm bigger than
Dreiser, but you have me looking like some ordinary little lizard
beside the huge dinosaur."

FORT WAS ANXIOUS to return home because his next book for
Sussman, *Wild Talents*, was being produced on an accelerated schedule. He was busy through 1931 arranging notes, writing the manuscript, and reading chapters to Anna for her opinion.

The book was a departure for Fort. "Talents" referred to
strange faculties—disappearing people, peculiar injuries, psychic
criminals, mysterious diseases, spontaneous human combustion,
religious miracles, even animals with unexpected abilities. Fort
broadly classified these phenomena as sorts of witchcraft. For *Wild
Talents*, Fort's sources were less scientific and more anecdotal than

his previous books; most seemed to be clipped from popular newspapers. The book was produced in less than a year, suggesting that parts of *Wild Talents* may have been adapted from other manuscripts—particularly the missing "W.W." and "M & F" that Fort mentioned in his notes. Much of his research had been taken from British newspapers while he was living in London.

Wild Talents shines with Fort's breezy commentary, connecting all his precious odds and ends, offering a more personal, self-effacing glimpse of the author than his previous books. This is the "comfortable, witty" Fort described by Dreiser, leading readers through his obsessions and concerns.

> *Conservatism is our opposition. But I am in considerable sympathy with conservatives. I am often lazy myself. It's evenings, when I'm somewhat played out, when I'm most likely to be conservative.*
>
> *I like to read my evening paper comfortably. And it is uncomfortably that I come upon any new idea, or suggestion of the new, in an evening paper. It's a botheration, and if I don't understand it, and it will cost me some thinking—oh, well, I'll clip it out, anyway. But where are the scissors? But they aren't. Hasn't anybody a pin? Nobody has. There was a time when one could maneuver over to the edge of a carpet, without having to leave one's chair, and pull up a tack. But everybody has rugs nowadays. Oh, well, let it go. We'd all be somewhat enlightened, were it not for easy chairs. One can't learn much and also be comfortable. One can't learn much and let anybody else be comfortable.*

Fort poked fun at his research. He admitted to trying his own hand at witchcraft. "The one great ambition of my life, for which I would abandon my typewriter at any time, is to say to chairs and tables, 'Fall in! Forward! March!' and have them obey me." He reported that, so far, his furniture hadn't responded. "I have tried this, because one can't be of an enquiring nature and also be very sensible."

He famously debated a report of a talking dog, defining the limits of his belief:

> *It was told in the* New York World, *July 29, 1908—many petty robberies in the neighborhood of Lincoln Avenue, Pittsburgh, detectives detailed to catch the thief. Early in the morning of July 26, a big, black dog sauntered past them. "Good morning!" said the dog. He disappeared in a thin, greenish vapor.*
>
> *There will be readers who will want to know what I mean by turning down this story, while accepting so many others in this book. It is because I never write about marvels. The wonderful, or the never-before-heard-of I leave to whimsical or radical fellows. All books written by me are of quite ordinary occurrences.*
>
> *It is not that I think it impossible that detectives could meet a dog who would say, "Good morning!" That's no marvel.*

Fort cited examples of dogs that said "Hello," or "Thank you." But the problem was the disappearance. He insisted that if he had similar examples—"Dated sometime in the year 1930, telling of a mouse who squeaked, 'I was along this way and thought I'd drop in, and vanished along a trail of purple sparklets' "—he'd consider admitting the phenomenon into his fold.

> *Some of us have taken Jehovah and some of us take Allah to despise, or to be amused with. To give us limits within which to seem to be, every mind must practice exclusions. I draw my line at the dog,*

who said, "Good morning!" and disappeared in a thin greenish vapor.
He is a symbol of the false and arbitrary and unreasonable and
inconsistent limit, which everybody must somewhere set, in order to
pretend to be. You can't fool me with that dog story.

As he composed *Wild Talents,* Fort bristled at Einstein's new-
found fame. His accounts of the scientist are unexpectedly vivid.

> *Einstein was said to be useful, and, in California, school chil-*
> *dren, dressed in white, sang unto him kindred unintelligibilities. In*
> *New York, mounted policemen roughly held back crowds from him,*
> *just as he, to make his system of thoughts, had clubbed many astro-*
> *nomical data into insensibility.*

There's no question where the first image originated: Fort must
have seen and heard the schoolchildren in newsreel footage of Einstein. We can picture Charles and Anna, sitting in the darkened
cinema in the Bronx during one of their nightly excursions. As he
squinted at the Movietone News, Fort reached into his pocket for
an ever-present scrap of notepaper.

He was equally critical of the latest scientific fashion, Professor
Bohr's Quantum Theory, which Fort called "the idea of playing
leapfrog without having to leap over another frog."

> *Belief in God, in nothing, in Einstein—a matter of fashion. Or*
> *that college professors are mannequins, who doll up the latest proper*
> *thing to believe, and guide their young customers modishly. Fashions*
> *often revert, but to be popular they modify. It could be that a re-*

dressed doctrine of witchcraft will be the proper acceptance. Come unto me, and maybe I'll make you stylish. It is quite possible to touch up beliefs that are now considered dowdy, and restore them to fashionableness.

I conceive of nothing, in religion, science, or philosophy that is more than the proper thing to wear for a while.

But overall, Fort's discussion of science was minimized. In *Wild Talents,* he suggested his cosmology with an elegant simplicity.

That everything that is desirable is not worth having—that happiness and unhappiness are emotional rhythms that are so nearly independent of one's circumstances that good news or bad news only stimulate the amplitude of these waves, without affecting the ratio of ups to downs. Or that one might as well try to make, in a pond, waves that are altitudes only, as to try to be happy without suffering equal and corresponding unhappiness.

The monistic relationship of all things, his theme developed from *The Book of the Damned,* was described with Fort's characteristic prose.

Not a bottle of catsup can fall from a tenement-house fire escape in Harlem, without being noted—not only by the indignant people downstairs, but even though infinitesimally, universally, maybe—

Affecting the price of pajamas in Jersey City, the temper of somebody's mother-in-law in Greenland, the demand, in China, for rhinoceros horns for the cure of rheumatism—maybe—

Because all things are inter-related, continuous, of an underlying oneness.

· · ·

FORT DASHED an amused note to De Casseres. A mutual friend
had solicited Fort's views on the solar system. "He asks what I am
going to do with the moons of Jupiter," Fort reported. "What do
people usually do with the moons of Jupiter? I hope that I shall do
right by them." He still visited with friends, and stockbroker Stan-
ley LeDoux came to the Bronx to share a game of Super-checkers.
But the last months of 1931 were devoted to completing *Wild Talents*. His manuscript included American newspaper sources from as
late as December 1931, suggesting that he was actively revising the
manuscript through the year. Fort's usual schedule was to work at
his desk until five in the afternoon, and then join Anna for dinner
and a movie, but he gradually worked later and later into the night.
"Sometimes he worked until it was time to go to the movies," Anna
said. "Sometimes I would even go to the pictures alone, and he
would follow. Then he could not go any more."

In a note to Dreiser, Fort wrote, "Breeze from you the other day,
but I was too feeble to fan back. I have had a breakdown. I'm pulling through all very well." Fort was aware of his aches and pains,
and was losing weight. He was determined to finish the manuscript.
When he worked late, he asked Anna, "Why don't you go to the
movies?" "But I would not leave him," she recalled. "I used to go
and get him ice cream every night."

Charles Fort realized that he was dying.

FORT HAD LOST his appetite. He had cut down on his smoking
and his beer, but now drank lemonade, ginger ale, and cider. Anna

thought it was not healthy to drink all that "sour stuff," and urged him to see the doctor again. He refused.

Aaron Sussman was hoping to generate some publicity for *Wild Talents*, and suggested having journalist Reed Harris and Dreiser "work up a battle" with conservative educators about Fort's views. Fort refused. He was uncomfortable that his friend Dreiser once again would be cast in the lonely role of his champion.

As he squirmed in his desk chair, growing more restless and impatient, Fort was determined to finish *Many Parts*. He kept track of his aches and pains on the handy rectangles of paper.

February 13: I have been half dead, so weak I couldn't go out walking, or felt weak walking a little, before today. Sat for the first time and read today.

February 19: Without being definitely ill I can't take walks. Can't smoke half as much, have cut down meals one-half, am sleeping poorly, have cut down beer. On Wild Talents *I can only do 4, 5 or 6 pages a day.*

February 20: Finished W.T. *today. I can't write more than mornings, but I don't see that my writing abilities affected.*

Beginning Anywhere

As my energy plays out, I become nobler. My last utterance will be a platitude, if I've been dying long enough. If not, I shall probably laugh.

I
n *Wild Talents*, Fort wrote, "To this day, it has not been decided if I am a humorist or a scientist." Theodore Dreiser always knew that his friend wasn't a scientist—or at least his credentials didn't hold up against established scientists. But he also never quite got the joke behind Fort's wild suggestions. To Dreiser, Fort was a magnificent philosopher and an explorer, with many lofty ideas yet to be recognized.

Dreiser was anxious to help with Fort's book. He finally settled on a long interview with Reed Harris, which would allow him to explain Fort's philosophy and generate interest for *Wild Talents*. As expected, Dreiser's interpretation was grimly overwrought.

> *Q: How do you account for the neglect heaped on Charles Fort by educators, scientists, theologians?*
>
> *A: Take the answer right out of his own books. He repeats over and over that for each period there is a mental acceptance and I know*

that this is true out of my own experience. He is faced with the limit of acceptance, which is all they know. There is no receiving station for his work, no office where you can take it, no door into any publishers, and there is no market. Eventually it will grow and gather more interest, and finally he will have a field, really something that never was there before. I have a feeling that sometime something substantial is to come out of this, and that it presages a great change. It presages a great change and it presages mental development and far greater scope of mind than we have yet.

Q: Charles Fort has been compared to Leonardo. Is there any aptness in this comparison?

A: Well, to one phase of Leonardo. Leonardo had the same intensive tendency toward creation. He saw fit to imagine things about life, and even tried to prove them. That is the really wonderful thing about the really creative mind, and out of that will come some kind of action on the part of a man like Leonardo or Fort.

When the entire interview was sent to Fort for his approval, he wouldn't give it. He vaguely complimented Dreiser—the "philosophic parts are enlightened"—but he objected to "so much about me and my personal affairs of years ago." Presumably this was Dreiser's recollection of Fort's early days as a short-story writer, and that he "lived on about five cents a day." Dreiser also described how *X* failed with science writers, how Fort tore it up in disgust, and Dreiser blackmailed Liveright into producing *The Book of the Damned:* "If you don't publish it, you'll lose me." Perhaps Fort also winced at the description of the author as an eccentric: "If you look at him, it is hard to believe it is the truth—he sticks in one room and eats rat trap cheese."

But Fort's discomfort may have had a simple explanation. Dreiser's breezy anecdotes about *X*, or Liveright, or cheese were a reminder of how much he actually knew about the author. Dreiser had seen Fort depressed, poverty-stricken, and helpless; he'd employed Fort, encouraged him, and then advocated for him. Those were embarrassing times that were best forgotten.

Dreiser wasn't surprised. He'd dealt with Fort's peculiarities, and he knew that Fort was ill. He wrote that he merely "intended it to be serious but interesting to readers." He promised that he would be coming up to the Bronx for a visit.

FORT KEPT TRACK of his latest phenomena on his paper slips:

February 23: Going to Loews last night, I could not keep up, or nearly up, to Annie's pace.

February 26: New difficulty in shaving—gaunt places in my face.

February 29: I sent W.T. to Sussman. I don't give it any thought.

March 3: New pains in a chair. My bones no longer padded. I have had no sense of illness, but of weakness.

March 3: I look almost frightfully ill. My appearance startled the LeDouxs. I have refused to have a doctor, not only on general principles, but because of way my own body is presenting to me—kind of good to have cut down food, cut smoke, drink.

Dreiser was shocked by his friend's appearance, as if "he'd endured a severe illness. His stocky body was considerably reduced in weight." Fort described *Wild Talents* and seemed especially satisfied with the result. Dreiser asked him if he'd been thinking about his next book, and Fort explained that there were still several areas of notes "that he hadn't interpreted." He was trying to decide.

For years Fort had been gathering clippings on the medical community—discussions of disputed medical procedures, mysterious diseases that went unsolved, germ theory, misdiagnoses, obsessions with tonsillectomies or appendectomies that seemed faddish. The newspaper clippings and scrawled paper notes were filed under "Medical." A few of these subjects had worked their way into *Wild Talents*. Fort's curiosity was spurred by his own maladies and his misgivings about physicians. He thought about assembling these phenomena in a book titled *Medi-Vaudeville*.

> *March 5: Saw Sussman. W.T. finally accepted. All seems well.*
> *March 6: Sussman, like LeDouxs, was shocked at my appearance. So many persons now know about me and no doctor that it is a challenge to me to get well.*
> *March 8: Annie has been almost fierce about getting a doctor.*

And then, a welcome diversion, another game of Supercheckers.

> *March 10: Thought with disgust having to see -113 again. 113 score. 8 + 30, 6 + 30.*

FORT WANTED ANNA at his side. When the downstairs neighbors visited, Anna escorted them into the dining room and offered a glass of beer. "Can't you cut out your afternoon entertainments?" Fort complained to her. Anna told him that "It is a very poor sort of entertainment, and I did it to save you."

One night, as he was lying quietly in the bedroom, Anna sat outside. "Who have you got there?" he called to her. She answered,

"I haven't got a living soul. I am all alone." "And he was pleased that I had no one with me," Anna remembered. "He just wanted me—him and momma—and no one else."

By April, Fort was confined to his bed. Dreiser and Helen went up to the Bronx to see him. "He fairly announced to me that he knew he had not long to live," Dreiser wrote. "He was convinced that he was incurable, whatever the doctor said, or didn't say." Helen recalled that Fort spoke of his leukemia "as a conscious, mysterious parasite which had seized on him, and there was no possible escape." Fort had written in *Wild Talents*, "I am God to the cells that compose me."

Fort was racked with pain, and could only rest in certain positions on his side. He needed assistance to turn in bed. Anna waited on him, feeding him meat broth, but he had difficulty taking food. When he reported to Dreiser that he couldn't sleep, his friend recommended narcotics.

> One of Fort's eccentricities was his stubbornness on certain subjects. Since he was so sure he was going to die, at least he could obtain the comfort of sleep by taking heroin, and it was foolish not to do it. He replied that he didn't believe in drugs. He finally became so tortured that he agreed to take the drug. And with the greatest astonishment he announced that it was unbelievable that a person could obtain that much relief from a drug. He was sorry he had not taken it before.

Dreiser left the Forts' apartment feeling helpless and depressed. He sent his own doctor, but received the report that "there was no hope whatsoever."

"One of the things that Fort said at this time," Dreiser recalled, "rather impressively, was that it was true that he had not known how to live, but that he would show me how to die."

• • •

ON MONDAY, May 2, 1932, Anna realized that she could no longer care for her husband; she called an ambulance. Fort was carried down the stairs on a stretcher and taken to the Royal Hospital on the Grand Concourse in the Bronx. Aaron Sussman rushed to Fort's bedside the following day with an advance copy of *Wild Talents,* holding it up so the author could see the finished product. Fort was unable to lift his hand to take the book.

On Tuesday night, with Anna at his bedside, Fort went in and out of consciousness. Shortly before midnight, he suddenly called out, "Drive them out, Dreiser, drive them out!" Then he repeated, "Drive them out!" At 11:55 p.m. on May 3, 1932, Charles Fort died. He was fifty-seven years old.

THE SERVICES were held at a local funeral parlor. A small group of Fort's friends, neighbors, and admirers was present. His younger brother, Raymond Fort, "the Other Kid," who had taken over the family business, came to the Bronx to arrange for burial at the Fort plot in Albany. H. Allen Smith arrived to write up a brief description for United Press.

Theodore Dreiser stood to say a few words, but felt that "to say anything of real import was impossible."

I contented myself with saying that the shadow of a great man— and as yet, an unrecognized genius—was lying there. That it would take time and much more understanding than he had encountered in

his life to bring even a partial recognition of the marvel of his tem-
perament and the work that he had done.

THE *NEW YORK HERALD TRIBUNE* obituary labeled Fort
the "Foe of Science" and mentioned that he was "a quiet man with
a dread of society" who had written "four astonishing and disturb-
ing books." The *New York Times* similarly used the headline "Foe of
Science," noting that he "refused to have a physician because of his
distrust of scientific men."

The *Times* obituary, published on May 5, noted that Fort's latest
book of oddities, *Wild Talents*, would go on sale in bookstores that
very day.

AT THE MOMENT of Fort's death, Alphonse Capone, America's
notorious hero-villain, was leaving for federal jail. Capone had
bribed juries and witnesses in the past, and the public wondered
whether he would escape these charges—but when the U.S. Supreme Court refused to hear his case, marshals quickly escorted
Capone to the Dearborn Street Station in Chicago. "I'm glad to get
started," the gangster told newsmen as he was hustled onto the late-
night train to the federal penitentiary in Atlanta.

The end of Capone's career symbolized the official end of the
1920s—when America's topsy-turvy sensibilities began righting
themselves again.

Ironically, Capone was not convicted for murder or bootlegging,
but only for income tax evasion—the minutiae of paper scraps and
records condemned the famous gangster. Frank J. Wilson, an investiga-

tor with the Bureau of Internal Revenue, moved to Chicago and spent years at a desk. "He will sit quietly looking at books eighteen hours a day, seven days a week, forever, if he wants to find something in those books," his boss boasted. Wilson sifted through accounting notes, receipts, and handwriting samples to finally pinpoint Capone's crimes.

CHARLES HOY FORT was buried at the family plot at the Albany Rural Cemetery, just north of the city, on May 6. His grave is just in front of his younger brother Clarence. Nearby are the graves of his father, mother, and stepmother.

The family's headstones are gathered around a tall monument, originally built for his grandfather, the grocery wholesaler of Albany. The classical figure atop the column is a robed woman who clutches a laurel wreath tightly in one hand. She stares out over a serene pond as if deep in thought, her chin poised over her fingertips. It's a curious pose, neither triumph nor grief. She is the perfect embodiment of doubt, or suspended judgment, or the hyphenated state of knowing-unknowing.

H. L. MENCKEN wrote to H. Allen Smith at United Press:

> *Your story describing the funeral of Charles Fort lists me as one of his customers. This was a libel of a virulence sufficient to shock humanity. As a matter of fact, I looked upon Fort as a quack of the most obvious sort and often said so in print. As a Christian I forgive the man who wrote the story and the news editor who passed it. But both will suffer in hell.*

· · ·

ABOUT A YEAR before his death, Fort had written a note instructing that "records of mine, such as notes, clippings and letters that constitute the collection" be given to the Fortean Society. "No more formal document is necessary because there will be no opposition to my wishes in this matter."

Anna Fort turned over her husband's treasured shoeboxes of notes and clippings to Tiffany Thayer, who had been in Hollywood, trying to find work as a screenwriter. She saved a handful of small slips—some of her husband's last penciled notes scattered next to his easy chair or atop his desk—for Aaron Sussman and Theodore Dreiser, as mementos of their friend.

ANNA AND CHARLES FORT had shared several weird, occult experiences—these had all been intrigues for Fort. Shortly after his death, one of Fort's aunts visited Anna and upset her by discussing Charles's money. "She said I had no right to it," Anna recalled.

> I went to bed crying, and in the night I thought he was sitting on a little bench, a couch which I have in the bedroom. He said, "Hello, Momma." I said, "Hello, Dad." And I was never so glad to see anybody in my whole life.

Several months later, she told Dreiser, there were raps on the door and she distinctly heard Charlie rushing through the rooms, calling "Annie, Annie!" "I was in bed in the back room," Anna recalled, "and he ran through the hall. I recognized his voice and knew it was he."

Anna shared these impressions when Dreiser interviewed her in 1933. She wasn't very talkative. She answered the questions in a perfunctory way, discussing the ghostly sounds in the apartment, early memories of her husband, their honeymoon trip, or his work schedule. According to the transcript, Dreiser interrupted the interview with an unexpected observation: "He said to me sometimes that he thought his whole life was wasted. I told him that was ridiculous." We can imagine the uncomfortable silence from Anna. She made no comment on her husband's self-doubt. Dreiser changed the subject and proceeded with another innocuous question: "What did *you* do in London?"

BEN HECHT had reviewed the original *Book of the Damned* with an approving roar of laughter. Years after Fort's death, he was still chuckling.

> When he was on earth not so long ago he went to a lot of work establishing the three great Fortean laws. These are, that man is a fool; that his soul is a swamp in a derby hat; and that his intellect is a fetus in a frock coat.
>
> I don't want to exaggerate the genius of Charles Fort. He was no philosophical comet. He was more of a roller coaster that took everybody for a ride. And for us Forteans the sciences have never quite recovered from this frolic. For us, the lights in the skies, the strange things cast up by the sea, the things that vanish from the earth without a trace, and the presence of all sorts of goofy dust rains every-

where will always take first place over Euclid, Eddington and even Einstein.

The folly of man is to be found spread out in his writings. They are writings that should be read today. You will see that man is no nearer the truth of life than are the sea shells. He only makes a little more, and a little less tuneful, noise.

THE AUTHOR and inventor R. Buckminster Fuller felt he may have met Charles Fort—a quiet man in the back of the room—during his own friendship with Theodore Dreiser. In later years, he was a card-carrying Fortean. "Charles Fort, as a man of true vision, purposefully inverted the equations," he wrote. "By getting the publishers to publish the absurd, he proved his point that the publishers published only the absurd."

There is something extremely inspiring about Fort's interest in his universe. His interest is very romantic. It isn't written in romantic terms at all, but the man is full of dreams—dreams of significance. Fort was in love with the world that jilted him.

Fort, like humanity, was looking for significance in experience. Fort is becoming increasingly popular with the university students who, all around the world, are looking for significance. Billions of young people are in love with a world whose complexity seems to be trying to jilt them. I don't think their love will be unrequited.

SOMETIME IN the late 1930s, Dreiser sat down to assemble an essay about his friend. He was still puzzled why Fort's particular genius had been lost on most people. Even the nature of their friendship—tentative yet profound—was difficult for him to put into words. The novelist noted that they shared "28 years of a most gratifying relationship." Astonishingly, Dreiser revealed that "in all of that time I saw him 20 or 25 times, if so much."

> *It was an intimate relationship, just as though he lived with me in my own home. He was never really out of my mind. Always he was one who seemed to be talking with my own voice, with my own moods. Not that I could present things as he felt them, and it thrilled me to know what he was doing.*
>
> *The people who were interested in him and in his work were intensely so. But the great majority, even of those who are interested in ideas and the poetry of life, never even noticed him.*
>
> *Fort was never truly at home in an ordinary world. He never accepted unthinkingly and without restraint the ordinary procedures of life, the ordinary conclusions, and ordinary interpretations. He looked on himself as if he were a creature from another planet, and he paid particular attention to the things that we neglect and ignore.*
>
> *Most would read Fort's books with repugnance and fear. Others would cast them aside with a smile and call them childish fairy tales. A few would shudder with delight, recognizing the poetry, the truth, insight and the marvelous intelligence of Fort's conception. So, though I think that Fort will continue to have an audience, and become a classic in his field, his audience will never be large. He will never be generally understood, not because of any defects in his approach, but because there are few who are able to, and can afford to, sympathize with him and appreciate him.*

Fall In! Forward! March!

The interpretations will be mine, but the data will be for anybody to form his own opinions upon.

Tiffany Thayer's Hollywood career had consisted of one acting role, assorted bits of dialogue in someone else's script, and several failed screenplays. He returned to the East Coast in the mid-thirties and resolved to revive the dormant Fortean Society. In 1935 he wrote to Dreiser, explaining his plans for a Fortean magazine so members would be able to keep in touch with each other, and Thayer could transcribe and reproduce some of Fort's cryptic notes. He thought that the raw notes would be of interest, but for anyone "to attempt to develop that material in imitation of Fort would smack of ghoulishness."

Thayer attempted to flatter Dreiser back into the fold, asking if he would provide a photograph and essay for the first publication—"the lead article can be about *you*, establishing the sort of intelligence Fort attracted."

Dreiser wasn't so easily charmed, and replied with an emphatic no. "At the time of his death I was interested to see the notes that

he left in order to estimate their volume and nature," he wrote to
Thayer, "but this was blocked by your taking them and disappearing with them up to this time. I believe I wrote you for information
but received no reply."

*Incidentally, it strikes me as presumptuous and ungracious for
the only person who seized upon his property and disappeared with
it, to indulge in thoughts concerning the ghoulishness of developing
material in imitation of Fort. Exactly who would be mentally capable of imitating Charles Fort?*

Thayer pushed back, writing, "Now, look. You're just angry."
Thayer pointed out that Fort had left his materials to the Fortean
Society, and he was now attempting to do the necessary dirty work
to make Fort's materials available. Dreiser stood his ground. "I do
not care to work with you. My decision is to remove my name from
the Fortean Society and I hereby formally request you to do this
at once."

After Charles Fort's death, Anna had moved to a smaller apartment on 125th Street in Manhattan. She turned over her husband's
letters, photographs, and books to Dreiser. Dreiser still was anxious
to see the mysterious boxes of notes. In 1937, Anna agreed to have
a legal request sent to Thayer. She asked that the notes be returned,
as Thayer had been treating them as personal property.

Before the issue could be settled, Anna Fort died on August 25,
1937, a victim of arteriosclerosis and myocarditis—the degenera-
tion of the heart muscle. She was buried alongside her husband
in Albany.

In her will, Anna left bequests to help fund scholarships for
deserving students at Harvard University, New York University, and
Washington Square College, in remembrance of her husband.

Raymond Fort, Charles Fort's remaining brother, died in Albany four years later, of lung cancer. He was survived by his wife, Theresa, and his daughter, Harriet.

THE FORTEAN SOCIETY MAGAZINE appeared in September 1937—the name was later changed to *Doubt*—and was issued erratically by Tiffany Thayer over the next twenty years. His caution about a ghoulish "imitation of Fort" was prophetic. Thayer "was an aggressive little man, contentious and rude," according to author Damon Knight. He was a facile writer who could transform outlandish arguments into prose, but possessed neither the wonder nor the warmth of Fort. He wrote most of the material himself, signing the stories "YS," for "your secretary."

In 1941, Thayer persuaded Henry Holt and Company to reprint Fort's four books of phenomena for the Fortean Society. The texts were collected in one volume as *The Books of Charles Fort*. Thayer contributed an introduction about Fort and the goals of his organization.

Thayer had a gift for exaggeration. When he began transcribing Fort's paper notes, he explained that they were "written in pencil, in a code known only to the author, a sort of personal shorthand." As Damon Knight pointed out, there is no code beyond an occasional abbreviation and Fort's terrible handwriting, which often can be discerned with a bit of head scratching.

In his introduction to *The Books of Charles Fort*, Thayer painted a surprising portrait of the author.

> *As we sat with home brew of his making, strong cheeses, coarse*
> *rye bread and whiskied grapes at a circular dining table, talking the*

night away, it often occurred to me that his frame called for leather
and buckles, that the board should have been bare and brown, washed
by slops from heavy tankards and worn smooth by heavy sword-
hands. The light should have been from flambeaux and, to match our
words, Faust and Villon should have stopped by in passing on their
way to murder, or conference with the devil.

The hyperbole said more about Thayer than Fort. Charles Fort was "built more like a walrus than a warrior, utterly peaceable and sedentary," author Damon Knight later observed. Writer Doug Skinner suggested that Thayer "felt hampered by our milquetoast, puny era; he longed to steep himself in the brawling world of Rabelais and Villon."

THEODORE DREISER and Helen Richardson moved to Hollywood, and they were finally married in 1944—two years after his first wife, Sarah, had died. With Helen's help, Dreiser finished his long-delayed novel, *The Bulwark*, in May 1945, and was hard at work at finishing another novel, *The Stoic*, when he died on December 28, 1945. Both books were published posthumously. He was buried in Glendale, California, the following month.

Tiffany Thayer diligently wrote to Helen Dreiser the following May.

Before anything else, please let me say with all the sincerity
any man ever felt, that I have regretted nothing in my life so much
as the inability of Mr. Dreiser and myself to work together amicably
in this effort which was so important to us both. Surely you will
agree with me that the place for the Dreiser-Fort correspondence is

*in the archives of the Fortean Society, which Mr. Dreiser helped to
found.*

*We could not concur with Mr. Dreiser's attempt to turn over the
Fort notes to a university. They would have been buried for all time.
Charles Fort fought scholasticism all his life.*

Thayer was unaware that Anna Fort, interpreting her husband's
wishes, had willed money to universities. Helen Dreiser didn't respond to Thayer's letter.

She died in 1955 and was buried next to Theodore Dreiser.

AS AN ADVERTISING MAN, Tiffany Thayer knew how to attract attention to his causes, and *Doubt* was propelled forward with
wild, pyrotechnic controversies. In the pages of his magazine, he
had forecast America's involvement in World War II—and called it
"The Great Hoax." He accused Roosevelt of colluding with Japan
and suspected that one of the president's political associates had
made a secret deal with Hitler. Thayer questioned civil defense,
tonsillectomies, the polio vaccine, and higher mathematics, and even
wondered if there was real gold at Fort Knox. He particularly annoyed his readers by proposing a new calendar (with a thirteenth
month named "Fort") and boldly suggesting Forteanism as a new
religion, "the religion of self-respect."

He even found a conspiracy theory in U.F.O.s, suggesting that
they were part of a plot by the government, to distract the public
and boost the defense budget.

Alexander Woollcott resigned from the organization in 1942,
perhaps angered by Thayer's charges against Roosevelt. Aaron Suss-

man resigned the following year, writing that Thayer was "perverting what I believe to be the real and only business of the society, spreading the word about Charles Fort." He felt that if Fort could have seen Thayer's recent issues of *Doubt*, obsessed with government conspiracies, "he would have expired from shock," and that Fort's name was now "a synonym for the dirtiest kind of subversive business."

Doubt, along with the Fortean Society, was a one-man show, a peculiar labor of love that made Tiffany Thayer no money but allowed him a forum for his colorful rants. Producing the magazine, he explained, occupied one week of his time every three months. In addition, he continued to write advertising jingles, specializing in cigarette commercials, and produced a number of successful, slightly smutty novels, like *Call Her Savage* or *One Woman*, both published in the 1930s. Of his prose, Dorothy Parker commented in the *New Yorker*, "Mr. Thayer, it is deplorably unnecessary to explain, has achieved great prominence in that school of American authors who might be described as the boys who ought to go regularly to a gym."

When Thayer and his wife visited the United Kingdom in 1952, Eric Frank Russell, a fellow Fortean who wrote for *Doubt*, was surprised at the Thayers' cynicism about the Fortean Society.

> *Mrs. Thayer picked up some of his attitude and, when in Dublin, took delight in nudging Thayer, pointing out some cross-eyed, crazy-looking Irishman and saying, "There's a member—go get him!"*

Through the forties and fifties, Thayer was busy with a three-and-a-half-million-word historical novel, a projected twenty-one-volume story about the Mona Lisa. The first three volumes, *The*

Prince of Taranto, were published in 1956. Thayer's inherent writing style worked against the historical setting. "Drool trickles from the wise-guy smoking car prose," wrote the reviewer for *Time.* "I am 'that dirty boy,' but I can't help it," Thayer explained in an interview. "I like to give my friends a laugh, that's all. Literature? To hell with literature."

The remaining eighteen volumes of the Mona Lisa story were never produced. Tiffany Thayer continued publishing *Doubt* until his death in 1959.

Vincent Gaddis, a popular writer on paranormal phenomena, wrote to a fellow Fortean:

> *Very few can understand the idea of suspended judgment, of being an absolute agnostic. They think Fort was a nut, who believed the yarns and theories (he called them suggestions) he wrote about. He didn't. Thayer was not a true Fortean, and very few of us are, anyway.*

A CONTEMPORARY of Fort's was author and cartoonist Robert L. Ripley, who concocted his first collection of sports oddities for a 1918 newspaper, and evolved the first "Believe it or Not!" cartoons around the time of Fort's first book, *The Book of the Damned,* in 1920. For millions of readers, Ripley's longtime newspaper feature provided their first encounters with such oddities—strange human abilities, bizarre or grotesque twists of nature, or puzzling historical facts.

Ripley's approach was purely commercial and his oddities were purely sensational: he was filling a newspaper column with engaging pen sketches and short captions, often punctuated with exclamation points. Ripley's short form allowed him certain liberties, and many memorable "Believe it or Not!" surprises relied on the cartoonist playing "gotcha" with the facts.

For example, Ripley was fond of recounting the thousands of letters of protest he received when his newspaper feature claimed "Lindbergh was the sixty-seventh man to make a non-stop flight over the Atlantic Ocean." (Lindbergh made the first non-stop solo flight. Alcock and Brown flew the ocean as a team in an airplane; the others were crews on various dirigibles.) Or, according to Ripley, "Buffalo Bill never shot a buffalo in his life." (Buffalos are found in Africa and India. Bill Cody killed North American bisons.)

A more complicated Ripley twist can be found in his headline "There are more than 4000 different ways of spelling the name Shakespeare." His article noted that Shakespeare himself always spelled his name differently—an astonishing fact, suggesting, "the Stratfordian was so uneducated that he could not write so much as his own name!"

Less obvious in Ripley's paragraph is the information that there were only three authenticated Shakespeare signatures: Shackspeare, Shakspeare, Shaxpr. This was not uncommon for the Elizabethan times, before spellings were standardized, and one Shakespeare signature was a clear abbreviation. Ripley's article then offered some of the four thousand possibilities that had been concocted by another author: "Chacsper, Shaxpere, Shaxespeyre, Schaxpeire. . . ." By stitching together these bits of trivia, "Believe it or Not!" seemed especially unbelievable. In recalling the article a day or a year later, the reader may easily misremember four thousand tortured spellings that Shakespeare had used.

Fort's process of collection meant that he was more careful and more discriminating with his facts. Then, too, Fort always had more oddities than he needed, and he never felt the necessity to stretch the truth. Existing correspondence demonstrates how Fort sought collaboration. In 1931, he wrote to a prosecutor in Newton, New Jersey, asking about a newspaper account of "the greatest mystery," a rain of buckshot that had supposedly fallen inside of a small office. In *Wild Talents*, Fort linked this to similar phenomena, but matter-of-factly ended the subject by quoting the letter he'd received from the prosecutor; "This occurrence turned out to be a hoax, perpetuated by some local jokesters."

Other letters from Fort had inquired about the mysterious "sword-shaped object," about six feet long and engraved with hieroglyphics, that had supposedly fallen from the sky and buried itself into the ground in Ulster County, New York, in 1883. Fort received a response that the boy who found it, named Bell, had a father who was a "crook, visionary and forger." Fort didn't include any mention of the mysterious sword in his books.

Later writers of the supernatural often followed the Ripley approach rather than the Fort model—choosing the best story for the greatest impact. But they also tried to copy Fort's idealized, agnostic attitude about the supernatural.

To understand Fort's legacy, it's important to remember that before *The Book of the Damned*, the supernatural was, by definition, special and unique. For thousands of years, supernatural events were used as evidence of a larger system—a mysterious force that could take control of our lives or offer temporary, extraordinary powers over nature. Miracles were interpreted as hints of god. Communication with the dead or a vision of the future was considered a special case, based on the skills of the medium or the blessings of the oracle.

There had always been a belief system woven into accounts of the supernatural. Even after Fort's death, the modern phenomenon of conspiracy theories—as exemplified by Tiffany Thayer's special brand of paranoia in *Doubt*—was a perverse view of an overarching system in control of our lives. The government can threaten us with fluoridated water, conceal the facts behind the Kennedy assassination, or deny the existence of an extraterrestrial crash in the desert of New Mexico. The conspiracy theory has the same religiosity as the supernatural, the same way that atheism requires faith. In a conspiracy theory, the explanation may not be god, but remains mysterious and all-powerful nonetheless.

Fort would have sneered at conspiracy theories, the same way he questioned whether scientists could add or subtract. For Fort, what we might identify as the supernatural is actually part of the natural world, forcing us to reconsider all of our definitions. He removes the lenses—religion, philosophy, or science—that have always tricked us into looking at the supernatural from extra far away or extra close-up. Now we see it in our own space, as a daily occurrence, and are challenged to shake hands with these oddities.

This is Charles Fort's legacy, copied and reinterpreted by generations of later writers. *Lo!*, in particular, formed the template for discussing the paranormal—the relentless arrangement of haunting facts to build suspicion, the ridicule of standard explanations, the trustworthy, disinterested, conversational tone. It is the modern approach to the supernatural.

Fifteen years after Charles Fort's death, when America was fascinated by accounts of flying saucers, Fort was included in one of the first books on the subject, Frank Scully's 1950 *Behind the Flying Saucers*. Scully included a chapter on Fort's accounts of early spaceships in the sky. These provided the pedigree for the latest craze, and Scully noted that Fort "gathered a lot of odd flowers from the field of science, and some were surely daisies." Scully also included an appendix labeled "The Post Fortean File," of saucer sightings

from 1947 to 1950. Like Fort, Scully had learned to build his case
by tweaking the establishment.

> *Men stay with what they believe, or fight for buggy whips in an*
> *era of automobiles for the simple reason that their livelihoods are all*
> *tied up with buggy whips. That racketeers should pooh-pooh the real-*
> *ity of flying saucers while giving painstaking details of trips to the*
> *moon in their imaginary rockets reveals how theories as well as*
> *worlds can suffer collision.*

Scully ridiculed scientist and author Willy Ley for his best-
selling accounts of future space travel. Ley, Scully wrote, "over-
whelms you with such a detail of engineering data, that you go with
him into areas where, if you thought about it, you would realize
that he had moved from fact into a strictly fictional field with more
laughable brass than any Jules Verne or flying saucers."

The construction became a standard formula for these books.
In Erich von Däniken's 1970 best-seller, *Chariots of the Gods?*, a speculation about ancient astronauts visiting earth, an early chapter
warned of science's prejudices.

> *Our historical past is pieced together from indirect knowledge.*
> *Excavations, old texts, cave drawings, legends, and so forth were used*
> *to construct a working hypothesis. From all this material an impres-*
> *sive and interesting mosaic was made, but it was the product of a*
> *preconceived pattern of thought into which the parts could always be*
> *fitted, thought often with cement that was all too visible. An event*
> *must have happened in such and such a way. In that way and no*
> *other. And lo and behold—if that's what the scholars really want—*
> *it did happen that way.*

In Charles Berlitz's 1969 *The Mystery of Atlantis,* the formula feels clumsy and self-defensive.

> *The established academic historical community, and to a some-what lesser degree the scientific world, has long regarded the question of Atlantis with skepticism, disbelief, and even a certain amount of hilarity. Serious consideration of the Atlantis theory would cause a number of established tenets concerning early civilization to tumble, with considerable rewriting of our early history.*

Berlitz continues, pointing out where science was wrong about just such things.

> *. . . The disbelief in the existence of the gorilla and the okapi before specimens of these "mythical" animals were obtained. . . . The dragon lizards of Komodo. . . . The possibility of transmuting metals, the efforts of alchemists now proved possible by modern science.*

By the time of his 1975 best-seller, *The Bermuda Triangle,* Berlitz was now needling science with the inevitable coelacanth.

> *The "extinct" coelacanth, a supposedly prehistoric fish with re-sidual limbs, was discovered to be very much alive and well in the Indian Ocean. Its last fossilized specimen, before the live one was found, had been dated at 18,000,000 B.C.*

The coelacanth, long considered an extinct species, was redis-covered in 1938, six years after Fort's death. It's a shame that we don't have Charles Fort's wry prose about it flopping back into existence in a South African fishing boat. Despite attempts at his formula, few authors have managed to match Fort's playfulness with these subjects. Even fewer have managed to emerge from discussions of the supernatural with their senses of humor intact.

SINCE THE REPUBLICATION of *The Books of Charles Fort*, the author's most famous texts have never been out of print. Today there is still an International Fortean Organization (INFO), and a popular British publication titled *Fortean Times* has managed to perpetuate Charles Fort's artistic tightrope dance, deftly pirouetting between belief and skepticism.

And the phenomena survive. Fort's interests became the canon of the supernatural, and his four gospels inspired subsequent books, including those of Berlitz and von Däniken, as well as Vincent Gaddis, Ivan Sanderson, John Godwin. Besides his accounts of early airships, many of Fort's phenomena have been rewritten and repeated—the devilish hoofprints in Devonshire, spontaneous human combustion, falls of blood, stones, fish, or frogs from the sky, Kaspar Hauser, and the *Mary Celeste*. In a 1964 magazine article, Vincent Gaddis took inspiration from Fort's calculation of the "London Triangle." Gaddis christened a small wedge of the Caribbean "The Bermuda Triangle," creating a renowned mystery.

Fort's writing has inspired numerous classic science-fiction stories. His phenomena have become shorthand symbols of the world's fascinating and unpredictable surprises. Evidence of Charles Fort has appeared in books like Eric Frank Russell's *Sinister Barrier*, Pauwels and Bergier's *The Morning of the Magicians*, Caitlín R. Kiernan's *To*

Charles Fort, with Love, Blue Balliett's *Chasing Vermeer,* and Paul Thomas Anderson's 1999 film *Magnolia.*

WHICH LEAVES one final problem to solve. Was Charles Fort a genius, or a crank?

The Books of Charles Fort is a dense brick, over a thousand pages of small type. Any reader who wants a fight can easily find a weapon from Fort's memorable phrases.

For example, in *Wild Talents,* Fort observed that the writer Ambrose Bierce disappeared in 1913. A few years later, a Canadian businessman named Ambrose Small had disappeared under mysterious circumstances. "Was someone perhaps collecting Ambroses?" Fort wrote. In reporting on Charles Fort, H. Allen Smith repeated this conclusion, adding, "He suspected as much." With this punch line, Fort becomes a dithering crank, examining newspaper clippings at the kitchen table, attempting to elevate rumors into cosmic theories. Smith didn't quote the paragraphs that followed, Fort's explanation of the joke.

> *There was in this question an appearance of childishness that attracted my respectful attention. . . . I'd not say that my question is so senseless. The idea of causing Ambrose Small to disappear may have had origin in somebody's mind, by suggestion from the disappearance of Ambrose Bierce.*

In his 1952 book *In the Name of Science,* Martin Gardner devoted a chapter to Fort, along with chapters on other fads and frauds perpetrated against the scientific establishment. Gardner was bewil-

dered by the author, but admitted that Fort "was far from an ignorant man."

> *His discussions of such topics as the principle of uncertainty
> in modern quantum theory indicate a firm grasp of the subject
> matter. Opposition to the notion that electrons move at random is
> not in fashion at the moment. Nevertheless, Fort's jibes are in har-
> mony with the more technical criticisms of Einstein and Bertrand
> Russell.*

Other researchers have pointed out that some of Fort's quibbles
with science may be explained by his reading too closely. Fort overstated several controversies that were then bubbling up in newspapers and scientific journals. Time and perspective have smoothed
over these debates.

Still, Gardner bristled at the end result of Forteanism. "More
meaning than meets the eye lurks behind Fort's madness," he hinted.
Gardner read Fort's musings on an "organism with intelligence" as
a nod to god. He was convinced that Fort was blind to the fact,
"or pretended to be blind to it," that scientific theories could be
given high or low degrees of confirmation. "It is this blindness
which is the spurious and unhealthy side of Forteanism." Gardner
continued:

> *In recent years, on top educational levels, there has been a minor,
> but observable, Fortean trend. Nothing official, of course, but if you
> know many Great Book educators* [this was a popular educa-
> tional movement at universities, emphasizing an active
> discussion of basic texts], *you will be struck by the fact that
> most of them regard scientists, on the whole, as a stupid lot. Stupid,
> that is, in contrast to liberal arts professors.*

Gardner's drum-beating for science was precisely the sort of thing that would have delighted Fort.

Critics may have been peeved at Fort's suggestion that scientific truths are "fashionable," but the word offends only by degree. He makes an essential point: the history of science is indeed full of buffoons, mistakes, miscalculations, changes of emphasis, arguments, and reevaluations. The public has done a disservice by ignoring these, elevating science to holiness—our salvation—and promoting scientists to a sort of priesthood.

Gardner worried that a "revival in religious orthodoxy," Fundamentalism, was caused by antiscientific movements like Forteanism. But an effective dose of Fort's philosophy may actually have prevented it. Fundamentalist movements of recent history seem to be the result of fear and isolationism, as well as an overreaction to the holiness of science in modern society—an effort to compensate. Just as it seems healthy to be able to laugh at priests to keep things in perspective, we need to be able to laugh at scientists.

BENJAMIN DE CASSERES felt that the strength of Fort was his balance of messages.

> Read Fort's astounding data and you will see you are living in a trick box.
>
> He says his cosmology of the universe is only his personal yarn. On the threshold of every room of his House of Affirmation stands Doubt. He is the enemy of all dogma. Here is wide-awake occultism, scientific clairvoyance, a shot into the dark—and a far-away scream as though Truth had been hit at last!
>
> Fort is not only a great, imaginative and revolutionary thinker

but he is also a literary artist and a vitriolic satirist of the first
water.

But a challenging criticism of Fort may be one of his sincerity.
Defenders of Charles Fort like Tiffany Thayer and Ben Hecht have
pointed out the author's pervasive sense of humor—that Fort is
continually joking with his readers. Thayer warned in his introduction to Fort's books:

> *Charles Fort packed a belly laugh in either typewriter hand. He*
> *laughed as he wrote, as he read, as he thought. Fort had the most*
> *magnificent sense of humor that ever made life bearable to a thought-*
> *ful man. Never forget that as you read him. If you do, he'll trick you.*
> *He'll make you hopping mad sometimes—remember, he's doing it*
> *purposely. He believed not one hair's breadth of any of his amazing*
> *"hypotheses" as any sensible adult must see from the text itself. He*
> *put his theses forward jocularly.*

But Thayer overstated his point. In Fort's writing, certain suggestions are given prominence and developed with sincerity. His *New York
Times* letters, discussing meteors or mysterious airships, are serious
requests for information, hinting at important research. Similarly,
each of his books on phenomena echo basic theories, and De Casseres
also listed the familiar cornerstones of Fort's contrary cosmology.
Fort's monism is expressed as a connection between all things—he
finds significance in seemingly unconnected occurrences and derives
meaning from this continuity. Fort also doubts the distances between
planets and stars, the distances that are commonly accepted by astronomers. He suspects that the earth is stationary, and his records
of objects falling from the skies are used to support this.

Admittedly, many other theories, as well as variations on his favorite themes, are playfully proposed to tease the reader. Fort's shyness about his own philosophy—continually suggesting theories and then denying them within his texts—matches his boyhood passions and punishments.

> *"Why do you do these bad things?"*
> *"Just for fun." Our stiff body was there; we were somewhere else,*
> *or had ceased to exist.*

The adolescent in Albany, accepting that he was a bad child, rubbed his bloody nose across the wallpaper and bedspread, deliberately dripping blood over the banister and onto the carpet. He insidiously punished himself and his authority figures at the same time.

> *We knew it was dirty work; had as much sense of decency as a*
> *grown person. Only, just then we were a little beast.*

The author of *The Book of the Damned, New Lands, Lo!,* and *Wild Talents* may have realized that his cosmology was the work of a delinquent. Playing the martyr, he took his punishment by simultaneously swinging at the scientific establishment.

When Tiffany Thayer asked Charles Fort what he called himself—"neo-astronomer or philosopher?" Thayer helpfully suggested—Fort answered simply, "I'm just a writer." Thayer interpreted this as a charming bit of modesty. But Fort was serious. From his earliest high school days and throughout his career, his primary intention was to be a writer.

● ● ●

CAN IT BE SOLVED? Was Fort a genius, or a crank?
In his final book, *Wild Talents,* he wrote:

> *Why this everlasting attempt to solve something? Whereas it is*
> *our acceptance that all problems are soluble-insoluble. Or that most*
> *of the problems we have were at one time conceived of as solutions of*
> *preceding problems. That every Moses leads his people out of Egypt*
> *into perhaps a damn sight worse: Promised Lands of watered milk*
> *and much adulterated honey.*
>
> *So, why these attempts to solve something?*

ACKNOWLEDGMENTS

For support and suggestions through my work on *Charles Fort, The Man Who Invented the Supernatural,* thanks to my wife, Frankie Glass. Her encouragement and ideas made this project possible and this story more interesting.

I am grateful to the late Roger Cox for his interest and friendship—generally and specifically. I also appreciate help and advice from David Britland, Richard Kaufman, Peter Lamont, and Ben Robinson. My agent, Jim Fitzgerald, was encouraging and enthusiastic. Thanks to Alban Miles, my editor at Heinemann, as well as Philip Turner, Joy de Menil, and Ravi Mirchandani for their support at the starting line. And thanks especially to Mitch Horowitz at Tarcher/Penguin, who got it all, and all at the right time.

Ian Kidd has been analyzing the twists and turns of Fort's beliefs, for his own book on Fort's philosophy, projected for next year. I was grateful for Kidd's critical comments and suggestions on my manuscript. Bob Rickard, the editor of *Fortean Times,* was helpful with references and suggestions. William Pack provided important research from the Chicago newspapers. Especially valuable was the assistance of Mr. X (his legal name), the respected Fort scholar; his research materials and personal insights were instructive.

Much of my research was conducted at the University of Pennsylvania, Philadelphia, Pennsylvania (the Theodore Dreiser Library and Dreiser papers); Cornell University, Ithaca, New York (the Dreiser letters, transcribed by Robert H. Elias); the New York Public Library, New York City (the Tiffany Thayer papers, Benjamin De Casseres papers); and Syracuse University (the Damon Knight papers). Additional research was conducted at the Albany Public Library, Los Angeles Public Library, and UCLA Library.

Charles Fort's books are:

Many Parts (manuscript fragments) (*MP*)
The Outcast Manufacturers (Dodd, 1909) (*OM*)
The Book of the Damned (Boni & Liveright, 1919) (*BOD*)
New Lands (Boni & Liveright, 1923) (*NL*)
Lo! (Claude Kendall, 1931)
Wild Talents (Claude Kendall, 1932) (*WT*)

The final four books were compiled in *The Books of Charles Fort*, with an introduction by Tiffany Thayer (Henry Holt, 1940), and this was later republished as *The Complete Books of Charles Fort*, with an introduction by Damon Knight (Dover, 1974).

There have been numerous editions of Fort's four last books; they are still in print and available to interested readers. All six of Fort's books in the above list are available in online editions published by Mr. X (www .resologist.net). Mr. X has annotated the phenomenon books, citing sources and making corrections.

Fort's quotations are distinctive and memorable; they were sometimes elaborately punctuated or spaced on the page. In quoting from his books or letters, as well as some other sources for my text, I've followed the lead of other writers, repunctuating and occasionally tightening the quotes without the usual ellipses (. . .). It's my hope that this produced a clearer, more readable text without altering the meaning or emphasis of Fort's words.

Charles Fort's previous biographer was the science-fiction author Damon Knight. His book, *Charles Fort, Prophet of the Unexplained* (Doubleday, 1970), is a concise and engaging portrait. I had the opportunity to speak with Mr. Knight about Charles Fort several years ago, before his death in 2002.

NOTES AND CREDITS

AUTHOR'S INTRODUCTION

Fort's quote is from *BOD*, Chapter 13.

Technopoly was written by Neil Postman (Alfred A. Knopf, 1992). Fort's quote on designs is from *Lo! The Morning of the Magicians* is by Pauwels and Bergier (Avon, 1968), and Benjamin De Casseres is quoted from the *Thinker*, March 1931. Fort's quote on coincidence is from *WT*.

Damon Knight's quote is from *Charles Fort, Prophet of the Unexplained* (Doubleday, 1970). This quote is often mistakenly attributed to Fort.

CHAPTER ONE. BUT THE DAMNED WILL MARCH

Fort's introductory quote is from *BOD*, Chapter 2.

The description of the 1920 book trade is taken from the contemporary pages of the *New York Tribune*, and the Boni & Liveright books are described in *Firebrand: The Life of Horace Liveright*, by Tom Dardis (Random House, 1995), and *The House of Boni and Liveright*, edited by Charles Egleston (Thompson-Gale, 2004). I have fragments of a dustjacket for Fort's *BOD*, but the quotes were described in the January 14, 1920, *Chicago Daily News*. Later editions had simpler dustjackets, without any pictorial images.

Fort's quotes are taken from *BOD*.

The *New York Times* review ran February 8, and Hecht's *Chicago Daily News* review on January 21, 1920. The *Life* quote is from February 26, 1920. Wells's letter to Theodore Dreiser is quoted in *Letters of Theodore Dreiser*, edited by Robert H. Elias (University of Pennsylvania Press, 1959). The Mencken letter and Dreiser's response were from *Dreiser-Mencken Letters*, edited by Thomas P. Riggio (University of Pennsylvania Press, 1986). Hecht's review was previously cited. The *New York Tribune* review ran January 17, 1920, and Booth Tarkington's review from the *Bookman* was quoted in *Charles Fort*, by Knight (Doubleday, 1970).

CHAPTER TWO. TODDY'S NOSE BLEEDS SO READILY

Fort's introductory quote is from *BOD*, Chapter 27.

The autobiographical material is from the unpublished pages of *MP*; the pages are in the Damon Knight papers at the University of Syracuse, and have been compiled and published online by Mr. X. A table of contents, in the Knight papers, suggests that that had been a different version of the manuscript.

The Fort family is discussed in *The Genealogy of the Fort Family in New York State*, by Jerome H. Fort (Edacra, 1993), and in *History of Saratoga County, New York*, by Nathaniel Bartlett Sylvester (Heart of the Lakes Publishing, 1979); some of this material can be found in online articles about the descendants of Jan La Forte and the history of Clifton Park. Additional family information is in *Charles Fort*, by Knight. Family tree and census records are online from ancestry.com. Addresses, names, and occupations were found in U.S. census records. Accounts of the Charles Nelson Fort family are from *Charles Fort*, by Knight; at the time Knight's book was written, Charles Fort's sister-in-law was still alive and could provide him with family memories—for example, the account of Agnes's death.

The Fort family was also discussed in Tiffany Thayer's "Prologue,

Notes and Epilogue," intended to accompany *MP* (published online by Mr. X), but Thayer misread a great deal, and his information is not always reliable.

In *MP*, the housekeeper is called Mrs. Lawson, but names have been changed in the manuscript; the 1880 census shows that her real name was Elizabeth Wassen.

Fort's memories of childhood and his quotations are from the manuscript *MP*.

CHAPTER THREE. LITTLENESS THAT WAS NO LONGER THERE

Fort's introductory quote is from *BOD*, Chapter 3.

Anna Filing's name is sometimes given as Filan, but I've taken the spelling from her marriage certificate. There is no clear record of her birth in the U.K. Family Records, nor an obvious Sheffield family listed, but it's possible that the name had alternate spellings, like Fallon or Phelan. Adding to the confusion, she may have misrepresented her age, as she did on one passenger ship crossing. I've been unable to trace her family in the U.K. or in America. An early portrait of her was taken in Manhattan, suggesting that her family settled there before she was in Albany.

Fort's accounts of his childhood and the quotations therefrom are found in *MP*.

I am grateful to Philip Kaminstein, Archives director of the Berkshire Farm Center, for information on the history of Berkshire Farm, although there are no remaining records from the time of Clarence Fort.

Anna Fort recalled her husband leaving home in Theodore Dreiser's interview of Anna Fort, conducted in September 1933, in the Dreiser papers.

CHAPTER FOUR. WE WRAPPED THE PIECE OF CAKE TO KEEP ALWAYS

Fort's introductory quote is from *BOD*, Chapter 7.

Fort's accounts of his childhood, including the account of his visit to

Clarence, are from *MP*. I've also used census information and cemetery records about the Fort family.

Fort's early writing career is from *Charles Fort*, by Knight; from "Raymond Fort's Recollections" of his brother (published online by Mr. X); and from the Knight papers.

The newspaper office accounts are from "The Short Stories of Charles Fort" (published online by Mr. X); from "Raymond Fort's Recollections"; and from *Charles Fort*, by Knight. Fort's memories of his newspaper days are from a letter to Dreiser (Knight papers).

The quotations from his childhood are from *MP*.

The quote about his days as a newspaper reporter, "collecting idealists' bodies," is from the *Chicago Daily News*, January 21, 1920. The quote about accumulating experience is from the *Albany Argus*, April 11, 1909.

CHAPTER FIVE. BLUE MILES, GREEN MILES, YELLOW MILES

Fort's introductory quote is from *NL*, Chapter 1.

The exhibits from the Columbian Exposition are taken from *The Official Guide to the World's Columbian Exposition* (The Columbian Guide Company, 1893).

The only account of Fort's travels appeared in the *Albany Argus*, April 11, 1909. I've been able to reconstruct his travels by linking this account to some ship records that show him returning to the United States.

Fort told the story about the South Africa ticket to Marguerite Tjader, Dreiser's secretary, and it was related in her book *Theodore Dreiser, a New Dimension* (Silvermine Publishers, 1965). She misremembered the story as happening years later, after his London researches, but the South Africa trip clearly was part of his world travels.

The story of the duel is from "Raymond Fort's Recollections," as cited.

Information on the Forts' marriage is taken from their marriage certificate and *A Parish Guide to The Church of the Transfiguration*, by Zulette Catir (Church of the Transfiguration, 1996).

CHAPTER SIX. WE, THEN A GREAT FAMOUS MAN

Fort's introductory quote is from *BOD*, Chapter 4.

Accounts of Anna Fort are from Sussman's recollections, quoted in *Charles Fort*, by Knight. Their honeymoon was recalled in Dreiser's interview with Anna in the Dreiser papers. Fort's account of drinking port is from *MP*.

Tiffany Thayer described Anna ("she never read his books") in his introduction to *The Books of Charles Fort* (Henry Holt, 1940). Dreiser also suggested that she was unaware of Fort's theories. But in Dreiser's interview with Anna, she recalled Fort reading chapters to her and asking her to comment on them.

Fort's addresses and his correspondence with Wallace are recounted in letters in the Knight papers. Knight also transcribed Fort's notebook entries, presumably from a family source. Tiffany Thayer speculated about the title *Many Parts* in Tiffany Thayer's "Prologue, Notes and Epilogue." But the title seems more than a literary allusion, and suggests an early representation of his philosophy. In later letters to De Casseres, Fort joked about his many "selves."

The letter to Anna, and accounts of hospital receipts, notebook entries about the rejections by publishers, his Employment Agency experience, and the pawnshop ticket are in the Knight papers. Some of these elements are also recounted in *Charles Fort*, by Knight. The table of contents for *MP*, the offer from Broadway Publishing, and Fort's failures, a notebook entry, are from the Knight papers. The *Evening Post* articles were accepted in a letter, in the Dreiser papers.

Fort's short stories are from "The Short Stories of Charles Fort" (published online by Mr. X), and a list of Fort's short stories is in the Dreiser papers. The Dreiser quote is from *My Life with Dreiser*, by Helen Dreiser (World Publishing Company, 1951).

CHAPTER SEVEN. ANYBODY COULD WRITE A TRUE STORY

Fort's introductory quote is from *Lo!*, Chapter 1.

Dreiser's quote is from an unpublished Charles Fort manuscript, in the Dreiser Papers. Presumably Dreiser intended this biographical chapter for a sequel to his book *Twelve Men*. Much of the material has never been quoted before. It seems to be an early draft and contains some incidents that are misremembered by the author.

The Dreiser material is taken from *Dreiser*, by W. A. Swanberg (Charles Scribner's Sons, 1965), *Theodore Dreiser: An American Journey*, by Richard Lingeman (John Wiley and Sons, 1993), *The Last Titan*, by Jerome Loving (University of California Press, 2005), Dreiser's *American Diaries*, edited by Thomas P. Riggio (University of Pennsylvania Press, 1982), and *A Theodore Dreiser Encyclopedia*, edited by Keith Newlin (Greenwood Press, 2003).

The Dreiser correspondence about Fort's stories is from Cornell University. These are copies of letters collected by Robert H. Elias. Some of these were reproduced in *Letters of Theodore Dreiser*, edited by Robert H. Elias (University of Pennsylvania Press, 1959), but the Elias papers at Cornell contain additional letters.

Dreiser described the collection of metaphors in the Reed Harris interview with Theodore Dreiser (Dreiser papers). I've taken my examples of Fort's metaphors from his short stories. He wrote about "the possibility of fire" in the *Chicago Daily News*, January 21, 1920.

Dreiser's correspondence to Fort is from Cornell University and the Dreiser papers.

CHAPTER EIGHT. LEAPING OUT OF A WINDOW, HEAD FIRST

Fort's introductory quote is from *WT*, Chapter 21.

The Coney Island tintype was in Anna Fort's possession and is now in the Dreiser papers. Fort's stories are quoted from "The Short Stories of Charles Fort."

Fort's journal is quoted in the Knight papers. Dreiser's recollection is from his Charles Fort manuscript (Dreiser papers). Wallace's letters and Fort's letter to Annie ("we are busted") are from the Knight papers.

Fort's experience with the golden light was described in Dreiser's *American Diaries,* edited by Riggio, and Dreiser's Charles Fort manuscript (Dreiser papers).

Dreiser's dramatic account of finding Fort hasn't been published before; it is from his Charles Fort manuscript (Dreiser papers). But Dreiser's biographers suggest that he was always an uneven reporter, juggling facts and dates. In this account, Dreiser describes finding Fort in the tenement with the manuscript *X.* But the dates aren't right, and letters confirm that this could not have been the book involved in the incident. *X* was written years later and discussed actively between them in correspondence, at a time when Fort was becoming financially comfortable. Dreiser was a fan of *X,* and may have elevated it to the starring role in this dramatic story.

In my research, I found that the details of Dreiser's account—Fort's silence and the couple's move to a cheaper apartment, Anna's work, and Dreiser's new job—perfectly match the time that Fort was writing *The Outcast Manufacturers.* I am assuming that this is the error in Dreiser's reporting, and I have quoted his story to describe this incident.

CHAPTER NINE. "TO WORK!" CRIED MR. BIRTWHISTLE

Fort's introductory quote is from *WT,* Chapter 5.

Fort's letters are from the Dreiser papers. The Dreiser letter criticizing Fort's manuscript is from Cornell University. Dreiser's recollections are from his Charles Fort manuscript (Dreiser papers), and Fort's letter about the waistcoat is from the Dreiser papers.

The Outcast Manufacturers was published by Dodd in 1909 and is also available online through the Web site of Mr. X. Quoted reviews are from clippings in the Dreiser papers. It seems that Fort subscribed to a clipping service for these reviews. Knight is quoted from *Charles Fort,* and Dreiser's praise is from his Charles Fort manuscript (Dreiser papers).

Dreiser's copy of the book, signed "To my partner," exhibits the pencil cuts, in the margins, that are later integrated into the *Pearson's* serialization, suggesting to me that Dreiser was the editor. Dreiser's copy is in the Dreiser Library, University of Pennsylvania. The Web site of Mr. X offers the *Pearson* chapters.

The *Albany Argus* article appeared on April 11, 1909.

I've reconstructed Fort's addresses from correspondence in the Knight papers, the Dreiser papers, and Cornell University. Dreiser's memory of Fort's collection of metaphors is from the Reed Harris interview (Dreiser papers). Fort's account of the "visualizing curtain" is from *WT*, chapter 26.

Fort's estimates of his writing are from the *Chicago Daily News*, January 21, 1920, and his journal entries are from the Knight papers. Dreiser's letter of criticism is from Cornell University. Destroying the notes is from the *Daily News* article, January 21, 1920.

CHAPTER TEN. X EXISTS!

Fort's introductory quote is from *BOD*, Chapter 8.

The Mencken and Dreiser friendship is taken from Dreiser biographies, as cited, and Dreiser's recollection, "Henry L. Mencken and Myself," reproduced in *Dreiser-Mencken Letters*, edited by Riggio.

The letters about his father's illness and death, and Raymond's letters about Clarence, are from the Knight papers. The portrait under his pillow is a memory of Raymond's wife, from *Charles Fort*, by Knight. Additional information on Clarence is from census records. Anna's recollection of Raymond, and the rapping sound in their apartment, are from Dreiser's interview with Anna (Dreiser papers).

Fort's notebook entries are quoted from the Knight papers. The account of "infinitesimal calculus" is a December 1, 1915, letter to Dreiser (misdated 1919) (Knight papers). Fort's accounts of his interests are from the *Chicago Daily News* article, January 21, 1920.

Fort's requests for library cards, and Dreiser's response, are in Dreiser's papers.

The missing manuscript for X has always been the Holy Grail for readers of Charles Fort. My account of it is reconstructed from Fort's May 1, 1915, letter to Dreiser—a three-and-a-half-page summary of the book—in the Dreiser papers. Dreiser captioned this letter "Concerning 'X' or 'The Trellis of Ether,' " suggesting that Fort may have considered an alternate title. Additional material on X is from Dreiser's Reed Harris interview, and Dreiser's Charles Fort manuscript (Dreiser papers). Fort's later film treatment for the book is also insightful. We have a good idea of what was in the book, and may assume that much of the phenomena cited in X were worked into Fort's later works. But the manuscript and Fort's stylistic touches had a hypnotic effect on Dreiser, who idealized it long after Fort had tired of it.

The account of Dreiser's party is from *Dreiser*, by Swanberg, and the Fort and Dreiser correspondence is from the Dreiser papers.

"The Dream" was later published in *Hey, Rub-a-Dub-Dub, or a Book of the Mystery and Wonder and Terror of Life*, by Dreiser (Boni & Liveright, 1920).

CHAPTER ELEVEN. A BATTLE IS ABOUT TO BE FOUGHT

Fort's introductory quote is from *NL*, Chapter 9.

The October 7, 1915, letter with the proposal for Y, a detailed manuscript describing the contents, is in the Dreiser papers. Their correspondence on the X manuscript and Kaempffert is from Cornell University and the Dreiser papers.

The proposal to dramatize X is from the Knight papers. "Spectators Interfere" is mentioned in a list of Fort works (Dreiser papers), as is Fort's correspondence about "love stories." Dreiser's involvement with Mirror Films is from Dreiser's biographies, as cited.

Information on *The "Genius"* is from Dreiser's biographies and *Dreiser-Mencken Letters*, edited by Riggio. Fort's letter to Dreiser ("High Priest of Evil") is published online by Mr. X. The letter about "protest" is from the Dreiser papers. Mencken's correspondence and the protest signers are from *Dreiser-Mencken Letters*.

Fort's letter about his uncle was published online by Mr. X. Information on Frank A. Fort is from census records and the Knight papers. Charles Fort's purchases are from the Knight papers, and the letter about Anna "becoming a snob" is published online by Mr. X.

Dreiser recalled the aunt's inheritance in his Charles Fort manuscript, but this reference isn't clear and, as mentioned, Dreiser's reporting can be spotty. For example, he also reported that the Forts took a trip to Puerto Rico around this time, even though this was denied in his later interview with Anna. The correspondence about Clarence is from the Knight papers.

Correspondence about X is quoted from the Dreiser papers and from letters published online by Mr. X. Dreiser recalled the difficulties in his Charles Fort manuscript and in *My Life with Dreiser* by Helen Dreiser.

Fort's correspondence is quoted from the Dreiser papers and from Mr. X's online material. Damon Knight is from *Charles Fort*, by Knight. Thanksgiving dinner is from online letters published by Mr. X; from Dreiser's Charles Fort manuscript; from the Dreiser papers; and from Dreiser's *American Diaries*, edited by Riggio. Additional information on the Bizozers is from census records. Fort's account about the can labels is from *WT*. The meal at Kubitz's apartment is from *American Diaries*.

The letter about Z is published online by Mr. X.

CHAPTER TWELVE. IT IS A RELIGION

Fort's introductory quote is from *Lo!*, Chapter 3.

The history of the library is from *The New York Public Library, Its Architecture and Decoration*, by Henry Hope Reed (W.W. Norton, 1986). I've examined Fort's notes, which are in twenty-nine shoebox-sized files in the Tiffany Thayer papers at the New York Public Library, and they include the dates and occurrences, a cross-referenced file of phenomena, obituary dates, and datelines of short news stories, letters, and clippings. His examples of categories are from the *Chicago Daily News* article, January 21, 1920.

Anna's recollections about her husband's eating habits and his schedule are from Dreiser's interview with Anna (Dreiser papers).

Fort's "cynical mind" is from a letter to Dreiser, published online by Mr. X. "I was a wizard" is from *WT*. "I wrote a book" is from the *Chicago Daily News* article, January 21, 1920.

Fort's letters, "topeacho," and "live tadpoles" are published online by Mr. X. His letter to Dreiser, "talking behind my back," is quoted in *Charles Fort*, by Knight, though the letter is misdated 1918.

Mencken on Dreiser is from *Dreiser-Mencken Letters*, edited by Riggio. Material on Liveright is from *Firebrand: the Life of Horace Liveright*, by Dardis, and from Dreiser biographies as cited. Information about the Fort-Dreiser correspondence about *BOD* is published online by Mr. X and is also from Cornell University. "X was even more wonderful" and the story of black-mailing Liveright is from Dreiser's Charles Fort manuscript (Dreiser papers), and from *My Life with Dreiser*, by Helen Dreiser. Curiously, in Helen Dreiser's book, Dreiser's recollection was that X was destroyed immediately, as Fort was "writing *The Book of the Damned,* and that he would rather I would interest myself in that." But correspondence demonstrates that Dreiser thought the manuscript still existed several years later.

The Maxwell book is mentioned in *Dreiser,* by Swanberg. Fort's "humbler discoverer" letter is published online by Mr. X.

The *American Quarterly* is discussed in Dreiser biographies as cited, in *Dreiser-Mencken Letters,* edited by Riggio, and in letters in the Dreiser papers. Fort's letter about the automobile accident is published online by Mr. X.

Fort's long letter to Dreiser about Dreiser's interest in metaphysics, dated June 4, 1919, is in the Dreiser papers.

The Hand of the Potter is discussed in Dreiser biographies as cited, and in *Dreiser-Mencken Letters,* edited by Riggio. Fort's letter is in the Dreiser papers.

Fort's signed copy of *BOD* is now in the Dreiser Library, University of Pennsylvania.

CHAPTER THIRTEEN. CHILDREN CRY FOR IT

Fort's introductory quote is from *BOD*, Chapter 8.

The history of this era was assembled from a number of texts and online sources; especially useful were *That Jazz!: an Idiosyncratic Social History of the American Twenties*, by Ethan Mordden (G.P. Putnam's, 1978), and *The Wicked City*, by Curt Johnson and Craig Sautter (Da Capo, 1998).

Mencken's quote, "hating knowledge," is from a June 29, 1925, column for the *Baltimore Evening Sun* during the Scopes Trial.

Mencken and Dreiser's correspondence about *BOD* is from *Mencken-Dreiser Letters*, edited by Riggio. Bernays's opinion of Fort is from *Biography of an Idea: Memoirs of Public Relations Counsel Edward L. Bernays*, by Edward Bernays (Simon and Schuster, 1965). Hecht's review is from the *Chicago Daily News*, January 21, 1920. Tarkington described his impressions in his introduction to *NL*.

Gardner discussed Fort in *Fads and Fallacies in the Name of Science*, by Martin Gardner (Dover, 1952), and Ian Kidd wrote of Fort's philosophy in "Who Was Charles Fort?" in the *Fortean Times*, January 2007. Fort's quote, "I had a theory," is from his short story "The Giant, the Insect, and the Philanthropic-Looking Old Gentleman," published online by Mr. X. The other Fort quotes, including the bridge analogy, are from *BOD*.

Bernays is taken from *Biography of an Idea*, by Bernays. The ad for *BOD* ran in the Feburary 8, 1920, *New York Times*.

The *New York Tribune* review appeared on January 17, 1920. Fort's additional quotes are taken from *BOD*.

Considering that Fort had tried to publish *X* and *Y*, there were coincidentally similar titles in the bookstores: *Station X*, an early science-fiction novel by G. McLeod Windsor, was published at the same time as *BOD*. Several months later, *That Damn Y* appeared; this was Katherine Mayo's account of the YMCA in France.

For Marconi and Lowell, see the *New York Tribune*, February 8, 1920.

Fort's letter about the response to *BOD* and the *Catholic World* review is from Dreiser papers, University of Pennsylvania. Fort's review appeared in the *Catholic World,* June 1920; Dreiser's appeared in May 1920.

CHAPTER FOURTEEN. THE LONDON TRIANGLE

Fort's introductory quote is from *NL,* Chapter 5.

Dreiser's letter to Fort is from Cornell University. Dreiser's letter to Mencken is quoted in *Dreiser-Mencken Letters,* edited by Riggio. Anna's recollection about the magazines is from Dreiser's interview with Anna (Dreiser Papers).

Pearson's story is from *Queer Books,* by Edmund Pearson (Doubleday, 1928). I've been unable to find Fort's published complaint about the library.

Fort's letter, "Forces are moving me," is from the Knight papers. Fort's quote, "Miserliness for notes," is from his story "The Giant, the Insect and the Philanthropic-Looking Old Gentleman," as cited. Dreiser's response about X and Y and the bottle of scotch is from Cornell University.

Anna's recollection of Charles's schedule and the Speaker's Corner is from Dreiser's interview with Anna (Dreiser papers). Fort's quote from the Speaker's Corner is from *WT.*

Fort's letter from London about singing "On the Banks of the Wabash" is from the Dreiser papers.

The letter to Raymond is from *Charles Fort,* by Knight. Anna's recollections of the night sky and about their shopping are from Dreiser's interview with Anna (Dreiser papers).

The information on *Chaos* is from a letter from Fort to Benjamin De Casseres (De Casseres papers, New York Public Library). Fort's letters to Dreiser are from the Dreiser papers.

Quotes are taken from *NL.*

The *Boston Transcript* is quoted in "Doubting Tiffany," by Doug Skinner, *Fortean Times,* Special Summer Issue, 2005.

The *New York Times* review appeared November 25, 1923.

CHAPTER FIFTEEN. THAT FROG WOULD BE GOD

Fort's introductory quote is from *Lo!*, Chapter 1.

Information on Tiffany Thayer is from "Doubting Tiffany," by Douglas Skinner, as cited; from Thayer's introduction to *The Books of Charles Fort*; from *Charles Fort*, by Knight; and from "A Talk with Tiffany Thayer," by Lewis Nichols, the *New York Times*, June 10, 1956.

A letter from the St. Clairs to Anna is in the Dreiser papers. "Rose Marie" is from Dreiser's interview with Anna (Dreiser papers).

DeFord is quoted in "Charles Fort, Enfant Terrible of Science," *The Magazine of Fantasy and Science Fiction*, January 1954, and in *Charles Fort*, by Knight. Reid's correspondence, from the Tiffany Thayer papers, is also published online by Mr. X. Hamilton's correspondence is quoted in *Charles Fort*, by Knight. The *Philadelphia Public Ledger, T.P.'s Weekly*, and information on the Dundas fish fall are published online by Mr. X. The Fort *New York Times* letters appeared on August 31, 1924, October 18, 1925, March 28, 1926, and September 5, 1926. Fort's letter about the clipping service is in the author's collection.

The stories of the dog and the falling pictures are from *WT*.

Fort's quote about spiritualists is from *Lo!*, the account of miracles from *WT*. The letter to Hamilton is quoted from *Charles Fort*, by Knight.

There are many accounts of the Scopes Trial. I've used *That Jazz!*, by Ethan Mordden, as cited; *The Constant Circle: H. L. Mencken and His Friends*, by Sara Mayfield (University of Alabama, 2003); and *Monkey Business: The True Story of the Scopes Trial*, by Marvin Olasky and John Perry (B&H Publishing, 2005).

Fort's quotes are taken from *Lo!* "The simplest strategy" is from *BOD.* "Canvasses that were daubed upon" is from *WT*; "I am not writing that God is an idiot," from *Lo!*; "Ideal is the imitation of God," from *WT*.

CHAPTER SIXTEEN. THE WORLD HAS CUT ME OUT—I HAVE
CUT MYSELF OUT

Fort's introductory quote is from *Lo!*, Chapter 1.

Fort's letter to Dreiser is from the Dreiser papers. Dreiser's response is from Cornell University. Mencken's review is from *Dreiser-Mencken Letters*, edited by Riggio. The account of Dreiser's lunch with Liveright is recounted in Dreiser biographies, as cited.

Fort's letters to De Casseres are in the Benjamin De Casseres papers. Mencken's opinion of De Casseres is from *Dreiser-Mencken Letters*, edited by Riggio.

Dreiser's visit to Marchmont Street is recounted in *My Life with Dreiser*, by Helen Dreiser. After this time, Dreiser stopped inquiring about X and Y.

The account of *Skyward Ho!* is from the De Casseres papers, from Fort's letter to John T. Reid, published online by Mr. X, and from *Charles Fort*, by Knight. Fort's account of his eyesight is from Fort's notebook entries (Knight papers). His depression, "plus sign or a minus sign," is from *WT*. Fort's evaluations of his writing and health are from notebook entries, as cited.

The account of Capone is taken from *The Wicked City*, by Johnson and Sautter, as cited. Fort's quote is from *WT*.

Fort's parrots' names appear in his notes. His letter about Super-checkers appeared in the *New York Sun*, December 20, 1928. The newspaper clipping says "400 squares," but on Fort's copy, in the Thayer papers, he corrects this to 800. His letter about Super-checkers was to Tiffany Thayer, recounted in the introduction to *The Books of Charles Fort*.

Fort's rent and neighbors are from census information. *A Book about Caciques* is quoted in *Charles Fort*, by Knight. "The Giant, the Insect and the Philanthropic-Looking Old Gentleman" is published in "The Short Stories of Charles Fort" online by Mr. X.

Tiffany Thayer is from "Doubting Tiffany," by Doug Skinner, as cited, and from Thayer's introduction to *The Books of Charles Fort*. The Sussman information is from *Charles Fort*, by Knight. A Fort manuscript, in the

Knight papers, records the title "Snoozers and Saps. . . ." The letter to Thayer discussing titles is from the Knight papers.

CHAPTER SEVENTEEN. A WELCOMING HAND TO LITTLE FROGS AND PERIWINKLES

Fort's introductory quote is from *Lo!*, Chapter 4.

Aaron Sussman's memories are from *Charles Fort*, by Knight. The first printing of *Lo!* had a conservative brown linen binding; the third printing was bound in a shiny purple fabric. Thayer's introduction appears in *Lo!* Fort's letter to "Ellsworth," the letter to Dreiser, and Dreiser's response are in the Knight papers. Fort's reply is in the Dreiser papers. The story of Sussman and the line in the galleys is from Thayer's introduction to *The Books of Charles Fort*.

Letters about visiting are in Cornell University and the Dreiser papers. The description of Fort is from *Dreiser: a New Dimension*, by Tjader. Anna's recollections about Lillian Gish and film stars are from Dreiser's interview with Anna (Dreiser papers).

The letter about Stern's interest in an organization and Fort's response to Thayer are from *Charles Fort*, by Knight, and the Knight papers. The letter to De Casseres is from the De Casseres papers. Fort's letter to Dreiser is from the Knight papers.

Dreiser writes of his plan in a letter that's at Cornell University. Fort's response is from the Knight papers. The *Cosmopolitan* article is discussed in letters at Cornell University.

The Fortean Society meeting is from "Transactions of the Founders at the First Meeting of the Fortean Society," in the Knight papers; from Thayer's account in the introduction to *The Books of Charles Fort*, by Knight; and from *Low Man on the Totem Pole*, by H. Allen Smith (Blakiston, 1945).

Fort's correspondence to De Casseres is from the De Casseres papers. *Mencken and Shaw* is by Benjamin De Casseres (Silas Newton, 1930). Mencken's letter is in the De Casseres papers.

Fort's quotes are from *Lo!*

CHAPTER EIGHTEEN. NOT A BOTTLE OF CATSUP CAN FALL
WITHOUT BEING NOTED

Fort's introductory quote is from *WT,* Chapter 6.

De Casseres's article, from the De Casseres papers, has not been quoted before; it is a wonderful description of Fort's work. Still, his colorful writing sometimes gets away from him. De Casseres suggests that Fort's philosophy is not relativity, but "irrelativity." It's a good turn of phrase, and suggests Fort's "pull-the-rug-out" theories, but it's also misleading. Fort always insisted on the interrelatedness of all things, a kind of "super-relativity."

De Casseres also ended his article on an odd note. "I thrill at [Fort's] pages as I do when I hear certain notes in *Lohengrin* or when I listen with eyes closed to Ravel's *Bolero* or when I re-read *The Shadow Eater* and *Anathema!*" The last two works were De Casseres's own books, and the self-reference sours a pretty analogy. Fort noted "the final line about yourself," writing simply "I so well know what you mean."

Fort on note-taking is from *WT*; notes are from the Knight papers, Dreiser papers, and Tiffany Thayer papers. Allen's chapter appears in *Low Man on the Totem Pole,* as cited.

The Sussman letter about the George Washington Hotel is in the Knight papers. Margaret Deland's letter is in the Thayer papers.

The Wells correspondence and comments are from Cornell University, the Dreiser papers, and *The Letters of Theodore Dreiser,* edited by Elias. Dreiser's comments on Fort are from Dreiser's Charles Fort manuscript (Dreiser papers).

Rascoe is quoted in "Doubting Tiffany," by Doug Skinner, as cited. Shipley's review appeared in the *New York Times,* February 15, 1931. Fort's response is from *Charles Fort,* by Knight. Fort to De Casseres is from the De Casseres papers.

Fort's adventure with pigeons is from *WT.* Dreiser wrote of Fort's health in his Charles Fort manuscript (Dreiser papers).

The visit to Iroki is documented in letters and photos; in the Dreiser papers; and in the Knight papers. It's also recounted in Dreiser's Charles Fort manuscript and in *My Life with Dreiser*, by Helen Dreiser. She suggests that Fort visited several times, but Dreiser's account, along with correspondence, disagrees.

Fort's quotes are from *WT*.

Fort's correspondence with De Casseres is from the De Casseres papers. Anna Fort's recollections are from Dreiser's interview with Anna. Fort's letter to Dreiser is in the Knight papers.

The Reed Harris interview is discussed in correspondence (Dreiser papers). Fort's notes are recorded in the Knight papers and in *Charles Fort*, by Knight.

Dreiser's biographer, W. A. Swanberg, wrote that, for Christmas, Dreiser visited Fort's "grubby Bronx apartment and gave him $100." But by this time, the Forts were quite comfortable financially.

CHAPTER NINETEEN. BEGINNING ANYWHERE

Fort's introductory quote is from *WT*, Chapter 6.

Dreiser's Reed Harris interview is from the Dreiser papers. Correspondence about the interview is from Cornell University and the Knight papers.

Fort's notes are from the Knight and Dreiser papers. Dreiser's account is from his Charles Fort manuscript (Dreiser papers). Fort's slips on medicine are in the Tiffany Thayer papers. The account of *Medi-Vaudeville* is from "Unforgettable Charles Fort," UFO Roundup, edited by Joseph Trainor (August 17, 2000, www.ufoinfo.com/roundup).

Anna's account of Fort's illness is from Dreiser's interview with Anna and from Dreiser's Charles Fort Manuscript, both in the Dreiser papers, and from *My Life with Dreiser*, by Helen Dreiser.

Fort's death is from *Charles Fort*, by Knight, and from the official death certificate. Additional information, from Dreiser's Charles Fort manuscript (Dreiser papers), has not been quoted before. The funeral is recounted in Dreiser's Charles Fort manuscript. Both newspaper obituaries appeared on May 5, 1932.

Capone's imprisonment is from *The Wicked City*, by Johnson and Sautter. Mencken's letter is from *Low Man on the Totem Pole*, by H. Allen Smith.

Fort's bequest is in a note in the Knight papers. Both Sussman and Dreiser had notes after his death, although Knight suggests that Sussman's notes were from Mrs. Tiffany Thayer.

Anna's experiences in the apartment after Fort's death are from Dreiser's interview with Anna.

Hecht's review of *The Books of Charles Fort* appeared in the *Fortean*, January 1942. Fuller's remarks are from the introduction to *Charles Fort*, by Knight. Dreiser's remarks are from his Charles Fort manuscript, Dreiser papers.

CHAPTER TWENTY. FALL IN! FORWARD! MARCH!

Fort's introductory quote is from *WT*, Chapter 25.

Thayer's career is from "Doubting Tiffany," by Doug Skinner, as cited. The Dreiser-Thayer letters appear in *Letters of Theodore Dreiser*, edited by Elias; in *Charles Fort*, by Knight; and in the Knight papers. Anna Fort's address is taken from correspondence (Dreiser papers). Dreiser wrote of the notes in his Charles Fort manuscript. I've also taken information from Anna's death certificate.

Anna Fort's bequests are recorded in the Knight papers. Raymond Fort information is from cemetery records.

Thayer and the Fortean Society is from "Doubting Tiffany," by Douglas Skinner, as cited; from *Charles Fort*, by Knight; and from the Knight papers, as well as Knight's introduction to *The Complete Books of Charles Fort* (Dover, 1974).

Thayer's letter to Helen is quoted in *Charles Fort*, by Knight.

Sussman's resignation letter and Gaddis's letter to Damon Knight are in the Knight papers.

Ripley's quotes are from the first edition of *Believe It or Not!*, by Robert L. Ripley (Simon and Schuster, 1929). Fort's correspondence is from the Thayer papers, New York Public Library, and his quote is from *WT*, Chapter 12.

Scully is quoted from *Behind the Flying Saucers,* by Frank Scully (Henry Holt, 1950). Other quotes are taken from *Chariots of the Gods?,* by Erich von Däniken (G.P. Putnam, 1970), *The Mystery of Atlantis,* by Charles Berlitz (Avon, 1969), and *The Bermuda Triangle,* by Charles Berlitz (Avon, 1975).

For Forteanism with twists, readers might wish to consult *Invisible Horizons,* by Vincent Gaddis (Chilton Books, 1965), *Invisible Residents,* by Ivan Sanderson (World Publishing, 1970), and *This Baffling World,* by John Godwin (Hart Publishing, 1968).

H. Allen Smith is quoted from *Low Man on the Totem Pole.* Martin Gardner is quoted from *In the Name of Science.* De Casseres is quoted from "The Fortean Fantasy" in *The Thinker,* as cited. Thayer is quoted from the introduction to *The Books of Charles Fort.* Fort is quoted from *MP.*

PHOTO CREDITS

Theodore Dreiser Papers, Rare Book & Manuscript Library, University of Pennsylvania: Fort at fifteen; Fort at nineteen; young Anna portrait; Dreiser with spyglass; Anna and Charles in Coney Island; Anna on sidewalk; Dreiser in Greenwich Village; Anna and Charles Fort, fingering paper; Dreiser and Liveright; Anna and Charles, early twenties; Anna and Charles, passport; Anna and parrots; Dreiser and Fort at Mt. Kisco; Anna on roof with cage.

Damon Knight Papers, University of Syracuse: Charles Nelson Fort; Charles, Clarence, and Raymond; Fort handwritten notes; Fort and Supercheckers.

Author's Collection: Frontispiece portrait; Albany home; Fort's New York apartment; Formal portrait; Bronx home; *Lo!* illustration; Fort newspaper portrait; Fort family grave.

INDEX

ABOUT THE AUTHOR

Jim Steinmeyer is a historian of stage magic and the critically acclaimed author of *The Glorious Deception* and *Hiding the Elephant,* a *Los Angeles Times* best-seller. He is also a leading designer of magic illusion who has done work for television, Broadway, and many of the best-known names in modern magic, such as Ricky Jay, Siegfried & Roy, Doug Henning, and David Copperfield, for whom he created the famous "Vanishing Statue of Liberty" illusion. A frequent writer on magic, Steinmeyer wrote the introduction for *The Book of the Damned: The Collected Works of Charles Fort.* He lives in Los Angeles, California.